Hand-Picked:
The Complete Guide to Finding and Hiring the Best Employees

By

Robert W. Wendover

National Press Publications
A Division of Rockhurst College Continuing Education Center, Inc.
6901 W. 63rd St. • P.O. Box 2949 • Shawnee Mission, KS 66201-1349
1-800-258-7248 • 1-913-432-7757

Hand-Picked: The Complete Guide to Finding and Hiring the Best Employees

National Seminars endorses nonsexist language. In an effort to make this Business User's Manual clear, consistent and easy to read, we've used "he" throughout the odd-numbered chapters and "she" throughout the even-numbered chapters. The copy is not intended to be sexist.

Copyright 1996, Robert W. Wendover
Published by National Press Publications
A Division of Rockhurst College Continuing Education Center, Inc.

All rights reserved. No part of this publication may be reproduced or utilized in any form by any means, electronic or mechanical, including photocopying, recording or by any information storage and retrieval system, without permission in writing from National Press Publications.

Printed in the United States of America.

ISBN 1-55852-176-3

About Rockhurst College Continuing Education Center, Inc.

Rockhurst College Continuing Education Center, Inc., is committed to providing lifelong learning opportunities through integration of innovative education and training.

National Seminars Group, a division of Rockhurst College Continuing Education Center, Inc., has its finger on the pulse of America's business community. We've trained more than 2 million people in every imaginable occupation to be more productive and advance their careers. Along the way, we've learned a few things. Like what it takes to be successful ... how to build the skills to make it happen ... and how to translate learning into results. Millions of people from thousands of companies around the world turn to National Seminars for training solutions.

National Press Publications is our product and publishing division. We offer a complete line of the finest self-study and continuing-learning resources available anywhere. These products present our industry-acclaimed curriculum and training expertise in a concise, action-oriented format you can put to work right away. Packed with real-world strategies and hands-on techniques, these resources are guaranteed to help you meet the career and personal challenges you face every day.

Legend Symbol Guide

Exercises that reinforce your learning experience.

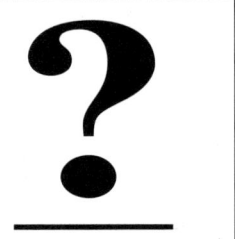

Questions that will help you apply the critical points to your situation.

Checklist that will help you identify important issues for future application.

Key issues to learn and understand for future application.

Table of Contents

Introduction i

Chapter One: Hiring the Best Employees 1
    I.   The Hiring Survival Checklist 4
    II. Alternatives to Hiring... 16

Chapter Two: The Legal Requirements of Hiring 23
    I.   What Laws Apply.. 24
    II.   Common Selection Issues 29
    III. Negligent Hiring.. 34
    IV. Enforcement and Record-Keeping 36
    V.   State Requirements 39
    VI. A Checklist for Hiring Law 41

Chapter Three: Job Descriptions and Compensation 43
    I.   Importance of Job Descriptions 43
    II.   Job Analysis and Audit 46
    III. Writing Job Descriptions 52
    IV. Determining Compensation 54
    V.   A Checklist for Job Descriptions and Compensation 61

Chapter Four: Recruiting the Best 63
    I.   Recruiting as a Hiring Tool 64
    II.   The Recruiting Plan 66
    III.   Budgeting for Recruiting 70
    IV.   Internal Recruiting and Referrals 73
    V.   Identifying Applicants' Motivations 74
    VI.   Enhancing Organizational Image 76
    VII. Exploring Sources of Labor 80
    VIII. Locating External Applicants 87
    IX.   Creating an Attractive Job Vacancy Notice 92
    X.   Developing Labor Pools for the Future 98
    XI.   A Checklist for Recruiting Basics 99

Chapter Five: Family and Friends — Dealing with Nepotism 101
    I.   Nepotism in Business 102
    II.   The Pros and Cons of Family and Friends 103
    III. The Legal Aspects of Nepotism 105
    IV. Devising a Nepotism Policy 106
    V.   Tips on Screening Family and Friends 107
    VI. The Nepotism Checklist 109

Chapter Six: Evaluating Resumes and Applications 111
    I.   Resumes and Applications: Where Should They Be Used?.... 112
    II.   Evaluating a Resume Effectively 113
    III. Evaluating Cover Letters 120
    IV. Development and Review of Applications 123
    V.   Evaluating the Resume/Application/Reference Package 126
    VI. The Resume/Application Checklist 128

Chapter Seven: Screening Applicants by Telephone 131
    I. The Value of Telephone Screening 131
    II. Preparing to Screen by Telephone 133
    III. Reception of Call-In Applicants 136
    IV. Conducting Telephone Screening 137
    V. Evaluating Callers 140
    VI. The Telephone Screening Checklist 142

Chapter Eight: Take-Charge Interviewing 145
    I. Detecting the Winners 146
    II. Establishing the Process 147
    III. Developing Questions 152
    IV. Conducting the Interview 154
    V. Alternative Interview Strategies 159
    VI. The Interview Checklist 165

Chapter Nine: Obtaining Reliable References 167
    I. Conducting a Reference Check 168
    II. Checking Credentials 173
    III. The Reference Checklist 175

Chapter Ten: Employment Testing — Dos and Don'ts 177
    I. Overview of Testing Issues 178
    II. Paper and Pencil Testing 179
    III. Selecting Integrity Tests 185
    IV. Polygraph Screening 186
    V. Genetic Screening 190
    VI. Drug and Alcohol Screening 192
    VII. Performance-Based Testing 196
    VIII. Screening for AIDS 197
    IX. The Testing Checklist 203

Chapter Eleven: Landing Performers — Making the Right Offer 205
    I. Final Selection 206
    II. Notifying Candidates 214
    III. Negotiating Offers and Compensation 217
    IV. The Decision-Making Checklist 219

Appendix A: Sample Interview Questions 221
Appendix B: Federal Record-Keeping Requirements 257
Appendix C: Sample Compensation Plan 261
Appendix D: Recruiting Strategies 267
Appendix E: Bibliography and Resources 275
Index 279

Introduction

"I can't believe this!" said Jack. "Do you mean to say that after three weeks of advertising in the newspaper and hanging that huge sign in the window, we only have 12 applications?"
"That's what's happened," replied Kate.
"I told everyone I know to refer the best people they know and we got no response."
"Unbelievable!" said Jack.
"What makes matters worse," replied Kate, "is that half of the people who applied can't pass the math test. We either train them or look for other applicants."
"I don't understand," sighed Jack. "This time last year, we were turning people away."

It is official. The recruiting race has begun! Where we could once merely open the door and receive an abundance of applications, in most every industry it is now necessary to search for applicants. This is especially hard on the high-turnover areas such as retail and fast food. But our concerns are not just limited to locating applicants.

With cutbacks and an emphasis on leaner organizations, every employee today plays a more critical role. As a result, poorly recruited staff means larger problems down the road. The traditional attitude about hiring has been, "When I need someone, I put an ad in the paper and hire, just like that," or "We need a warm body right now. If it doesn't work out, we can always get rid of him later."

But hiring is no longer what it used to be. Potential applicants have to be sold on the idea of working for a firm and then, once they have applied, they have to be screened carefully to ensure they will be productive.

> *"The people who get on in this world are the people who get up and look for the circumstances they want and, if they can't find them, make them."*
>
> George Bernard Shaw

Introduction

> *A host of new legal considerations also have evolved, making employees harder to hire and almost impossible to fire.*

To accomplish all of this in an efficient and cost-effective way, some old hiring habits have to be changed. Those who are used to waiting for candidates to walk in the door will have to go outside and drum up interest. Those who are accustomed to hiring teen-agers will have to explore alternative sources of labor. And those who are used to having qualified applicants may find themselves spending more time on training.

Many times little attention is paid to the hiring process with so many other tasks to be taken care of. But such haste can produce endless headaches. Someone hired in a rush to work in customer service, for example, may alienate a number of patrons before it's discovered she doesn't get along well with people. A new line manager may slow production because he was hired for a job that is over his head.

A host of new legal considerations also have evolved, making employees harder to hire and almost impossible to fire. For example, the practice of "employment-at-will," where an employer does not have to justify an employee's termination, has almost become a dead issue. Employers are now required by law to pay more attention to the needs and rights of employees and applicants.

In addition to the legal and practical aspects, other factors can influence the hiring process.

> *"I failed to get this job because I answered one question wrong on the application. The question asked, 'Do you advocate the overthrow of the U.S. government by revolution or violence?' I chose violence!"*
>
> Dick Cavett

For example, because hiring appears to be simple, few plans are made to predict its patterns and expansion. But many times the needed labor pools do not exist when openings occur. Also, many changes are taking place in the labor force. Traditional pools such as teen-agers and college students are decreasing in size. Meanwhile the number of senior workers (those 55 and over) has increased dramatically. "Help Wanted" signs have appeared in the windows of businesses that traditionally had more than enough applicants.

While the labor force will decrease in size, prospective employees must still be chosen carefully. Better personnel planning is needed to anticipate business demands.

Part-time employment is another growing issue. Seniors are not often willing to work full time. Women comprise more than half the workforce. There is also an increased emphasis on leisure activities instead of long hours. Now, more than ever, employers must make the work environment both stimulating and satisfying.

Finally, decisions on disabilities, psychological screening, drug and AIDS testing, along with new interpretations of the anti-discrimination acts, have all affected the procedures for acquiring new employees.

"Success is a journey, not a destination."
Ben Sweetland

Why this book? To save you time and money!!

Hand-Picked has been written to provide a quick, easy-to-read manual to assist any business in hiring effectively and legally. It is designed as a tool that can be referred to daily as hiring occurs.
- Use the principles in this book to pick the best applicant for the job.
- Understand the employment laws outlined here to avoid the common mistakes made when hiring.
- Place this book in the hands of your managers so they too will hire the right person for the right job.

Hand-Picked is specifically designed for the manager who has little or no experience in dealing with employee selection and its issues. Each chapter begins with an outline of what the reader will learn and concludes with a checklist of important guidelines. The text is outlined for easy reading and location of necessary principles along with sample forms and illustrations.

"Remember, nothing blocks insight more than your own ego."
Mark McCormack

To get the most from this book, read it completely. Then place it in an easy-to-reach location for future reference. Treat this as a handbook. Use it the same way you would the Yellow Pages, as a daily resource for hiring effectively.

CHAPTER 1

Hiring the Best Employees

"If each of us hires people who are smaller than we are, we shall become a company of dwarfs, but if each one of us hires people who are bigger than we are, Ogilvy & Mather shall become a company of giants."
— David Ogilvy, Chairman
Ogilvy & Mather

Here's What You'll Learn

I. The Hiring Survival Checklist
II. Alternatives to Hiring

> *"If you pick up a starving dog and make him prosperous, he will not bite you. This is the principal difference between a dog and a man."*
>
> Mark Twain

How well do you perform the task of hiring? What characteristics make one candidate more attractive than the others? Do you hire giants or dwarfs?

The job you have is all-consuming. You work day and night making sure that every detail is attended to. If a new employee is needed, your urge might be to hire the first reasonable person who walks through the door. You might call around to friends, acquaintances and colleagues to see if they know someone reliable. But it's not that simple.

Chapter 1 Hiring the Best Employees

THE CHANGING WORKFORCE

A tremendous change is taking place in our nation's workforce. According to recent studies, four key trends will shape the next 10 years in the workplace:

1. The U.S. economy should grow at a healthy pace boosted by a rebound in U.S. exports, renewed productivity growth and a strong economy.
2. Despite its international comeback, U.S. manufacturing will have a much smaller share of the economy. Service industries will create virtually all of the new jobs and most of the new wealth.
3. The workforce will grow slowly, becoming older, more female and more disadvantaged.
4. The new service industry jobs will require significantly higher skill levels than the jobs of today. Few new jobs will be created for those who cannot read, follow directions and use mathematics. Ironically, the demographic trends in the workforce, coupled with the higher skill requirements of the economy, will lead to both higher and lower unemployment, more joblessness for the lower skilled and less for the higher skilled.

Regardless of the size of your organization, these changes will have an impact on you. In hiring lower-skilled workers, for instance, you will discover an increasing need to provide training in basic skills. In higher-skilled jobs, the competition will be keener for qualified applicants. Applicants will come from more diverse backgrounds and experiences. Some will present language barriers and many more will be female.

Your organization's ability to adapt to these changes and use them to your advantage will determine your ability to compete successfully in the world economy. Hiring competent workers is no longer an option. It is a requirement for successful business. It requires anticipation of local markets in your community, long-term planning of labor force movement, education, cultural balance and work ethic. How much do you know about these factors within your present labor force?

> *"A musician must make music, an artist must paint, a poet must write, if he is to be ultimately at peace with himself. What a man can be, he must be."*
>
> Abraham Maslow

> *"Nothing endures but change."*
>
> Heraclitus

CULTURAL DIVERSITY

In addition to numbers, the attitudes and culturalization of new workforce entrants are becoming significantly different. The Hudson Institute has estimated that between now and the year 2000, the total number of native white male entrants to the workforce will represent only 15 percent. Women will account for 67 percent and nonwhite and immigrant men will account for 20 percent. These figures have impacts on language, work ethic and social barriers with which you, the employer, will have to deal. Workforce entrants born after 1964 have known relative affluence and have not experienced the turmoil of previous generations. These attitudes, combined with an abundance of jobs and a shortage of workers, will enable them to be more choosy about the positions they take, whether higher or lower skilled. Also, job security, which so obsessed earlier generations, now seems to mean little to these younger entrants.

With the shortage of labor, the expected abundance of applicants will not appear. This may further your urge to hire any warm body. But with the expense of turnover cutting into profits, staff selection without proper care is not an option. According to the Saratoga Institute, the average cost of hiring a first-level supervisor was $7,488 in 1990. For nonexempt employees, it was $652. How much does it cost you?

You may have hired employees before. Some worked out. Some did not. How can you do a better job of selecting peak performers?

Chapter 1 Hiring the Best Employees

Rate Your Hiring History

List the last four people you hired and rate the quality of each hiring decision:

	Low				High
1. _____	1	2	3	4	5
2. _____	1	2	3	4	5
3. _____	1	2	3	4	5
4. _____	1	2	3	4	5

What did you do well?
_____
_____
_____
_____

What did you do poorly?
_____
_____
_____
_____

Compare your hiring decisions above. Are there common strengths or faults?
_____
_____
_____
_____
_____

I. The Hiring Survival Checklist

Before we go on, it is important to understand your present position. What are your typical hiring practices?

Answer the questions below. There is no grading or rating scale attached, it is just an inventory of the process that should be practiced.

1. Do you hire "tens"?

According to management consultant I. Martin Jacknis, there is a tendency among supervisors to hire individuals who will not challenge their authority or influence. In other words, the "tens" (superior supervisors) will hire "nines."

The nines will hire "eights" and the eights will hire "sevens." As David Ogilvy observes at the beginning of this chapter, continuing this practice makes the company an organization of dwarfs.

Encourage managers to look for the best person for the job regardless of the potential threat. It is commonly held that no one moves up until he has found someone to fill his present position. Finding an expert to do your job puts a feather in your cap.

> *Think BIG!*

2. **Have you defined the kind of person who makes a good employee in your organization?**

    Whether you're a company of three or 300, you have your own culture. How do the other employees act? How hard do they work? How well do they get along? Is this a serious atmosphere? Does it lighten up? Is it downright fun?

    What motivates these people? Do they share the company dream? How do you know? How did you select these people? What qualifications did these individuals have when they entered the company? Are there definite skills or experiences that all your employees have that are necessary for the manufacture or marketing of the product? Are "people skills" essential for marketing the product?

    > *There is a tendency among supervisors to hire individuals who will not challenge their authority or influence.*

    All of the above, in addition to other considerations specific to your situation, will assist you in determining with consistency who might "fit in." After all, performing the task is just part of the job. The manner in which new employees communicate with others, for example, is also critical.

3. **Do you communicate your hiring goals to the rest of the company?**

    If the remainder of the organization is aware of the company's hiring needs, other employees will recruit suitable candidates. Informing employees of hiring policy creates and enforces an impression that everyone is involved in the process. This might be accomplished through a quick, two-page newsletter from the president that examines the issue of "Where we are and where we're going." Something chatty and inspirational is usually effective.

1 Chapter 1 Hiring the Best Employees

The Digi-Lectronics Circuit
A monthly update of what's happening
Volume 34

New Distribution Jobs

Supervisor

Due to the increase in sales over the past six months, we will be hiring an additional distribution supervisor. This person should have a minimum of one year's experience in shipping (nonsupervisory), knowledge of accounts receivable and payable, and a demonstrated high-energy work ethic. This is a second-shift position and will pay an 8 percent differential. Interested employees should contact Alex Raski's office ASAP. Referrals encouraged.

Shift Work

In addition to the supervisor's position, we are also seeking to fill a second shift of warehouse workers. These positions provide excellent opportunities for training and advancement to supervisory jobs. Those interested should apply to Rosemary Crena in Shipping. Referrals encouraged.

Parking Lot Details

As petty as this sounds, we must insist that you park on the south side of the building for the rest of the time we are under construction. We know your cars are hot in the afternoon, but haphazard parking has cost the company a number of dollars.

Take Me Out to the Ballgame

We have purchased a block of tickets for the Reds and Mets game on June 30. If you qualify for two tickets from the incentive program, pick them up at Jean Simmons' desk by June 20. Tickets not redeemed by that time will be raffled off.

New Manuals Are in!

Those of you who requested personal copies of the circuit design for APA-36 can pick them up from Hank Evers' office any time. Digi-Lectronics will split the cost with you. Your share is $12.50.

continued on the next page

Callouts: New Opportunity! · Common Concern · Point of Interest · Great Offer!

Sample Newsletter Page

---

4. Can you explain the procedures that are used when hiring new employees?

Consistency is vital to the employee selection effort. As the organization grows and the occasional crisis takes place, there is a temptation to bend the rules to get a vacancy filled. This practice may have dire consequences in several ways: discrimination-related litigation, bad public relations both inside and outside the company, unacceptable turnover and declining employee morale. If the company is perceived as one that hires only people with an "inside track," other excellent candidates may not apply. Such impressions are easily created through one or two questionable actions. In a small community, for example, rumors travel quickly if something is perceived to be wrong. Correcting impressions could take years.

There is a temptation to bend the rules to get a vacancy quickly filled. This practice may have dire consequences.

5. **When was the last time you examined the hiring procedures your company follows? Have the recommendations that resulted from that examination been implemented?**

    Who has time for something like this, right? But a cursory review of the procedures now in place may reveal some "interesting" items.

    If you suspect that some practice now in place might be improper, check your facts. Can someone really ask "that" question? Can we really say "this" in the job announcement?

    Examine the entire process. What is being written in the classified ads? Does the standard application contain improper questions? Is the record-keeping being maintained to satisfy government requirements? (See Appendix B for a complete list of federal requirements.)

    Consider the decision-making process. How was the last employee hired? Sit in on candidates' interviews to get a feel for what is occurring. What other details can you examine in your organization? One simple slip can be costly. "That's an interesting accent," observed one interviewer. "Where did you grow up?" Innocent question? Yes. Job-related? No. Discriminatory? It could be viewed that way.

6. **When was the last time you updated yourself on employee selection law and hiring technologies?**

    In this litigious society, the laws concerning employment change daily. It is not enough to rely on your attorney and accountant to warn you about potential liabilities. A solid working knowledge of these regulations is important, especially if you are responsible for most or all of the organization's hiring. (A thorough explanation of employment selection regulations is provided in Chapter Two.)

    The technology surrounding employee selection has grown more exacting. Many of the traditional strategies and questions have been replaced with more accurate procedures. These strategies provide an employer with additional "surefire" means for selecting the best applicant. Even preemployment testing is making a comeback. (See Chapter Ten.)

> *"The successful man will profit from his mistakes and try again in a different way."*
>
> Dale Carnegie

> *"Ignorance of the law excuses no man."*
>
> John Selden

Chapter 1 Hiring the Best Employees

COST OF HIRING WORKSHEET

Count the costs as you weigh your hiring decision. Please use this worksheet to gain an appropriate perspective about this hiring investment. By estimating your hiring investment, you'll have a better idea of how expensive a bad hiring decision is!

Cost Estimates

Exit Interview of Former Employee _____ (hours) x _____ (rate) = _____

Paperwork/Administrative Support _____ (hours) x _____ (rate) = _____

Last day of work (unproductive hours) _____ (hours) x _____ (rate) = _____

New hire selection process:

    Advertisement Costs _____

    Phone/Resume Review _____ (hours) x _____ (rate) = _____

    Interview Time _____ (hours) x _____ (rate) = _____

Hiring/Interviewing Expenses:

    Travel _____

    Entertainment _____

    Moving/Relocation _____

Training Time _____ (hours) x _____ (rate) = _____

                                Total _____

SELECT CAREFULLY — *You've made a significant investment!*

Hand-Picked: The Complete Guide to Finding and Hiring the Best Employees

7. **How much does it cost for you to hire someone?**

    If you have not done so, calculate the cost of hiring for the various levels of employees within your organization. Are there ways to reduce these expenses by using different strategies or sources of applicants? For example, are you advertising every position in the newspaper when a number of these positions could be filled if you pressed your colleagues for additional referrals?

8. **How much does it cost when an employee needs to be replaced?**

    This figure should include the cost of replacement, the additional training and staff commitment, and the lost work on the job. Seeing these expenses proves to be an effective motivator for reexamining your recruiting and training process.

> *When asked what he thought of Western civilization, Gandhi replied, "I think it would be a good idea."*

MEMORANDUM

TO: Alex Raski, Vice President

FROM: John Tutor, Customer Service Manager

These are the estimated costs for replacing a receptionist as we did last week. It's obvious that this could get to be an expensive process.

Exit interview with manager @ $15/hr	$15
Administrative paperwork @ $12/hr	12
Last day of work (exit interview, clean out desk, party, etc.) 8 hours @ $10/hr (incl. benefits)	80
New hire selection costs (this has been our average)	482
Training time (unproductive for 16 hrs @ $10/hr)	160
Total	$749

Note: This does not include unemployment compensation if necessary.

The Cost of Turnover

Chapter 1 Hiring the Best Employees

9. **Do you regularly refine the descriptions of vacant positions?**

    The average company, large or small, does not have a complete set of job descriptions covering all positions. However, these documents are important. In addition to providing focus for the job, they may also serve as protection against litigation. A fired employee, for example, may sue for wrongful discharge. If the company is unable to produce even the most basic job description, it will be difficult to prove that the individual was released for not performing adequately on the job.

    Finally, job descriptions serve as a road map for new employees. Supervisors can also benefit by familiarizing themselves with the "official" job descriptions of all those within their purview.

10. **Are you considering the versatility of the candidates?**

    The average employee wears multiple hats. Will the person you hire be able to handle more than just the original responsibility? Are the skills of the final candidate too narrow to allow such a broadening?

    It is not unreasonable to assume you will be able to find individuals with a myriad of talents. It just takes longer to find them. That's the reason for planning.

11. **Are you selling the advantages of working for your company?**

    In a job shortage, everyone applies and you have no difficulty finding suitable applicants. But will the best ones stay when things get better?

    Applicants need a "sales pitch" just as much as they need to make a good impression. Individuals on both sides should be on their best behavior. Explain how working in your company can benefit them. Discuss opportunities they might not have in other organizations. Explain the downside to make sure they understand the risks involved. If all of this is discussed during the hiring process, employees' understanding and commitment to the company will become apparent during crises and hard times.

"To understand everything makes one tolerant."

Madame de Staël

One caveat here is to make sure you're selling the *right* person. Don't get so caught up in the "wonderfulness" of your company that you lose track of whether the candidate is suited for the job. Also be careful not to imply that the opening is a "permanent" or "career" position.

MEMORANDUM

TO: All department managers

FROM: Alex Raski, Vice President

RE: Some thoughts on marketing the company to applicants

As we add a number of people to our organization over the next six months, I believe it is important to put our best foot forward. With regard to this, I have listed a few facts below to assist you in "selling" the applicants we want on coming to work for us.

Let's continue to build a great team!

- We are the "fastest growing" electronics firm in the region, according to *Daytona Business Journal* (April 6 issue).
- Our sales have increased a minimum of 30% every year for the past five.
- Our turnover rate among professionals is currently 4.5% (the lowest in the area for electronics firms, according to our research).
- With the current Titan package being approved by Congress, we estimate that the contract alone will be responsible for $3 million in income next fiscal year.
- Our assembly technicians rated supervisory personnel 4.7 on a scale of 5.0 for attention to concerns.
- We will be debuting a new product on the market in the next three months, which should significantly change production schedules of printed circuit boards.
- Our rejection rate on circuit assemblies is presently .6%, far below industry averages.

Just thought you'd like to know!

Marketing the Company to Applicants

Chapter 1   Hiring the Best Employees

12. Have you analyzed the sources of your applicants?

Are some more fruitful than others? Could some means of recruiting be eliminated and others increased in order to improve effectiveness? Are there sources from which you do not want applicants? It is always a good idea to start from the inside with referrals and proceed outward as the need warrants.

Recruiting Evaluation Worksheet

Position_____ Closing Date_____ Total # of Applicants_____

Targeted Applicant Groups: _____

_____

_____

	Expense	Resulting Applicants	Comments
In-House Posting:	_____	_____	_____
Employee Ref.:	_____	_____	_____
Classified Ads:	_____	_____	_____
Agency:	_____	_____	_____
Job Service:	_____	_____	_____
Other #1:	_____	_____	_____
Other #2:	_____	_____	_____

Recommendations:_____

Do you keep statistics on your best resources? Do you really know where your best applicants come from?

13. Do the right people do the hiring?

As organizations grow, the owners and executives sometimes retain crucial day-to-day duties that are best delegated. Too often the founder hangs on to the responsibility for all hiring, even though he may not be in touch with the actual needs of a particular function. It is best to relinquish the responsibility to someone more directly related to the vacant position, like an immediate supervisor, provided that person is skilled in hiring.

A president in one company of 250 employees insisted on reviewing all applicants, including receptionists and dock workers. When he was not consulted before an offer was made, he would rescind the offer. While no litigation was initiated, he succeeded in losing the respect of most everyone in the organization. His intent may have been sincere, but the result was discouraging.

You have to let go at some point. The key to a smooth transition is adequate training of all involved.

14. If you have delegated hiring tasks to others, have they been properly trained to handle the responsibility?

Too often, a supervisor is given permission to fill a vacant position but has little or no training to do so. This is where much litigation arises. Everyone with hiring power or influence should be properly trained for the task. The initial investment is outweighed by the savings in lost time, turnover and legal problems. Consider the employee selection training outline on page 14.

> *"He who has no faith in others shall find no faith in them."*
>
> Lao-Tzu

Chapter 1 Hiring the Best Employees

Employee Selection Training Session

September 1, 19XX
7:30-10:30 a.m.

OUTLINE

I. Employment Law
   A. Laws to be aware of
   B. What you can or cannot say or do
   C. Common pitfalls

II. Reviewing Resumes and Applications
   A. What to look for
   B. Common applicant "tricks"

III. How to Check References
   A. What to ask
   B. How to ask
   C. How to read a reference

BREAK

IV. Interviews
   A. What to ask
   B. What to look for
   C. Pointers to conducting an interview

V. Making the Decision
   A. What to evaluate
   B. How to compare

VI. Record-Keeping
   A. Records we must keep
   B. What you may ask after the person has been hired

15. **Have you checked on your competitors to discover their secrets of hiring?**

What are other organizations doing to ensure optimum hiring? There is usually an abundance of information available (such as this book) to gather ideas for improving your system. Check with trade associations, chambers of commerce and libraries for the latest information on salary data and related information.

> *"Wise men don't need advice. Fools don't take it."*
>
> Benjamin Franklin

Competitor Hiring Analysis Worksheet

Watch the local classified ads and gather competitive data on positions similar to the ones you manage. As your awareness of the competition expands, so will your confidence in what you offer applicants.

Yes No
- ❏ ❏ 1. Do you have a "clipping file" of competitors' job postings?
-       2. Have you "secret shopped" your competitors' ads?
- ❏ ❏   Do you know what they pay? Benefits?
- ❏ ❏   Do you know how long they take to respond?
- ❏ ❏   How do they handle rejections?
- ❏ ❏   Do you know what their correspondence says and looks like?
-       3. Have you compared job descriptions?
- ❏ ❏   Are they including/excluding key accountabilities?
- ❏ ❏   Do they have incentives/disincentives built into the job?
- ❏ ❏ 4. Are there modifications that should be made to your job offer based on what your competitors are offering?

16. **How "user friendly" is the overall hiring system? Could anyone understand it?**

There are many unwritten laws in most organizations about who has influence over what function. This type of authority should be clearly defined to ensure consistency and accuracy. Written procedures should be developed for all hiring, and these documents should be updated as needed.

This does not have to be a manual 3 feet thick. Investing the short amount of time it takes to prepare a document like this will eliminate hours of questions and possible lawsuits later.

> *Written procedures should be developed for all hiring — yet this does not have to be a manual 3 feet thick.*

II. Alternatives to Hiring

Hiring new employees may not always be the best way to go. More than one employer has experienced the frustration of recruiting new people only to let them go six months later when the business slowed down. An uptick in sales is not necessarily long term.

In addition, some organizations choose to staff their ranks with people contracted in a variety of ways. Such employees can be divided into four categories:
- Temporary employees
- Contracted managers and professionals
- Job shops
- Leased labor

Temporary employees

The traditional idea of a "temp" is one who fills in for the receptionist when that person is sick. This practice has radically changed and expanded over the past few years. Temporary help can be found in all departments within a company, performing all sorts of work.

Employing temporaries in place of full-timers offers several advantages:
- It provides the needed staff assistance without the burden of having to pay benefits.
- There are fewer layoffs involved, especially in seasonal businesses.
- It offers an opportunity to try out employees whose qualifications may be borderline for a full-time position.
- There is less of a personnel paper trail since the person is not working for you, but for the agency.
- Discipline problems can be resolved by asking that the temporary be replaced.
- Temporary individuals are already screened for necessary qualifications and experience.

The disadvantages of temporary workers can be lack of training, little investment in the organization, and a constant turnover, which can negatively influence morale. Costs must also be watched carefully, since a disorganized use of temporaries can be more expensive than hiring full-time staff.

> *"Behold the turtle; He only makes progress when he sticks his neck out."*
>
> James Bryant Conant

In addition to the listing of temporary services in the phone book, you might contact the local chapter of the National Association of Temporary Services (703-549-6287) or the Association of Part-Time Professionals (703-734-7975). Ask plenty of questions of these services. What to ask? Check the following table.

Selecting a Temporary Service

✔   Is it a member of the National Association of Temporary Services?

✔   Does it adhere to the NATS code of ethics?

✔   Does it have a formal policy on evaluating each temp's assignment?

✔   Does it provide temps with instruction on office equipment?

✔   Can it provide references from other clients?

✔   Does it check references and background on the people it provides?

✔   Does it have a professional staff that develops client relationships so they know your needs?

✔   Does it have a formal contract you can take away and have reviewed by an attorney?

✔   What are their policies for turning the temp into a permanent position?

Chapter 1 Hiring the Best Employees

Contracted managers and professionals

The concept of contracted managers and professionals has grown in popularity as organizations are increasingly cautious about hiring full-timers. Only in existence for the past few years, companies offering this service provide a professional who assumes a particular role within the organization for a defined period of time.

The contracting organization pays the agency and the agency pays the professional. This concept offers several advantages:
- These professionals can be contracted for a day, week, month or more.
- They generally have at least 10 years' experience in their field of expertise.
- They can be paid as contractors, eliminating costly paperwork.
- The agency brings qualified candidates to you, eliminating the search.
- The agency will, if asked, help coordinate the project or responsibilities.
- You retain supervisory control.
- This is a great way to "try before you buy" when hiring for critical positions.

How to find contract employees

Agencies handling contracted professionals are few in number at present, but starting in many cities. To locate them, you might check with the local chamber of commerce or with a chapter of the Society for Human Resource Management.

Another alternative is to consult local professional organizations in the relevant area of expertise. If they are not aware of a service like this, some members might be interested in making an arrangement on their own.

Contracted managers are a great way to "try before you buy" when hiring for critical positions.

"In the long run, men hit only what they aim at."

Henry David Thoreau

"From the highest to the humblest tasks, all are of equal honor; all have their part to play."

Winston Churchill

Determining Independent Contractor Status

There is a temptation among employers to classify certain individuals as independent contractors rather than employees. In the short run, this practice can appear to save on paperwork and payroll taxes. In the long run, however, it can cost back taxes, penalties and unwanted attention from the Internal Revenue Service.

The IRS examines the means and manner of the work rather than the results. In other words, if the worker acts like an employee, then he probably is an employee. This misclassification is commonly detected when the worker in question applies for unemployment after leaving the organization. When the worker is not found to be listed in the organization's employ, the state investigates.

The IRS has issued form SS-8 to assist in determining the status of workers performing a particular function. An abbreviated form of these 20 essential questions can be found below. In general, it is better to err on the side of treating the worker as an employee.

1. Is the individual providing services required to comply with instructions concerning when, where and how the work is to be done?
2. Is the individual provided with training to enable him to perform a job in a particular manner or method?
3. Are the services performed by the individual integrated into the business operations?
4. Must the services be rendered personally?
5. Does the business hire, supervise or pay assistants to help the individual performing services under the contract?
6. Is the relationship between the individual and the person for whom he performs services a continuing relationship?
7. Who sets the hours of work?
8. Is the person required to devote full time to the person for whom he performs services?
9. Does the individual perform work on another's business premises?
10. Who directs the order or sequence in which the work must be done?
11. Are regular oral or written reports required?
12. Is the method of payment hourly, weekly, commission or by the job?
13. Are business or travel expenses reimbursed?
14. Who furnishes tools and materials necessary for the provision of services?
15. Does the individual performing the services have a significant investment in facilities used to perform the services?
16. Can the individual providing services realize both a profit and loss?
17. Can the individual providing the services work for a number of firms at the same time?
18. Does the individual performing services make his services available to the general public?
19. Is the individual performing services subject to dismissal for reasons other than nonperformance or contract specifications?
20. Can the individual providing services terminate his relationship at any time without incurring a liability for failure to complete a job?

> *"Be not simply good, be good for something."*
>
> Henry David Thoreau

Job shops

Job shops are temporary help agencies that specialize in specific tasks. A good example of this would be so-called "letter shops," which handle direct mail for catalog distributors. Rather than hiring individuals to stuff and seal envelopes, the distributor contracts with a letter shop that handles the entire process. This eliminates the employer's recruiting, training and payroll processes.

In professional areas, job shops can provide everyone from accountants to systems analysts to engineers. These individuals serve on long- or short-term assignments.

For certain defined projects, this alternative may represent significant cost savings along with less time and effort.

Jobs shops are located in every city. To find them, look up the type of industry or service you need in the Yellow Pages. You might also check with trade or professional associations for recommendations and additional ideas on how to work with these agencies.

Employee leasing

Staff leasing is a relatively new concept. After you have contracted with a leasing company, your employees are discharged and hired by this firm and then leased back to your organization. Everyone retains his original position. You retain supervisory control, but the leasing company is now the employer. The leasing company issues paychecks, provides benefits and handles the necessary paperwork normally maintained by a personnel department. Hiring, firing and discipline are a joint effort.

A major advantage of leasing employees is better benefits and human resources management for your staff. Since a leasing firm may be handling thousands of employees, it can take advantage of large group insurance discounts to which a smaller organization does not have access.

The downside of this strategy is lack of continuity and loyalty. With their newfound relationship, employees may not stay in one company as long, moving from leasee to leasee. Additionally, pension legislation has complicated the process for employers using this service by adding special paperwork and compliance.

Since employee leasing is not widespread, the best way to locate this service is through the National Association of Professional Employer Organizations or the Society for Human Resource Management. Once again, ask plenty of questions before proceeding, since leasing employees will have a major impact on your staff relations.

> *The best way to find an employee leasing service is through the National Association of Professional Employer Organizations (703-524-3636) or the Society for Human Resource Management (1-800-283-7476).*

Where do we go from here?

The checklist should give you a working knowledge of the considerations necessary to conduct an effective employee selection program. The next chapter covers the myriad of laws and regulations surrounding employee selection. Be sure to examine this information thoroughly, since significant portions of it have changed in the past few years.

Chapter 1   Hiring the Best Employees

Questions for Personal Development

1. What is the major emphasis of this chapter?

2. What are the most important things you learned from this chapter?

3. How can you apply what you learned to your current job?

4. How will you go about making these changes?

5. How can you monitor improvement?

6. Summarize the changes you expect to see in yourself one year from now.

Chapter 2

The Legal Requirements of Hiring

"My client says he took one look around your company and realized that everybody was white," said the attorney. "He says he's perfect for the job and that you rejected him because he's Hispanic."

"That's not true!" insisted the owner. "We hire anybody who's qualified for the job."

"I hope you can prove that in court," retorted the lawyer.

> *In this litigious society, the need for a solid knowledge of employment law has become critical for large as well as small business managers.*

Here's What You'll Learn

I. What Laws Apply
II. Common Selection Issues
III. Negligent Hiring
IV. Enforcement and Record-Keeping
V. State Requirements
VI. A Checklist for Hiring Law

Twenty thousand dollars! That's how much the American Bar Association has estimated it costs in legal fees alone to defend a discrimination lawsuit that goes to trial.

In this litigious society, the need for a solid knowledge of employment law has become crucial for large as well as small business managers. In addition to the myriad of federal laws, each state maintains its own set of statutes.

Chapter 2   The Legal Requirements of Hiring

Federal and state labor laws have been enacted to protect those living in the United States from discrimination in hiring. There are currently over 400 federal laws pertaining to employee rights and selection. While it would be counterproductive to address each and every one in this chapter, the major laws and applications will be covered.

> *"The worst bankruptcy in the world is the person who has lost his enthusiasm."*
>
> H.W. Arnold

I. What Laws Apply

The Civil Rights Act of 1964 is the cornerstone of anti-discrimination legislation in the United States. Title VII of this act pertains to labor and employment. Its purpose is to require the removal of artificial, arbitrary and unnecessary barriers to employment when such impediments discriminate against individuals on the basis of race, sex or religious beliefs. Other related acts include the following:

- **The Pregnancy Discrimination Act of 1978** amended Title VII to prohibit discrimination on the basis of childbirth, pregnancy or related medical conditions.
- **The Age Discrimination in Employment Act** (as amended in 1978) prohibits discrimination in hiring of individuals age 40 and older.
- **The Rehabilitation Act of 1973** prohibits job discrimination against otherwise qualified individuals with handicaps. This statute applies to all employers that have federal contracts in excess of $2,500 or that receive financial assistance from the federal government.
- **The Immigration Reform and Control Act of 1986** prohibits the employment of illegal aliens, except under certain specified conditions.
- **The Fair Labor Standards Act**, as amended by the Equal Pay Act, sets minimum wages as well as overtime and equal pay standards.
- **The Polygraph Protection Act of 1988** prohibits the use of polygraphs and voice print devices with certain exceptions.
- **The Americans with Disabilities Act of 1990** prohibits discrimination against qualified individuals with disabilities in employment, public services, transportation, public accommodation and telecommunications.

> *"Any man who has had the job I've had and didn't have a sense of humor wouldn't still be here."*
>
> Harry S. Truman

Who's affected

Title VII and the Americans with Disabilities Act apply to all private employers, state and local governments, educational institutions and labor organizations that have 20 or more employees. Those individuals must have been employed for each working day in each of 20 or more calendar weeks in the current or preceding calendar year. These same parameters apply to the Age Discrimination in Employment Act and the Pregnancy Discrimination Act of 1978.

The exception to these guidelines is the Immigration Reform and Control Act (IRCA). Under this legislation, all newly hired employees are required to show proof of their eligibility to work in the United States within the first three days of employment. Unlike Title VII and other antidiscrimination laws, IRCA includes all employers. If you hire a housekeeper, for example, that person must show proof of eligibility to work in the United States.

In addition to the federal government, many states have passed laws governing employment that parallel federal legislation. Since state laws are often broader, more comprehensive and more stringent than federal statutes, it is paramount that those performing the hiring function be familiar with them. The most stringent law, whether federal, state or local, is the one that applies. (A discussion of state hiring laws can be found at the end of this chapter.)

Enforcing agencies

The Equal Employment Opportunity Commission (EEOC) was created to enforce Title VII of the Civil Rights Act of 1964. In addition, it currently enforces the Pregnancy Discrimination Act, the Age Discrimination in Employment Act, the Equal Pay Act and the Americans with Disabilities Act.

The commission consists of five members who are appointed by the President with the advice and consent of the United States Senate. The EEOC has established district offices throughout the nation and collects and publishes data on discriminatory practices in addition to investigating violations of employees' civil rights.

The Rehabilitation Act of 1973 is enforced by the Office of Federal Contract Compliance Programs and each federal agency. The Immigration Reform and Control Act is enforced by the Immigration and Naturalization Service, although the law is written so that employers are each responsible for enforcement within their own companies.

> *"I believe every person has a heart, and if you can reach it, you can make a difference."*
>
> Uli Derikson

Chapter 2 The Legal Requirements of Hiring

> *Bona fide occupational qualifications have been narrowly interpreted by the courts and are a rare form of defense in a discrimination suit.*

Selection guidelines

To assist employers in abiding by the federal antidiscrimination laws, the Equal Employment Opportunity Commission developed the *Uniform Guidelines for Employee Selection Procedures* in 1978. The purpose of these guidelines is to help those hiring employees to interpret the federal statutes. It is not the questions asked by an employer that are unlawful. It is what the employer might do with the answers that comes into question.

It is perfectly acceptable, for example, to ask a question like "That's an interesting accent. Where did you grow up?" However, the employer must realize that the question infers that the applicant's nationality is of concern in the hiring process. Unless there is job-related reason, this question could lead to charges of discrimination. Even if there is a legitimate reason, such as a U.S. Defense Department requirement, the correct question is "Are you a U.S. citizen?"

Bona fide occupational qualifications

In certain instances, an employer will have a legitimate reason for setting standards that restrict the hiring of particular groups. A warehouse job, for example, may require workers to be able to lift 75 pounds. This may appear outwardly discriminatory toward women or individuals with certain physical disabilities. If this requirement can be demonstrated to be a "business necessity," however, it will be considered a bona fide occupational qualification (BFOQ). BFOQs have been narrowly interpreted by the courts and are a rare form of defense in a discrimination suit.

> *"I am not young enough to know everything."*
>
> J.M. Barrie

The best advice concerning exceptions to the antidiscrimination laws is to assume there are no exceptions. Approach each hiring requirement as if all individuals are eligible, regardless of age, sex, race, religion, national origin, disability and marital status.

Adverse impact

Under Title VII of the Civil Rights Act of 1964, an employer's hiring practices become illegal when the company operates to the disadvantage of certain protected classes of individuals. While the employment practices may be neutral in appearance and intent, the company's hiring practices must reflect the characteristics of the surrounding community.

A number of variables enter into this equation, such as the ratios of existing employees within the organization and the population of certain protected classes within the surrounding community. It is best to keep accurate records of hiring patterns, no matter what your company's size is.

Hand-Picked: The Complete Guide to Finding and Hiring the Best Employees

Standard Form 100
(Rev. 12/81)
O.M.B. No. 124-R0011
Approval
100-210

EQUAL EMPLOYMENT OPPORTUNITY
EMPLOYER INFORMATION REPORT EEO-1

Joint Reporting Committee
- Equal Employment Opportunity Commission
- Office of Federal Contract Compliance Program

SAMPLE

Section A — TYPE OF REPORT
Refer to instructions for number and types of report to be filed.

1. Indicate by marking in the appropriate box the type of reporting unit for which this copy of the form is submitted (MARK ONLY ONE BOX).

   (1) ☐ Single-establishment Employer Report

   Multi-establishment Employer
   (2) ☐ Consolidated Report
   (3) ☐ Headquarters Unit Report
   (4) ☐ Individual Establishment Report (submit one for each establishment with 25 or more employees)
   (5) ☐ Special Report

2. Total number of reports being filed by this Company (Answer on Consolidated Report only)_____

Section B — COMPANY IDENTIFICATION (*To be answered by all employers*)

OFFICE USE ONLY

1. Parent Company
   a. Name of parent company (owns or controls establishment in item 2) omit if same as label

   a.

   Name of receiving office | Address (Number and street)

   b.

   City or town | County | State | ZIP code
   b. Employer Identification No.

2. Establishment for which this report is filed (Omit if same as label)
   a. Name of establishment

   c.

   Address (Number and street) | City or town | County | State | ZIP code

   d.

   b. Employer Identification No. | | | | | | | (If same as label, skip.)

3. Parent company affiliation (Multi-establishment Employers Answer on Consolidated Report only)
   a. Name of parent-affiliated company | b. Employer Identification No.

   Address (Number and street) | City or town | County | State | ZIP code

Section C — EMPLOYERS WHO ARE REQUIRED TO FILE (*To be answered by all employers*)

☐ Yes ☐ No 1. Does the entire company have at least 100 employees in the payroll period for which you are reporting?

☐ Yes ☐ No 2. Is your company affiliated through common ownership and/or centralized management with other entities in an enterprise with a total employment of 100 or more?

☐ Yes ☐ No 3. Does the company or any of its establishments (a) have 50 or more employees AND (b) is not exempt as provided by 41 CFR 50-1 5. AND either (1) is a prime government contractor or first-tier subcontractor, and has a contract, subcontract, or purchase order amounting to $50,000 or more, or (2) served as a depository of Government funds in any amount or is a financial institution which is an issuing and paying agent for U.S. Savings Bonds and Savings Notes?

NOTE. If the answer is yes to ANY of these questions, complete the entire form; otherwise skip to Section G.

Sample EEO-1 Form

Chapter 2 The Legal Requirements of Hiring

Affirmative action requirements

If a company is found to be in violation of Title VII statutes by the EEOC or courts, it may be required to establish an affirmative action plan to integrate its workforce. This action may *require* the employer to hire applicants from protected classes, and to recruit them if insufficient numbers apply.

Employers working under federal contract rules have even more stringent requirements. Under Presidential Executive Orders 11246 and 11375, all employers with more than $50,000 in federal contracts and 50 or more employees are required to establish affirmative action plans regardless of whether they have been forced to do so because of adverse impact. The Executive Orders take precedence over Title VII legislation.

In addition, employers with more than $10,000 in federal contracts are required to establish an affirmative action program for qualified Vietnam-era veterans under the Vietnam-Era Veterans Readjustment Assistance Act of 1974. Failure to do so can result in loss of eligibility for federal contracts.

Key Components of Affirmative Action

An employer is not required to establish an affirmative action plan unless it has shown discrimination in the past. (The exceptions to this are federal contractors with $50,000 in federal work and more than 50 employees.)

There must be a clear assignment of direction for the program.

The plan must contain clearly stated procedures.

The plan must contain a clearly stated equal opportunity policy.

The plan must contain specific goals and timetables for hiring protected groups who are underrepresented.

II. Common Selection Issues

Job relatedness is the key determinant in deciding whether a particular requirement can be considered a hiring condition. Job requirements that have a disparate impact on certain protected classes are prohibited by the federal government and most states. Some of the more common job requirements and their allowability are listed below:

Accents: Candidates may be excluded from a position if that position requires substantial communication with customers and/or employees and the person's accent is found to be so strong that it would impair that person's performance.

Age: Employment discrimination due to age is prohibited under the Age Discrimination in Employment Act of 1967 (as amended in 1978) except in situations where there is a bona fide occupational qualification. Other statutory exceptions, such as the positions of airline pilot and senior corporate executive, are also made.

> *"I am a citizen not of Athens or Greece, but of the world."*
>
> Socrates

Employment of aliens: The Immigration Reform and Control Act along with many state statutes prohibits the hiring of aliens unless they have obtained permission to work in the United States. It is now an employer's legal responsibility to check an employee's working status within three days of hire.

Alienage: It is unlawful, according to Title VII, to require citizenship as a standard for hire if the result is discrimination against individuals on the basis of national origin. The major reasons for requiring citizenship usually center around national security.

> *An employer may set standards of dress if these are substantially related to the employer's needs.*

Appearance and dress: An employer may not reject an applicant for employment on the basis of appearance and dress if that appearance and dress is typical of the applicant's culture. However, an employer may set standards of dress if these are substantially related to the employer's needs. Common reasons for this would be safety and commonly accepted social norms. Some locales have passed ordinances prohibiting discrimination because of personal appearance, especially related to religious custom.

Chapter 2   The Legal Requirements of Hiring

Arrest and criminal records: The EEOC prohibits the requirement that applicants have no previous arrest record. It is also unlawful to reject an applicant on the basis of conviction of a crime unless that crime was substantially related to job responsibilities. An applicant who has been convicted of embezzlement, for example, could be refused a job as a bookkeeper.

An employer can also ask about pending indictments since the answer can be relevant to job performance. One of these factors would be crimes related to the job, such as an indictment for embezzlement in a cashier's position, or a charge of theft for a warehouse supervisor. Another factor would be the length of time the person may need to pursue her defense.

Blacklisting: It is unlawful, in most states, to maintain a "blacklist" of applicants for any reason.

Credit: It is against EEOC guidelines to require a good credit rating as a condition of employment unless the employer can demonstrate business necessity. This is a reasonable qualification, for example, in the hiring of a credit manager or cashier.

Dependents' status: Employers are prohibited from rejecting a female applicant because she has children of preschool age when no such requirement exists for male applicants. Nor can she be refused because she is an unwed mother, since this condition has no relation to business necessity.

Disabilities: Employers are subject to the Rehabilitation Act of 1973 if they receive grants from the federal government or have federal contracts in excess of $2,500 annually. Under this Act, an employer is required to provide reasonable accommodation to applicants with disabilities. This may include wheelchair access, removal of architectural barriers, adjustments of furniture and equipment, and special aids for telephones.

As of July 26, 1994, employers with 15 or more employees are subject to the Americans with Disabilities Act of 1990 (ADA). ADA requirements mirror those of the Rehabilitation Act.

The courts have held that handicaps are not limted to physical disabilities. They may also include obesity, suicidal tendencies, borderline personality, posttraumatic stress syndrome, diabetes and allergies to tobacco smoke. Alcoholics and drug addicts are also considered handicapped unless their condition currently prevents them from performing a job adequately. Thirty states have also decided that AIDS is a physical handicap entitled to protection.

Education: An employer may use education as a requirement only to the extent that the education can be demonstrated to be a business necessity. A high school diploma, for example, cannot be used as a condition of employment unless it can be shown that the skills provided in a high school education are substantially related to job duties.

Fingerprinting: Fingerprinting of employees is generally accepted in all states with the exception of New York, where authority to do so is limited.

Hair: It is generally considered a violation of Title VII to have a hair requirement that differs from men to women. However it has not been a major issue in the courts as long as there has been no disparate impact on either sex.

Health: An applicant may be refused employment if he fails a physical examination as long as the requirements in the exam demonstrate that the applicant would not be able to perform on the job. For example, an employer can reject an applicant for an electronics assembly position who fails a coordination test.

Height/weight: Applicants protected by Title VII can be refused employment on the basis of a height or weight requirement provided the employer demonstrates job relatedness. An applicant who is 6'5" tall, for example, may be refused a flight attendant position due to safety restrictions.

Language: Proficiency in English may not be required as a condition for employment under Title VII due to disparate impact unless the employer can demonstrate business necessity. A retail clerk, for example, can be required to be proficient in English.

> *"Many strokes overthrow the tallest oaks."*
> John Lyly

> *"The average person thinks he isn't."*
> Father Larry Lorenzini

> *"Most of our future lies ahead."*
> Yogi

> *"One man that has a mind and knows it can always beat 10 men who haven't and don't."*
> George Bernard Shaw

> *Employers must make reasonable accommodation for applicants' religious convictions.*

Marital status: An employer may not have a policy prohibiting the hiring of married women unless this same policy prohibits the hiring of married men.

Military record: Unless the employer can demonstrate that the decision was related to job performance, an applicant may not be rejected on the basis of having received a less-than-honorable discharge from the military.

National origin: Unless a bona fide occupational qualification has been established, an applicant may not be rejected on the basis of national origin.

Nepotism: An employer's policy of prohibiting nepotism may be in violation of Title VII if it has a disparate impact on a protected class. In a small town, for example, a company's prohibition on nepotism may have a disparate impact on women due to the number of jobs available in the community. This same adverse impact might exist in a community with a large minority population.

Polygraph/lie detector: As of January 1, 1989, private sector employers are prohibited from using polygraphs, voice print devices and other related technologies in the selection of employees. The three major exceptions to this law are certain defense, security or pharmaceutically related jobs. (See Chapter Ten for a full discussion.)

Pregnancy: The Pregnancy Discrimination Act of 1978 (Title VII) prohibits discrimination against women affected by pregnancy, childbirth and related medical conditions.

Recruitment: There are no specific prohibitions concerning the recruitment of certain applicants. However, an employer who grants preferential treatment to friends and relatives may be in violation of Title VII guidelines if one or more protected classes are underrepresented in the firm. This also holds true for referrals from other company employees.

Religious conviction: Employers must make reasonable accommodation for applicants' religious convictions and may not reject them on that basis unless it would create undue hardship on the employer's business. An applicant should not suffer in being considered for a job, for example, because she asks that an interview be moved due to the observance of a religious holiday.

Sex: An employer may not limit a job to "females only" or "males only" unless a bona fide occupational qualification is evident. An example of this might be the role of a male or female character in a theatrical production.

No-spouse: It is lawful to have a rule prohibiting the hiring of a spouse as long as the rule is neutral. In other words, if the wife of a male employee cannot be hired, the husband of a female employee cannot be hired.

Strength: An employer can require that applicants pass a strength test provided the requirement is a business necessity. A stocking position in a warehouse, for example, could have a lawful strength requirement if the employer can demonstrate its legitimacy.

> *An employer can require that applicants pass a strength test provided the requirement is a business necessity.*

Testing (aptitude/psychological): The requirement that applicants submit to aptitude or psychological testing is unlawful unless the employer can demonstrate relatedness to job performance. In all cases, the tests must be validated and approved by the EEOC. In addition, they must not have an unequal impact on protected classes. (See Chapter Ten for additional information.)

Testing (drug): There are several debates revolving around the legal use of preemployment drug testing. These include accuracy, invasion of privacy and relatedness to job performance. It is best to tread lightly in this area. (A full discussion of this topic can be found in Chapter Ten.)

> *"I probably can't play for me. I wouldn't like my attitude."*
>
> John Thompson,
> Georgetown University

Work experience: An employer may require previous work experience provided that relatedness and business necessity can be demonstrated. The amount required must be reasonable according to the job duties. For example, a grocery cashier's position requiring two years' experience is unreasonable.

Chapter 2   The Legal Requirements of Hiring

III. Negligent Hiring

A new concern for employers is the expanding concept of negligent hiring. Under this theory, employers who know or should have known that an employee is unfit for a position may be liable for the employee's criminal or devious behavior. Negligent hiring is now recognized a "cause of action" in more than 30 states.

Generally, an employer has a duty to exercise reasonable care when hiring employees who, if incompetent or unreliable, might cause a risk of injury to the public or fellow employees by reason of their employment. Examples of this theory have been illustrated by court cases such as an employee who used a passkey to enter an apartment and attack a tenant and a taxi driver who raped a rider in his cab.

A plaintiff has to prove three things in negligent hiring cases:

(1) The employee who caused the injury was unfit for hiring or retention

(2) The employer's hiring or retention of the unfit employee was the cause of the plaintiff's injuries and

(3) The employer knew, or should have known, about the unfitness.

> *"I never forget a face, but in your case I'll be glad to make an exception."*
>
> Groucho Marx

> *An employer has a duty to exercise reasonable care when hiring employees who, if competent or unreliable, might cause a risk of injury to the public.*

How to avoid negligent hiring

To protect against negligent hiring, several steps should be applied in screening candidates. These steps include:

- ✔ Review applicable federal, state and local laws to ensure your process conforms to all such laws.

- ✔ Comply with federal, state and local fair credit reporting laws if a credit check is conducted.

- ✔ Look for gaps in employment and suspicious or unusual entries in candidates' applications.

- ✔ Call each reference listed on the application.

- ✔ Obtain a signed waiver and consent form from each applicant to conduct a full reference check.

- ✔ Document all information received, including licenses, diplomas and certificates, as well as efforts to obtain this information if it was not available.

- ✔ Require all employees who have served in the armed forces to provide a copy of their DD-214 stating they were discharged honorably.

- ✔ Decide whether it is appropriate to conduct a criminal records search in view of the job being filled.

- ✔ Carefully review the background and experience of applicants for jobs that involve public safety and operation of motor vehicles, aircraft, trains and the like.

- ✔ Do not offer employment until screening and testing has been completed.

- ✔ If appropriate, require a physical examination of the applicant. Make sure the applicant consents to the examination.

- ✔ Even if an employee is transferring within the organization, reexamine her fitness for the new position.

IV. Enforcement and Record-Keeping

The federal government has detailed specific procedures and remedies for failure to comply with the guidelines for antidiscrimination under Title VII, the Pregnancy Discrimination Act, the Age Discrimination in Employment Act, the Rehabilitation Act and the Immigration Reform and Control Act. The Equal Employment Opportunity Commission is responsible for enforcement of all except IRCA.

Procedures

If an applicant feels she has been the victim of discrimination in a company's hiring process, that person may choose to file a complaint with the Equal Employment Opportunity Commission along with state and local authorities. A claimant has 180 days from the day of the action to file a complaint with the EEOC. If the state or locale in which the discrimination allegedly took place has its own antidiscrimination laws, then federal guidelines allow a filing time of 300 days. This extension is allowed to give the state or locale ample time to act on the complaint.

After the investigation has been completed, the commission will issue a determination that either no discrimination took place or that discrimination did take place. If the commission finds that no discrimination took place, it will issue a "right-to-sue" notice to the claimant, explaining that the claimant may still pursue the matter in district court.

If discrimination is found, both parties will be invited by the commission to join in a conciliation process. An EEOC conciliator will attempt to get the two parties to come to an agreement regarding the alleged discrimination. If the respondent (company) refuses to enter into conciliation or the parties fail to come to an agreement, the EEOC will terminate the proceedings and issue another "right-to-sue" notice to the claimant.

Under certain circumstances, the EEOC itself may bring suits against companies it feels are engaged in a pattern of discrimination. It may also enforce the Title VII conciliation agreement in district court if it believes the respondent is not performing.

If discrimination is found, both parties will be invited by the EEOC to join in a conciliation process.

"I don't make jokes. I just watch the government and report the facts."

Will Rogers

Remedies

The remedies for Title VII judgments are varied and depend upon the severity of discrimination. A main determinant is the employer's intention at the time the act took place.

When the action is blatant, as in a rule such as "no women need apply," the remedies are apt to be severe. In a situation where the employer is guilty of disparate treatment, the remedies may be less severe. Disparate treatment can be described as discrimination as the result of neutral hiring rules. If, for example, an employer has been advertising for laborers and the requirements listed could be construed as male when a female could perform the job, then discrimination may result.

Once an employer has been found liable of discrimination, a number of reliefs may be made to the plaintiff. These include the hiring of individuals who have successfully sued for discrimination, allotment of back pay with interest, attorneys' fees, health and disability benefits, and retroactive seniority and pension benefits. Employers may also be required to locate past victims of bias. In some cases, hiring goals and ratios are established to make up for past inequities.

Defenses to Title VII and the Age Discrimination Act

There are several typical defenses that employers can use for Title VII claims. The most prevalent of these is *business necessity*. In this situation, the court will look at legitimate business purpose and whether there is truly no alternative policy or practice.

A second defense is a jurisdictional defect in the plaintiff's claim. The most common of these is failure to file within the prescribed period (180 days).

A third is a bona fide occupational qualification. The courts have severely limited these defenses.

Other defenses include seniority systems, testing that demonstrates the employer's reasoning for action, and reasonable accommodation in which the employer made an attempt to address the applicant's situation.

Typical defenses to age discrimination are legitimate seniority systems, bona fide occupational qualifications, and rejection on the basis of other factors not involving age.

The most prevalent defense for a Title VII claim is business necessity.

"In life, as in a football game, the principle to follow is: Hit the line hard."

Theodore Roosevelt

Classifying Exempt and Nonexempt Employees
Fair Labor Standards Act — 1936

Exempt employees are determined by two factors:
1. Duties and responsibilities
2. Salary paid

Each person must meet all of the criteria in their category below:

	Executive	Administrative	Professional	Outside Sales
Primary Duties	Manager of the enterprise or a subsidiary. Customarily supervises at least two. Authority to hire/fire.	Nonmanual work directly related to policy-making and operations. Duties related to education or training. Customarily exercises independent judgment and authority.	Specialized knowledge requiring instruction, or original and creative work in an artistic field, or certified or recognized instructor. Customarily exercises discretion and judgment.	Customarily works away from place of business selling or taking orders.
Time Requirement	20% of time can be spent on nonmanagerial duties, 40% in service or retail.	20% of time can be spent on nonmanagerial duties, 40% in service or retail.	20% of time can be spent on nonprofessional duties.	20% of time can be spent doing work normally performed by nonexempt employees.
Salary Requirement	Minimum of $155/wk other than room and board. At $250/wk, 20% rule changes to majority of time must be spent on management.	Minimum of $155/wk other than room and board. At $250/wk, 20% rule changes to majority of time must be spent on administrative duties.	At least $170/wk other than room and board. At $250/wk, 20% rule changes to majority of time must be spent on professional duties.	NONE

The Equal Pay Act of 1963

Although the Equal Pay Act of 1963 does not apply to hiring practices per se, *all employers* should make sure their compensation policies treat all employees equally. A violation of this act may be triggered by the hiring of a new employee with compensation inequitable to others who are doing comparable work with comparable experience.

The Fair Labor Standards Act exempts employees from hourly pay regulations provided they meet certain requirements concerning duties, responsibilities and salary paid.

Record-Keeping

The Equal Employment Opportunity Commission requires all employers falling under the jurisdiction of Title VII to preserve employment records for a period of six months. This includes application forms and all other data relating to the hiring process. This six-month period begins on the day the record was made and/or the personnel action was taken.

Employment records relevant to any charge of discrimination must be kept until the disposition of the complaint or litigation.

Record-keeping that pertains to the Age Discrimination in Employment Act requires employers to preserve all materials relating to the hiring process for one year from the date of action or record being made. The Equal Pay Act requires all employers to maintain and preserve wage and compensation records for two years. *The bottom line is that employment records should be kept for one year and compensation records should be kept for two.*

To ease your understanding of these laws, a matrix detailing the requirements can be found in Appendix B.

> *"Justice often satisfies neither side."*
> Richard M. Nixon

V. State Requirements

State laws regarding equal employment are generally broader in scope than federal statutes. With the exception of Alabama, all states now have laws protecting certain classes of individuals in the employment process. Employers must comply with all state and federal laws affecting their locale.

It is critical for employers to be aware of all state employment laws that affect the hiring process. While the federal government, for instance, does not enforce Title VII until an employer has reached 15 employees, individual state laws may be triggered with

> *"No problem can stand the assault of sustained thinking."*
> Voltaire

Chapter 2 The Legal Requirements of Hiring

In an Ohio Study, 73 percent of 94 applications collected were found to contain at least one illegal pre-employment inquiry.

a lesser number. In fact, laws in 13 states and the District of Columbia provide that employers are subject to the state's statutes if they employ one or more persons. Other states require compliance from employers that employ two or more to 25 or more.

Some local ordinances provide additional protection to certain individuals. These generally include homosexuals, people with disabilities and those with Acquired Immune Deficiency Syndrome (AIDS). Check with your attorney to be sure you are within the local laws.

Be aware of more restrictive rules in recruiting, interviewing, testing and use of applications. In an Ohio study, 94 applications were collected for analysis. Seventy-three percent were found to contain at least one illegal preemployment inquiry according to state law.

Although all complaints must be filed with the Equal Employment Opportunity Commission in addition to the state agency, EEOC defers investigation to the state for 60 days. After that time, its jurisdiction to investigate returns unless the state agency has begun an investigation. In that case, the EEOC will wait for the outcome of that inquiry.

The states follow procedures that parallel those of the federal agency. In fact, the EEOC has a written agreement with each state concerning these practices.

While the state laws can vary, there are several excellent references available to assist you in understanding your company's obligations. These can be found in Appendix E.

Do You Know the Numbers?

	Address	Phone
• Civil Rights Commission	_____	_____
• Wage and Labor Office	_____	_____
• Dept. of Immigration & Naturalization	_____	_____
• State Dept. of EEOC	_____	_____
• Federal Dept. of EEOC	_____	_____
• Office of Mediation and Conciliation	_____	_____

A Checklist for Hiring Law

☐ 1. Have you developed a strong working knowledge of:

    Title VII of the Civil Rights Act of 1964
    Age Discrimination in Employment Act
    Equal Pay Act (pertaining to hiring)
    Pregnancy Discrimination Act of 1978
    Rehabilitation Act of 1973

☐ 2. Can you explain affirmative action and adverse impact?

☐ 3. Can you explain a bona fide occupational qualification?

☐ 4. Have you developed a working knowledge of the applicable employment laws in all states in which your company operates?

☐ 5. Can you explain the laws and decisions regarding the job relatedness of the following:

☐ Education	☐ No-spouse requirement
☐ Health requirements	☐ Language requirement
☐ Strength requirement	☐ Dependents' status
☐ Height/weight requirement	☐ Marital status
☐ Work experience	☐ Sex status
☐ Appearance and dress	☐ Pregnancy
☐ Hair requirement	☐ National origin
☐ Credit requirement	☐ Religious convictions
☐ Arrest and criminal records	☐ Disabilities
☐ Alienage	☐ Age requirements
☐ Military record	☐ Nepotism

Chapter 2 The Legal Requirements of Hiring

Questions for Personal Development

1. What is the major emphasis of this chapter?

2. What are the most important things you learned from this chapter?

3. How can you apply what you learned to your current job?

4. How will you go about making these changes?

5. How can you monitor improvement?

6. Summarize the changes you expect to see in yourself one year from now.

CHAPTER 3

Job Descriptions and Compensation

Writing job descriptions can be tedious, yet it provides an excellent opportunity to define the exact requirements for each job.

The applicant asked for a written job description. "We don't have it written down," responded the owner, "but let me tell you what the person does." "Are you telling me what the person does or what they're supposed to do?" she asked. "Jobs evolve," said the owner. "All I can give you is a rough sketch." "So you really don't know what you're hiring for," the applicant said.

Here's What You'll Learn

I. Importance of Job Descriptions
II. Job Analysis and Audit
III. Writing Job Descriptions
IV. Determining Compensation
V. A Checklist for Job Descriptions and Compensation

I. Importance of Job Descriptions

Most Americans have never seen a written description for their job. The average company cannot provide written job descriptions for all existing positions.

Chapter 3   Job Descriptions and Compensation

> *"The quality of a person's life is in direct proportion to their commitment to excellence, regardless of their chosen field of endeavor."*
>
> Vince Lombardi

The task of analyzing jobs and writing descriptions can be tedious. Yet it provides an excellent opportunity to define the exact requirements for each job. As a small company grows, positions may be added without much thought to the design of duties. This evolution tends to be haphazard and disorganized. Therefore, when a position needs to be filled, no one seems to know *exactly* what the incumbent did.

A job description provides definition and focus. Parameters within which the person will work are identified. It describes day-to-day responsibilities, levels of authority and the person to whom the new employee reports.

A job description can be used in a variety of ways. For the purposes of hiring, it:

1. Assists in explaining the job to applicants.

2. Serves as a basis for writing job postings and developing a list of criteria for a successful candidate to meet.

After the person has been hired, it:

1. Gives the new employee a direction and basis from which to start.

2. Serves as a tool in the measurement of performance.

Some people view a job description as limiting. It may hinder their creativity by setting defined boundaries. Those holding the position might be hesitant to step beyond its scope. Employees with brilliant ideas, for instance, may bury them because they believe they will be told to stick to the job at hand.

Consider the position of office manager. While the duties may be straightforward, you also want to encourage this individual to use creativity in solving daily problems. Outlining too many job specifications will work against you.

On the other hand, it is hard to get some workers to do the job assigned, let alone granting authority to wander. A balance has to be developed between defining the job and welcoming creativity. Encouraging a dock foreman to think creatively while loading trucks may end in more bureaucracy than productivity.

Do you need the job?

1. What is the purpose of this new job?
2. Who is presently performing these tasks?
3. How long have the employees who presently perform these tasks been overloaded?
4. Is this added business the result of a cycle or is the pace more permanent?
5. What will be the initial goals of this position and how long will it take to accomplish them?
6. What is the best that can happen if we fill this position with a good person?
7. Is there enough work for a full-time position? Can it be performed by a part-time employee?
8. Can some of the overload duties be switched to another area within the same department or location?
9. Is this a true need or can the systems in this function be streamlined for better productivity?
10. How much will this new position cost?
11. Is there a sufficient labor market to choose from?
12. Will this position exist 24 months from now?
13. Have you checked with all the parties involved to determine if everyone feels there is a need?
14. How will other departments view the addition of this new position? (They may feel their need is just as important.)
15. What impact will the creation of this new position have on the jobs from which the tasks are being removed?
16. What is the worst that can happen if we don't create this position?

Chapter 3 Job Descriptions and Compensation

In some cases, job descriptions are being enhanced by videotapes of employees at work to show applicants what jobs are really like. Current employees are taped at work and asked to talk about their day-to-day duties and responsibilities, the most rewarding and stressful aspects of their jobs and why they like working for the organization. These videos are featured at job fairs and other recruiting events.

A final consideration is potential litigation. While there are no specific legal requirements for having these documents, organizations unable to produce descriptions of jobs in question face an uphill battle in wrongful discharge and discrimination suits.

Do you need the job?

Before proceeding with the development of a job description, determine whether the position is actually necessary. In the rush of newfound business or expansion, it is easy to imagine the need for a new person to assume some of the responsibility. On the other hand, this same person may be unnecessary six months hence when business slows. While the work may overload existing employees for the moment, be careful not to create a new position that will have to be eliminated later. Consider the questions on the previous page.

Once you have decided there is justification for creating this position, the next step is to analyze the actual needs and functions.

II. Job Analysis and Audit

Before a job description can be developed, an analysis of the position, existing or proposed, must be conducted. While this can be involved, it does not have to be. The key is to ask the right questions. All job audits should answer the eight questions on page 48.

Audits should be performed for existing jobs in addition to those newly created. Turnover is an unpredictable creature. The occupied position today may be the vacancy of tomorrow.

Clear communication is essential while conducting a job audit. Any time someone starts "inspecting" jobs, rumors abound, even in a small company. A short memo or mention at a staff meeting should quell concern.

> *"Man is still the most extraordinary computer of all."*
>
> John F. Kennedy

MEMORANDUM

To: All Staff

From: Bill Bradley, Production Manager

Subject: Job Audit Plan

Have you noticed that things have changed around here?

In order to staff our department appropriately and hire the best people, we will be conducting a production inquiry to best determine our output compared with customer demands.

We will also be reviewing each job description to ensure that what you are doing daily matches what is written.

Please rest assured, this is designed to make us more effective and profitable. You are not being appraised or personally assessed.

Once we have a clear picture of what we do and what we are doing, we will staff accordingly. Please keep your eyes open for new job postings.

Chapter 3 Job Descriptions and Compensation

Job Audit Questions

1. What duties does the person perform to complete the job? (Be specific in description.)

2. What tools, services and/or accommodations does the person need to complete these duties?

3. Who supervises the person in this position?

4. With which other people does this person interact, both in and out of the organization?

5. Is the person performing the job able to complete all duties in the time allotted?

6. What formal training does a person need to perform this job, if any?

7. What skills does the person need to complete this job? (Include technical, interpersonal, organizational and problem-solving skills.)

8. How is the person performing this job evaluated?

Existing jobs

To properly audit an existing job, you must first develop a questionnaire covering the general categories of work. It might be designed in the manner of the example on the following page.

Anyone can perform the analysis, although it is not a good idea to have the present jobholder do so. This person may tend to exaggerate the responsibilities. It is better to have an objective staff member interview the jobholder and record the information.

The descriptions in an audit should be specific and measured. A duty such as "takes care of all the inventory paperwork" is not acceptable. A better way of relating the same thing might be:

"Is responsible for the completion of all paperwork on incoming inventory. This includes, but is not limited to, checking manifests against actual counts, recording and assigning storage for all incoming freight and maintaining accurate control over all internal distribution of inventory. This responsibility entails 60 percent of average weekly time."

While the second description is more involved, it is also more accurate and gives the readers a realistic picture of what the job entails. Since responsibilities change on a constant basis, it is best to reassess all job descriptions on a periodic basis.

A completed job audit form can be found on page 51. Note the informality and easy-to-read descriptions.

New jobs

While it is impossible to determine the actual duties in a newly created job, you can usually make an accurate estimation. The same questions asked about an existing job need to be asked in this case.

The analysis is best performed by the person who will supervise the position. It may then be reviewed by others for modifications and corrections. Before proceeding, ask whether the job is "do-able." While the amount of time necessary to complete the new job cannot be thoroughly determined, one should be careful not to overload the job, especially if the company is expanding at a rapid pace.

It is better to begin the job with duties that will not fill the time alloted than to overload a new employee. Otherwise, it will result in high turnover. Other duties may be added to a new job as the person becomes acclimated. The illustration on page 51 provides an example of what the completed form may look like.

The descriptions in an audit should be specific and measured.

"In America, anyone can become president. That's one of the risks you take."

Adlai Stevenson

Job Audit

Audit conducted by _____ Date _____

Job title _____

Major duties:

Minor duties:

Is supervised by (state relation):

Number of employees supervised (state relation):

Training required:

Education required:

Certificates/licenses required:

Experience required (identify specific skills):

Physical requirements:

On-the-job hazards/working conditions:

Source of job audit information:

Job Audit

Audit conducted by _____John Jennings_____ Date ___Sept. 3, 19XX___

Job title _____Assistant Store Manager_____

Major duties:
- Opens and closes store including cash register
- Schedules employees
- Participates in design of store displays
- Serves as a salesperson 50 percent of time
- Maintains inventory control

Minor duties:
- Trains new employees in company policies and sales
- Hires new employees as needed
- Constructs store displays

Is supervised by (state relation): Store Manager

Number of employees supervised (state relation): Supervises all employees in store. Has authority to hire new employees. Provides input to manage or discipline.

Training required: Primary training in supervision. Additional training in sales promotion.

Education required: High school graduate. College course work — helpful especially if in business administration.

Certificates/licenses required: Valid driver's license

Experience required (identify specific skills): Previous management experience preferred. Ability to operate an NCR cash register. Open and close cash drawer.

Physical requirements: Must be able to lift 50 lbs. Corrected vision to 20/100

On-the-job hazards/working conditions: Must lift and move inventory and furniture correctly to avoid risk of back injury.

Source of job audit information: Interviews with two assistant managers and one other store manager. Research with neighboring stores in mall.

III. Writing Job Descriptions

Based on the completed analysis, a job description can now be written.

The basics

The description should include the following components:
1. A brief overview of the position (two to three sentences) describing its basic function and the role it plays within the rest of the organization.
2. A list of functions, as delineated in the job analysis.
3. An explanation of the reporting structure for the position. (To whom does the position report and whom, if anyone, does the position supervise?) Describe how the new hire will be interacting with other employees and what the job means to the progress of the company. Understanding of these roles may very well be the deciding factor in whether or not your top candidate accepts the position offered.
4. Necessary qualifications required for the position. Be careful to identify only those requirements actually necessary, e.g., licenses, certifications, technical degrees, etc. Requiring a college degree does not reflect what is actually necessary and may be construed as discriminatory.
5. Possible sources of job satisfaction and dissatisfaction. Listing satisfiers and dissatisfiers and reviewing this list prior to interviewing candidates will help you better evaluate candidates' suitability for the position.
6. Training necessary. This might involve specific training on a piece of equipment, a particular procedure or set of standards. Having this information in the description ensures an accurate assessment of what will be needed before the new person can become productive.
7. How performance will be appraised. Include specific measurements and accomplishments.
8. What job opportunities would probably become available to the holder of this job if it is performed well. This will help you weed out the candidates who are not really suited to the organization's growth needs.

> "Every man is a damn fool for at least five minutes every day; wisdom consists in not exceeding the limit."
>
> Elbert Hubbard

> "Man's mind, once stretched by a new idea, never regains its original dimensions."
>
> Oliver Wendell Holmes

Hand-Picked: The Complete Guide to Finding and Hiring the Best Employees

Sample Job Description

Job Title: Traffic manager

Job Summary: Coordinates and supervises all shipping and receiving by common carrier.

Major Duties: Schedules all shipping by common carrier and overnight delivery. Ensures that freight is properly packaged and labeled. Inventories all incoming freight against manifests and bills of lading. Schedules shipping and receiving personnel. Submits annual department budget. Supervises mail distribution.

Minor Duties: Trains new department personnel. Responsible for maintenance/housekeeping of department. Serves on _____ committee.

Relationships: Reports to plant super_____ and receiving employees.

Qualifications: Solid working know_____ including common carrier practices_____ experience in supervision of others_____ including staffing costs. (Should be_____

Compensation: Commensurate w_____ charts for actual salary and benefi_____

Description prepared by: D. R_____

Sample Job Description

Job Title: Senior assembly technician, circuit boards

Job Summary: Assembles and inspects printed circuit boards for use in computer components. Trains others.

Major Duties: Checks all components prior to installation on circuit board. Assembles board according to specifications. Runs check on every board assembly to ensure quality. Maintains speed and accuracy to ensure constant inventory.

Minor Duties: Trains new technicians on circuit board assembly. Maintains workbench tools.

Relationships: Reports to shift assembly manager. Trains junior technicians, but supervises no one.

Qualifications: High school graduate. Must be able to read and interpret printed circuit board specifications. Effective communication skills for training. Minimum on_____ nted circuit boards. Trade school _____ mandatory.

_____ ith experience. Check current _____ package.

Sample Job Description

Job Title: Receptionist

Job Summary: General reception duties and light typing.

Major Duties: Receives and directs all incoming calls. Greets visitors. Performs light typing duties for office manager.

Minor Duties: Performs light housekeeping duties in reception area. Maintains coffee service and orders coffee supplies.

Relationships: Reports to office manager. Supervises no one.

Qualifications: High school graduate. Excellent verbal communication skills. Adept at troubleshooting and able to deal effectively in a fast-paced plant environment. Type 60 words per minute.

Compensation: Hourly wage commensurate with experience. Check current compensation chart for actual wage and benefit package.

Description prepared by: D. Resnick

Chapter 3 Job Descriptions and Compensation

Additional considerations

In addition to the basics of writing a job description, consider these points:

- All titles and language should be nonsexist.
- The descriptions should be about the job, not about the present jobholder.
- Factors included should outline in detail what needs to be done, not what is being done presently. In some cases, the present jobholder may be doing more or less than necessary.
- Take care not to include discriminatory requirements (age, sex, physical characteristics, education, etc.). If you think something might be discriminatory, it probably is discriminatory.

After the description has been written, it should be reviewed for clarity, specificity, accuracy and possible discriminatory requirements. These descriptions should be reviewed on a periodic basis to ensure their accuracy and to save valuable time when hiring.

Compensation should not be listed on job descriptions since it changes frequently, which would necessitate constant updating of the descriptions. A salary and compensation schedule can be established for all positions. This practice also helps maintain consistency between individuals holding the same and comparable jobs.

IV. Determining Compensation

Before setting compensation for any position, it's best to develop a compensation philosophy. For example, a company may decide to pay less and be a "training ground" for other larger companies in the area; or it may decide it wants to beat the competition by paying a percentage higher than the going rate. While the first will result in increased training costs, the latter will increase compensation values. Before defining your salary schedules, step back and consider your philosophy.

"When a person says it ain't the money but the principle of the thing ... it's the money."

Abe Martin

Factors to consider

In developing a compensation strategy, you must research several areas. These are:
1. Compensation ranges within the industry
2. Cost-of-living factors in the local community
3. Supply and demand for labor
4. Alternatives to traditional compensation

Compensation ranges within the industry

Every industry conducts periodic compensation studies. Traditionally, the professional associations connected to an industry are responsible for this information. If the field is unionized, these organizations will also serve as a reliable source for such statistics.

Cost of living in the community

The cost of living within the local community will need to be taken into consideration. Some communities vary as much as 10 percent from those 10 miles away. The chamber of commerce and government offices will be able to provide up-to-date information.

Supply and demand for labor

Research the labor pool for the various positions you normally fill within your organization. Once again, the chamber of commerce, State Department of Labor and local job service will be able to provide estimates. You might also try local chapters of trade associations. Compare this information while looking for consistency. Also, compare notes with colleagues in like situations.

Alternatives to traditional compensation

A wide range of alternatives should be considered when calculating compensation. Perks such as memberships, special equipment and subscriptions should be examined for their tax benefits.

Factors affecting working conditions such as flextime and additional staff support, especially at the upper levels, are sometimes most welcome. In addition, on-site day-care centers, athletic facilities, cafeterias and other such services contribute to the feeling of being well compensated and may not be as expensive as straight salary.

> *Perks such as memberships, special equipment and subscriptions should be examined for their tax benefits.*

> "The reward of labor is life."
> William Morris

More and more firms are turning to cafeteria-style benefit programs, where each employee chooses benefits according to need. Some companies give each employee a certain amount to spend on benefits per year with the unused portion going directly into the employee's pocket. In this way, single individuals are not paying for benefits they don't need. Investigate these options. They are becoming increasingly popular.

Incentives can also play a role at all levels of an organization. Rather than granting raises, more and more organizations are giving bonuses, prizes and nonsalary incentives to improve productivity. You might, for example, provide deep discounted trips for two to a nearby resort or present the "employee of the month" with six months of gasoline. Examine the possibilities of this area thoroughly.

Assembling the information

Once the research has been completed, the compensation for each type of position will have to be calculated. While the considerations for top levels may vary from those of production or line personnel, all factors need to be considered.

With a senior-level position, for instance, one might include more alternative forms of compensation such as travel expenses, professional memberships and profit sharing. While production compensation may be based more on straight salary, perhaps a say in working conditions and incentives might be included. In all cases, however, every factor must be weighed and considered.

> "You're only as good as the people you hire."
> Ray Kroc

Compensation Profile
Comparison of Coverage

Position_____ Date Surveyed_____

Source of Survey Data:_____

Type of Compensation	Present Company Policy	Competitor's Policy	How We Compare	Plans and Recommendations
Wages				
Salary increase				
Bonuses				
Profit sharing				
Flexible hours				
Paid vacations				
Paid holidays				
Paid sick leave				
Paid disability				

Other leaves
  Jury duty
  Funeral
  Military
  Marriage
  Pregnancy				

Health ins.				
Dental ins.				
Disability ins.				
Life insurance				
Pension plan				
Savings plan				
Credit union				
Education ben.				
Children's ben.				
Other				
Other				

Chapter 3 Job Descriptions and Compensation

SAMPLE HOURLY WAGE RATE TABLE

COLORADO DIVISION OF EMPLOYMENT AND TRAINING
JOB BANK   JULY 1985 -   JUNE 1986
STATE OF COLORADO
TABLE V

HOURLY WAGE RATES FOR SELECTED OCCUPATIONS

OCCUPATION CODE	EMPLOYER JOB TITLES	MINIMUM	JOB OPENINGS RECEIVED PAYSCALE AVERAGE	MAXIMUM
317381010	BAKER (HOTEL & REST)	3.35	5.06	7.25
313671010	SHORT ORDER COOK II	3.35	4.05	5.00
313684010	BAKER HELPER (HOTEL & REST)	4.50	4.75	5.00
318361010	MESS COOK	2.31	4.43	7.62
316684018	MEAT CUTTER	3.50	5.28	8.00
317684014	PANTRY-GOODS MAKER	3.35	4.32	5.75
317684018	SANDWICH MAKER	3.35	3.73	5.25
317687010	COOK HELPER	3.25	3.76	6.85
318487010	KITCHEN HELPER	2.40	3.74	7.50
319137010	FOOD-SERVICE SUPERVISOR	3.45	4.97	6.00
319474010	FOUNTAIN SERVER	2.50	3.74	5.50
320137014	LODGING-FACILITIES MANAGER	2.88	4.71	7.70
371137010	HOUSEKEEPER	2.50	3.75	6.38
323687010	HOSPITAL CLEANER	2.00	4.41	7.00
373687014	HOUSEKEEPING CLEANER	1.92	3.91	7.50
332271010	COSMETOLOGIST	3.35	3.81	5.00
392647010	RECEPTIONIST	3.35	4.20	5.50
354374010	PRACTICAL NURSE	2.03	5.38	6.50
355377014	PSYCHIATRIC AIDE	3.50	5.44	7.50
355674010	CHILD-CARE SCHOOL ATTENDANT	3.35	3.44	4.35
358674014	NURSE AIDE	2.03	3.78	8.00
353674018	ORDERLY	3.35	4.22	6.19
355677010	HOSPITAL-FOOD-SERVICE WORKER	3.35	3.60	4.14
359677010	CHILDREN'S INSTITUTION ATTDNT	2.00	4.08	7.50
361665010	MACHINE WASHER (LAUND)	3.35	4.19	5.00
361685018	LAUNDRY WORKER II	3.35	4.16	6.00
341687014	CLASSIFIER (LAUND)	3.90	3.90	3.90
341687018	LAUNDRY LABORER	3.35	3.68	6.38
343687018	MACHINE PRESSER	2.75	3.69	5.00
343684018	HANDPRESSER	3.35	3.90	5.00
372647018	CORRECTION OFFICER	3.35	5.45	6.50
372687022	TRAFFIC-CONTROL FLAGGER	3.35	5.69	7.91
372647034	SECURITY GUARD	2.52	4.61	7.25
372647038	MERCHANT PATROLLER	2.31	4.37	8.00
373364010	FIRE FIGHTER	2.86	6.84	7.50
373263014	POLICE OFFICER I	5.50	6.16	6.92
361137010	JANITORIAL-SERVICES SUPERVISOR	3.75	5.08	6.90
381687014	COMMERCIAL OR INSTL CLEANER	3.35	4.04	7.23
381687018	INDUSTRIAL CLEANER	3.35	4.65	7.75
387464010	JANITOR	2.50	4.18	7.84
389684010	EXTERMINATOR	6.00	6.00	6.00
481683010	GRAIN FARMWORKER I	4.00	5.04	6.92
482687010	VEGETABLE FARMWORKER II	3.35	3.52	4.00

Sales compensation

While sales drive any for-profit company, it is difficult to calculate a balance in compensation that is both equitable and attractive. Salespeople are motivated by various factors. However you pay, it must be satisfying and yet provide incentives.

One company set sales compensation for a new product at a particular rate. It was soon discovered that a hard-working salesperson could earn more in nine months than the vice president would earn in one year. When commissions were cut, however, the company promptly lost three-quarters of its sales force.

This scenario is not uncommon. But it's difficult to pinpoint a level of compensation that is both attractive and yet retains some incentive for a salesperson to work harder.

When developing a sales compensation plan, consider the following:

- Examine the motivations of individual salespeople. What incentives have they responded to in the past? Ask them what they would find most attractive as compensation. Individuals are motivated differently.
- If you are hiring new sales people, ask them about compensation at their last job. How were they paid? What kinds of incentives did they receive? Why did they leave? Was it due to compensation? Their responses will help you discover their motivations.
- Research your competitors. How do they compensate? Are there established industry standards? Have you checked industry trade studies? No matter what you are selling, someone else, somewhere, is selling the same thing or something close. Find out who that is and what they're paying.
- Consider all options. Once again, motivations differ. Be creative with your incentives. Make the earning fun and exciting. Trips to Tahiti are more interesting than an additional $2,000 per year, and the trip won't cost you as much. Besides, the scuttlebutt about the trip will go on for years.

Increased benefits, perks around the office, better job titles, even the possibility of equity, are all options to examine.

> *"Coming together is a beginning; keeping together is progress; working together is success."*
>
> Henry Ford

Chapter 3 Job Descriptions and Compensation

The *best policy* for organizing a sales compensation plan is to start with a small base and commission representing the lower end of industry standards. You can always increase commissions, add incentives and give big bonuses. But you can never retreat from a compensation plan that pays too much. Regardless of reasoning, a reduction in commissions will be perceived as a cut in pay.

Compensation policy

Developing a compensation policy for a large company can be a difficult task. But for most small- and medium-sized concerns, development of this policy is fairly easy. The policy should be straightforward and updated on a periodic basis. This is particularly important as the organization grows. It is assumed that when the organization grows to 100 employees, a personnel department will be created to address these concerns.

A sample compensation plan can be found in Appendix C. Notice that it is aimed at the needs of employees.

Two final hints:
- If you are filling a vacancy, do not base the new employee's compensation on that of the former. For whatever reason, that salary may have been higher or lower. How you pay should be based on the merits of this new individual.
- Assume that everyone's compensation will be public knowledge. While you may wish to keep this information confidential, it's impossible to do. The rumor mill will always discover hidden inequities in salary. Be prepared to justify them to anyone who asks.

"Men of genius do not excel in any profession because they labor in it, but they labor in it because they excel."

William Hazlitt

"Money can't buy happiness, but it certainly doesn't discourage it."

French proverb

A Checklist for Job Descriptions and Compensation

☐ 1. Have you developed written job descriptions for all positions within your organization? (If "yes," skip to question #4.)

☐ 2. Have you developed a checklist for determining whether a new position is needed?

☐ 3. Have you developed a quick and efficient system for auditing positions within your organization?

☐ 4. Have you developed a formalized compensation plan including all positions within the organization?

☐ 5. Does all compensation within the organization reflect accurate pay rates throughout your industry and community?

☐ 6. Are all forms, titles, job descriptions and compensation policies written in a nondiscriminatory way?

Chapter 3 Job Descriptions and Compensation

Questions for Personal Development

1. What is the major emphasis of this chapter?

2. What are the most important things you learned from this chapter?

3. How can you apply what you learned to your current job?

4. How will you go about making these changes?

5. How can you monitor improvement?

6. Summarize the changes you expect to see in yourself one year from now.

CHAPTER 4

Recruiting the Best

"I can't believe we've only received three applications for these positions," he said. "Does this mean we have to hire everyone who walks in the door? We may get some real dorks!"

"I don't see how we have any choice," she responded. "Maybe you can shift some of the more experienced people around and give these new people the easy jobs. The new production run starts tomorrow."

"In Indianapolis, we'd unlock the door and they'd come rushing in," he said. "I just don't get it."

Here's What You'll Learn

I. Recruiting as a Hiring Tool
II. The Recruiting Plan
III. Budgeting for Recruiting
IV. Internal Recruiting and Referrals
V. Identifying Applicants' Motivations
VI. Enhancing Organizational Image
VII. Exploring Sources of Labor
VIII. Locating External Applicants
IX. Creating an Attractive Job Vacancy Notice
X. Developing Labor Pools for the Future
XI. A Checklist for Recruiting Basics

Finding the right person for the job is a complicated process. It can be hounded by impatience, favoritism, inadequate training in employee selection, poor labor pools and a host of other barriers.

Chapter 4   Recruiting the Best

I. Recruiting as a Hiring Tool

As organizations continue to monitor costs more closely, each employee recruited becomes more critical. While a so-called "bad hire" may have gone unnoticed in the past, the same person now stands out due to the increased burden on every employee. It has been estimated that a position with a $30,000 annual salary over 10 years ultimately costs the organization $480,000, including recruiting costs, health benefits and cost-of-living increases. Everyone knows who is making a contribution.

The quality of the hire is also a reflection on the person making the decision.

The way you approach the process is very important. Traditionally, we have looked at recruiting through the organization and procedures surrounding it. While there are antidiscriminatory guidelines to be followed, the remainder of the process can be conducted in any way you wish.

All too often we rely on the standard list of questions or commercially bought application blanks to determine what information we should seek. Unfortunately, these tend to be shallow and generic.

Instead, someone in the position to hire should be identifying what is important to her. Many times we hesitate to dig deep enough into what we want for fear of not being able to find a person who fits the entire bill. The chances are good that you never will. But it is better to aim for perfection than to settle for mediocrity at the outset. As long as it's job related, you can ask any question you wish. So get specific in your expectations. Turnover or low productivity are expensive prices to pay for not defining your needs up front.

"Think ...we can develop a soda can that will last forever, and a car will rust out in a year or two."

Paul Harwitz

"It is one of the most beautiful compensations of this life that no man can sincerely try to help another without helping himself."

Ralph Waldo Emerson

Remember that candidates are screening you as much as you are screening them. Employees are much more concerned about their ability to control their environment within the workplace than they have been in the past. If your employees feel unable to control their surroundings, the growing scarcity of workers will allow them to simply vote with their feet and move to another employer.

A key ingredient for effective recruiting is being able to offer better work environments coupled with flexible benefits and generous training opportunities. Companies able to effect these changes become flexible work sites and have become the most successful employers in the 1990s.

> *"If you have a job without aggravations, you don't have a job."*
> Malcolm Forbes

Determining needs

Consider the following ideas when developing your list of needs:

1. Consult the job description for the position. In addition to identifying actual duties, look for other attributes that might be helpful.
2. Determine the characteristics of your organization's culture. What attributes might a person need to fit in?
3. Who will be supervising the position? What attributes should a person possess to serve as a complement to this boss?
4. With what other individuals will this person have day-to-day contact? Are there certain group characteristics that need to be taken into account?
5. Look around your environment. What other factors might have to be taken into consideration to ensure a thorough assessment of position characteristics?

> *"The highest reward for a person's toil is not what they get for it, but what they become by it."*
> John Ruskin

This type of procedure should be followed with every hire. While it can be time-consuming, it tends to ensure effective hiring, low turnover and higher productivity.

II. The Recruiting Plan

While there is no exact way to determine optimum strategies for recruiting for every position, you should develop a plan prior to approaching applicant pools. Comparing the actual results with the original estimates will provide an approximate picture of your effectiveness.

Here are some considerations:
- What positions are you presently seeking to fill?
- Which of these jobs can benefit from the same advertising?
- Which of these jobs should not be advertised with others? (I.e., don't cluster shop foremen with accountants.)
- What is the expected turnover? If you are expecting high turnover, as in retail, your standards for acceptable applicants may be lower than for a long-term professional.
- Who are your targeted applicant pools? Applicants for different positions will be recruited from different sources.
- What are the best strategies for approaching the pools selected?
- What staff resources will be necessary to complete this project?
- How far in advance will you have to recruit to fill upcoming vacancies? Develop a time line.
- What are the recruiting messages being used with different applicant pools? Try not to mix these strategies. It will confuse people.
- Does your plan include the recruiting of minorities and other protected classes?
- Are the strategies proposed consistent with your organization's image? Would you advertise for bank tellers, for instance, on bumper stickers?
- What will the project cost? Be sure to include expenses such as staff time, postage and phone charges.
- What approvals are necessary for this project to begin? Be cognizant of building support among those who hold the necessary influence.

Develop a functional chart to organize the actual process. Keeping an eye on the flow graphically will help you stay on top of the plan's implementation.

> *"Too many people quit looking for work when they find a job."*
>
> J. Paul Getty

MEMORANDUM

TO: Alex Raski, Vice President

FROM: Janet Forthright, Human Resources

After surveying all departments, I have established the following recruiting plan. We will be using a few rather nontraditional techniques this time. Hopefully, they will improve our applicant base, especially for assembly technicians.

Note: The numbers next to each job title are the number of individuals we expect to hire this quarter.

1. Assembly technicians (32)
2. Quality control technicians (21)
3. Shipping clerks (9)
4. Customer support clerks (15)
5. Billing specialists (7)
6. Secretaries (7)
7. Assembly supervisors (6)

Recruiting Technique	1	2	3	4	5	6	7
Direct mail to selected customers	●	●					●
Newspapers	●	●	●	●	●	●	●
Employee referral campaign	●	●	●	●	●	●	●
Local JTPA program	●	●	●				
Signs on local transit	●	●		●		●	
Morning TV spots	●		●		●	●	
Posters at all 7 community colleges	●	●	●	●	●	●	●
Letters to churches and senior center			●			●	●

Alex, we really need to get a handle on this turnover problem. We can only go to the well so many times. It's costing us a fortune!

Plan evaluation

Recruiting plans can be measured in several different ways:

Cost per hire is determined by dividing the total expense of the plan by the number of hires. Be sure to include all indirect expenses such as clerical and planning time. Calculating cost per hire enables you to analyze your effectiveness in hiring quality candidates economically.

Vacancy rates allow recruiters to evaluate the patterns of frequency in the turning over of employees. It is calculated by dividing the number of open positions by the total number of positions when the organization is fully staffed. This information can be instrumental in discovering escalating turnover among certain jobs.

Selection rates enable you to see the ratio between the number of people interviewed and the number hired. This information is obtained by dividing the number of interviews by the number of hires. Selection rates help you to determine the quality of the candidates being interviewed. If your selection rate is low, your preinterview screening techniques may need to be evaluated.

Referral rates illustrate the return on recruiting advertisements. A low return means that the effectiveness of the ad needs to be improved. Referral rates are calculated by dividing the number of people who responded to the ad by the number who were actually qualified for the position. If, for example, you receive 200 responses to a particular campaign and only 25 are qualified, the targeting of the ad probably needs adjustment.

Recruiting plans, if carefully developed, can be extremely valuable in conducting a quality and cost-efficient recruiting campaign. In addition, plans such as this ensure compliance with equal opportunity and affirmative action requirements.

MEMORANDUM

TO: Alex Raski, Vice President

FROM: Janet Forthright, Human Resources

We have completed evaluating the results of our first quarter recruiting campaign. While we did not receive the number of applicants we would have preferred for certain positions, we did meet our targets.

Job Title	Hiring Target	Appli. Target	Appli. Respon	Actual Hires	Best Method
Assembly Technicians	32	120	69	30	Local JTPA program
Quality Control Sup.	21	100	42	21	Posters at comm. coll.
Shipping Clerks	9	30	27	8	Signs on local transit
Customer Supp. Clerks	15	70	61	15	Posters at comm. coll.
Billing Specialists	7	28	20	7	Newspapers
Secretaries	7	21	15	7	Letters to senior center
Assembly Supervisors	6	30	37	6	Posters at comm. coll.
TOTALS	97	399	271	94	

Comments: Morning TV spots did not work as planned. Most were aired before 7 a.m., against our wishes. The results did not justify the expense.

The open house was a tremendous success. The trouble is, we can't do it four times a year. It also played havoc with the Saturday shift.

The JTPA program worked fine. I was skeptical of the first five applicants, but they have a better attendance rate than everybody else. I think we have discovered something!

The new ideas such as transit signs and that balloon giveaway at the mall appear to be bettering our image. On to the next quarter!

Chapter 4   Recruiting the Best

III. Budgeting for Recruiting

Recruitment of employees can be an expensive process. Most surveys published on hiring indicate the average professional hire costs approximately $5,000. Studies covering the trades and unskilled labor show averages around $700.

With the coming labor shortages, it is even more important to monitor the recruiting budget closely. It is easy, for instance, to overspend in a particular area simply because there is a sudden need for labor. A little planning will reduce the number of times this happens. This, in turn, will help keep the recruiting budget within limits.

There are, of course, the expenses of training, along with the occasional executive hire, which will cost more. But for the most part, recruiting expenses should be carefully watched.

Look for innovative, inexpensive ways to get the recruiting word out. Participating in or sponsoring local school events can be a great way to garner attention for your company and attract teen-age applicants. You might attempt trades of service or products with organizations that have the ability to promote your need for applicants. In both of these cases, the actual costs should be minimal.

What's included

There are several areas that need to be taken into consideration, including overhead, staff time, phone expenses and managerial time. The table on the facing page illustrates a typical method for hiring one professional and one receptionist. Your costs may vary slightly, depending on your location. Occasionally calculate your company's hiring costs to remind everyone of the substantial expense resulting from careless selection and improper training.

Saving money

How can you save money in the recruiting process? Be practical and creative. Ask plenty of questions and approach the process with a commonsense perspective.

Costs can be reduced significantly if more attention is paid to the overall investment of time and expenditures. In many organizations, the recruiting process is not mobilized until a position needs to be filled. If a supervisor is hired in January, for instance, it's possible that those hiring for the same type of position three

---

Look for innovative, inexpensive ways to get the recruiting word out. Sponsoring local school events can be a great way.

"If you spend money on it, it's a hobby, if you make money on it, it's a business."

Samuel Johnson

MEMORANDUM

TO: Alex Raski, Vice President

FROM: Doris Resnick, Administrative Manager

Here are the comparisons between hiring the new customer service manager and and the customer service receptionist we just replaced.

	Manager	Receptionist
Cash expenses		
Classified advertising	$500	$100
Postage, phone, miscellaneous (est.)	75	10
Labor & management time		
Search planning meetings	415	0
Develop and place classified ads	35	15
Administration of search	350	0
Review of applications	70	15
Phone interviews	175	0
Interviews	420	75
Second interviews	280	30
Decision-making	175	15
Negotiation	70	0
Orientation and planning	350	30
Training	1,650	150
Secretarial support	120	27
Miscellaneous administration	175	15
GRAND TOTAL	$4,860	$482

Note: These totals do not include the unproductive training time on the new hires' part.

"Beware of little expenses. A small leak will sink a ship."

Benjamin Franklin

months hence will begin a new campaign to collect applicants for the current opening. A one-hour investment in calling those candidates involved in the process last time may reveal two or three prescreened individuals who are still interested.

A policy of "we are always looking for good people" even though there may be no openings at the time can save back-breaking work when someone is needed in a hurry. Encouraging employees to be on the lookout for possible applicants not only builds candidate pools, but investment in the organization. Besides, it doesn't cost a thing!

It is best to start from the beginning when developing recruiting procedures. Examine every step and ask, "How can I save money and still accomplish this task effectively?" Here are a few hints to help you:

- Look to internal referrals first, whenever possible. This could save the majority of recruiting costs. (See Part IV in this chapter.)
- Concentrate on local hiring. There is no reason to pursue out-of-state candidates if someone suitable can be found in your own back yard.
- Be extremely judicious in the use of headhunters and employment agencies. You are not necessarily saving money or getting the better candidate. Check references and reputation before proceeding. (More about this later in this chapter.)
- Keep a constant eye on costs. Remind those doing the hiring that recruiting is a cost center. Cut corners when you can.

IV. Internal Recruiting and Referrals

Recruiting from within is the most cost-effective way to fill vacancies. While there can be drawbacks, these strategies offer several benefits.

If you promote from within, the employee already knows the organization and is a proven worker. In addition, overall employee morale will be improved since employees realize that it is possible to advance within the organization.

Personal referrals from employees offer information of a more personal nature on an applicant. They also carry more weight because the organization already knows and believes in the person who provided the referral.

The drawbacks of using this strategy can be a limitation in your choice of candidates. There is also the potential for rancor within the company if the job opening isn't posted and discussed internally in an open, forthright manner; or if it isn't posted for a long enough period of time. There may be understandable disappointment if the insider is not selected. It is also difficult to discharge someone who was recruited for the position from inside the company if that person doesn't work out.

Defining the plan of action

In order to conduct an effective and fair selection process by either of these methods, you must have a defined plan of action. Consider the following:

- Ensure clear communication about openings within the organization. Make sure that everyone knows what's going on. This eliminates rumors, misinformation and hard feelings.
- Develop a workable system. Posting a position for five days, for instance, does not allow enough time for people to think about it. Be sure there are no hidden barriers. Standards that are too high or too specific can be disheartening as well as discriminatory.
- When you are considering a person in a certain department, make sure that the supervisor is aware of your interest. Marching in and "stealing" someone, even though it may be a promotion, will create animosity.

> *"If everyone is thinking alike, then somebody isn't thinking."*
>
> George S. Patton

- Be open to new ideas in referrals. When we start looking for likely candidates, we tend to have a picture in our heads about what we would like. As a result, when something unusual comes up, we tend to ignore it. Test out new ideas. Consider individuals who did not become apparent right away. You may be pleasantly surprised.
- Keep a record of referrals and the people who made them. If the referral worked out, you may want to go to that person again for help. If it didn't, you may want to avoid future referrals from that person. Be sensitive, however, to the possibility that an unequal amount of influence may result from these lists if the referrals are coming primarily from a small group of employees.
- Provide incentives for referrals. Incentives could include a bonus, time off, a prize, plaque or something else; these types of carrots can get everyone looking for good applicants.
- Remember to make sure that you clearly state what type of person you're seeking. Otherwise you may be swamped with unmatchable candidates.
- Consider how much encouragement you and the executive level give to employees about moving up. If staff sees that management is encouraging promotion, they will be more interested in applying for the vacancies.
- Set goals for hiring internally. This will demonstrate to employees that you really mean it. While there is a chance of becoming an inbred company, this possibility is slight. Ten to 20 percent of your annual hires should be in-house. Otherwise, turnover will increase because employees decide that there is nowhere to go within the organization.

> *"Drive thy business; let it not drive thee."*
>
> Benjamin Franklin

V. Identifying Applicants' Motivations

Before developing any strategy for approaching applicants, it is important to examine the motivation of those you want to attract. This can be accomplished in several ways.

The most basic strategy is to simply list those attitudes likely to appear in your target audience. If you have the same experience, age and background, you should be able to develop an accurate profile of recruiting materials and approaches.

WHAT TO ASK
When surveying your applicant pools

Ask each individual these questions:

1. What is the most important feature to you in a job?

2. What was your last job? *(If employed, where are you working now?)*

3. Why did you accept that job?

4. What did you like best about the last job you held?

5. What did you like least about the last job you held?

6. Please rank the following from most to least important:

    a. Distance from work

    b. Hours

    c. Job duties

    d. Pay

    e. Work environment

7. What is the most important feature you look for in a supervisor?

8. How did you find out about your last job?

> *"A message for businessmen: 'Whatever happens, never happens by itself.'"*
>
> Sally Rand

In many cases, however, those doing the recruiting and those being recruited vary significantly in age, values and experience. While you may have passed age 18, that does not mean you can identify with the attitudes of today's teen-ager. A means for getting more accurate information is to ask the teen-agers already working for you. This not only provides useful input, but also involves them in the process. Their ensuing interest may result in more enthusiasm for the job and even referrals of qualified applicants.

A final method is actually surveying those in your target group. This means getting on the phone and asking them what they want out of a job opportunity. While this can be time-consuming and expensive, it may result in good referrals and useful information. Going directly to the market will also help enhance your organization's image.

VI. Enhancing Organizational Image

Before implementing a recruiting program, you should examine how your organization is perceived by the community. It is difficult to attract applicants when those in the targeted groups are not aware the company exists. It is even more difficult when they have a negative perception of what it is like to work for your organization.

You might conduct an informal survey to discover how those in the community feel. Explain what you're doing and ask broad, open-ended questions:

"What have you heard about our organization?"

"Do you use our products? What do you think of them?"

"Do you know people who work here? Do they like it?"

These surveys will provide information on what's being said about your company, both positive and negative. While much of this is probably based on rumors and gossip, you still need to address those concerns that are having a bad influence on organizational image.

This type of information will also reveal other concerns that can be used in the recruiting process to attract candidates. These include attitudes about working conditions, hours, compensation and the like.

> *"When the well's dry, we know the worth of water."*
>
> Benjamin Franklin

Recruiting Brochures

Just as brochures are necessary to sell your products, it is imperative that you have brochures and support material to assist applicants in understanding the value of your organization and why they should work for you. These brochures should speak to the applicant's concerns. The applicant is not the only person involved. Applicants usually consult with family and friends before making a decision. Those individuals will ask them about the job. Applicants' ability to answer those questions and, in the end, feel like they are making the right choice has a tremendous bearing on whether they accept the position and the pride they have after they accept the position.

Designing the brochure:

- Begin by listing the possible questions the typical applicant will have. These items will probably include a brief company history, the company's role in the industry, the products you provide, image in the community and organizational structure.

- Collect as many corporate recruiting brochures as possible and look for ideas that relate to your organization. Be sure to comment on the work environment and reporting structures within the firm. If there is one thing an applicant wants to know, it is what it is like to work in the company.

- Prepare the brochure for easy reference. Lay it out so that different concerns can be located quickly and be shown to other individuals. Address the text to candidates and write it in easy- to-understand terms. Use photographs to communicate the job content. Action pictures of the work environment and the people tend to lend credibility to the idea of working for you.

- Include quality-of-life information. Help applicants understand that your firm has the employees' best interests at heart. Stress opportunities for personal and professional growth, extracurricular activities. Include evidence of long-term career potential. Provide employee testimonials and third-party endorsements that give candidates the idea that employees who work there enjoy what they do. Aim these remarks at candidates for the front-line positions since that is where you experience the greatest turnover.

- Summarize basic business facts about the company. Help candidates understand the company's position within its industry along with its strengths and future. Create a forward-looking brochure that helps candidates see that yours is a forward-looking company with potential for the future.

Chapter 4   Recruiting the Best

There are several areas to monitor when assessing and enhancing an organization's image:

Overall company public relations: Consult with those responsible for public relations. Provide them with information on new endeavors such as training programs, recruiting outreaches to special groups and affiliations with local schools. These all demonstrate the organization's citizenship in the community. The media can have a tremendous impact on an organization's image. It is best to maintain good relations with them at all times.

Recruiting literature: Take a close look at the literature being used for recruiting. Does it accurately represent what the company does? Is it written for the prospective employee? Does it discuss working conditions, expectations and opportunities? Even for the most menial positions, a powerfully written brochure will make applicants want to work for you.

Recruiting approaches: Have you examined the strategies you are using to approach applicants? Are they tailored to address the values of the targeted populations? To retirees, advertising exciting advancement opportunities, for example, will not have the same impact as offering flexible schedules.

Front-line reception of applicants: When applicants make contact, how are they treated? Is the phone answered courteously? Does the receptionist have the correct information? Are there individuals available to speak to the applicant? A positive first impression goes a long way toward selling the job.

"A bad workman never gets a good tool."

Thomas Fuller

"Chance favors the prepared mind."

Louis Pasteur

Handling of the selection process: Is the process simple and straightforward? Are deadlines met? Are candidates handled professionally? Are interviewers prepared? Is an effort being made to "sell" to the top candidates?

Employee turnover: After employees have left an organization, they are bound to talk about their experiences. While there are some who will have been discharged, the vast majority leave on their own. Their comments about long hours, difficult supervisors, lack of opportunity and so on can seriously damage your organization's image. This is another good reason to work toward reducing turnover as much as possible.

The "sales" pitch

Everyone associated with the organization's hiring should be able to discuss this topic at a moment's notice. Some of the best candidates come through referrals and informal introductions. Managers able to take advantage of these situations by speaking intelligently about openings and opportunities will acquire some top performers.

The best approach for this is a "30-second commercial." Prepare what you would say in advance. Include information describing the company and its opportunities, and tailor the rest to what you think would attract the person in question.

You might mention tuition reimbursement to a college student, for example, or research and development funding to a computer specialist. Constant attention to organizational image will help you land the best people.

> *"A wise man will make more opportunity than he finds."*
>
> Francis Bacon

VII. Exploring Sources of Labor

The major change in recruiting has been the evolution of labor sources. For the past 20 years, employers have taken the ample supply of inexperienced labor for granted. Much of this supply has consisted of students and homemakers looking for part-time work.

But as the baby boom has grown up and the number of career women has exploded, employers have found themselves short-handed. Every industry is experiencing the crunch for applicants.

Now that these sources are in short supply, we need to pay more attention to groups that have received a prejudicial eye in the past. These include:

- Senior workers (those 55 and over)
- Displaced homemakers
- Moonlighters
- Retired or exiting military
- Career changers
- Individuals with physical disabilities
- Individuals with mental disabilities
- Ex-offenders
- Economically disadvantaged

Senior workers

The largest and most influential of these groups is senior workers. Where 20 years ago most individuals retired at 65, many are now continuing in their jobs or taking early retirement to pursue a new endeavor.

According to a survey conducted by the American Association of Retired Persons, 48 percent of those who said they were retired indicated that they would consider employment if the right situation appeared. As our population matures, the influence this group will exert in the workforce will be enormous.

While myths surround the capabilities of older workers, most employers are finding these individuals work just as hard and efficiently as their younger counterparts. Due to maturity and experience, they are able to adapt quickly to new responsibilities, deal with crises and get along with co-workers. Their loyalty to the company also tends to exceed that of younger employees.

> *"The secret of business is to know something that nobody else knows."*
>
> Aristotle Onassis

The myth that you have to pay an older worker more money has also been found to be untrue. While there are some who command a superior wage, many choose other forms of compensation such as more time off, flexible hours and health benefits. Some may choose to limit their hours and/or compensation to avoid losing government aid such as Social Security and Medicare.

Concerns about older workers tend to revolve around their ability to adapt to technology, their inflexibility and a lack of aggressiveness. While some employers are also troubled about lost time due to illness, statistics show that older workers and younger workers lose about the same number of days. Retirees and older workers in general may be just what your company needs to maintain a reliable and relatively inexpensive staff.

> *Statistics show that older workers and younger workers lose about the same number of days.*

Accessing the senior-worker market

To recruit older workers, the message must be tailored to their way of thinking. Appealing to job qualities they value will attract attention. These include flexible hours, flexible benefits, autonomy, opportunity to meet new friends and working with people their own age. You might also stress that you value their maturity and experience.

The vehicles for reaching this group are varied:
- Advertising in banks and post offices on the first of the month
- Community or church publications
- Bargain newspapers found at grocery stores
- Bulletin boards in communities where there is a concentration of older individuals
- Testimonials of older workers within your organization
- Posters with tear-off coupons in malls
- Advertising in newspaper sections that appeal to older individuals
- Local senior centers

> *"When we have done our best, we should wait the result in peace."*
>
> J. Lubbock

There are also an increasing number of retiree pools to be found in cities around the United States. You cannot advertise for "older workers" since this is discriminatory. The best means for locating these individuals is through the local chapter of the American Association of Retired Persons along with churches and civic organizations.

> *"By and large, mothers and housewives are the only workers who do not have regular time off. They are the great vacationless class."*
>
> Anne Morrow Lindbergh

Many cities have Forty-Plus clubs to assist members in pursuing employment. The individuals within these groups have generally been laid off by other companies.

The Small Business Administration's Senior Corps of Retired Executives (SCORE) might also be able to assist. These individuals are generally retired from business, having started their own companies in the past. Not only do they meet with likely candidates every day, but they themselves might be interested in working on at least a contract basis.

Examine the possible sources in your local area and discover how senior workers might fit into your organization.

Displaced homemakers

Displaced homemakers are those women who choose to reenter the workforce after a long period of separation or those who are forced to work due to hardship. In some cases, these individuals have substantial skills and expertise. In others, they are inexperienced and may be entering the workforce for the first time.

Depending on organizational need, the individuals in this group may be able to fill valuable roles. In most cases, training will be necessary to teach new skills for both job duties and for coping with the balance between business and family.

Women Work: The National Network for Women's Employment (202-467-6346) provides nationwide assistance to these individuals for training and placement. In addition, local agencies such as the YWCA will be able to identify other organizations that provide assistance.

Moonlighters

While many employers have discouraged moonlighters in the past, this group offers a pool of part-time labor to fill a variety of jobs. The key to attracting these individuals is stressing flexibility in schedules. They can best be reached through advertising aimed at groups such as teachers, police officers, firefighters, skilled trade workers, retail clerks and other hourly employees. If you are especially interested in part-time workers, you might also try college students, homemakers and individuals who can spare only part of their day.

An alternative to flexible schedules is job sharing. This allows two individuals to complete the job by arranging their schedules and, at the same time, assuring the employer of a full-time worker.

Some companies have also begun to offer part-time positions to their full-time employees. This allows these individuals to earn extra cash and saves the employer the trouble of hiring other individuals. In addition, full-time employees are already invested in the organization and do not require training and orientation on company policy.

Retired or exiting military

While employers look upon those leaving the military as an excellent source of skills and experience, many of these individuals find landing a civilian job difficult. Much of this is due to the adjustment into a civilian environment along with the challenge of translating skills into business terminology.

To attract these individuals, you have to approach them in ways with which they can identify. These include such things as testimonials from former military personnel who have joined your firm or holding an open house for retiring military if you are located in an area with a high military concentration.

Advertisements should be written with slogans and terminology that will catch their eye. Phrases such as "Join our team" or "We need your discipline" will attract that split second of attention you need to convince them to read on.

Put military applicants at ease and make them feel welcome when they contact you. Helping them to adjust to an unfamiliar environment will win them over. You might offer a free workshop to help them with their job search in the civilian world. Include some information on opportunities within your organization and how they might fit in.

"Hitch your wagon to a star."

Ralph Waldo Emerson

To reach exiting military personnel, you must advertise in areas they frequent and publications they read. You might, for instance, distribute fliers in stores and housing complexes where there are concentrations of military personnel. A billboard outside a local base will also attract attention.

There are also a number of military publications distributed nationwide. These provide an excellent means for contacting these highly qualified individuals. Call an installation near you for more information.

> *"Most people like hard work. Particularly when they are paying for it."*
>
> Franklin P. Jones

Career changers

Those contemplating a change in careers can be another good source of labor. The average person switches fields three to four times, and these individuals may be tapped to fill roles in your organization.

While there are plenty of these people outside your organization, there may also be a number inside who are growing restless. Look for better ways to keep those already on board more satisfied with the firm. Cross-training, professional development and educational assistance will all help prevent the loss of key individuals.

One of the best means for attracting career changers is to advertise "little or no training necessary." Many of those contemplating a move may look upon this as an opportunity to gain a foothold in their new area of interest.

Target your recruiting messages to those populations you feel will yield the largest number of respondents. These might include teachers, clerical workers, retail clerks and manual laborers. There are a number of individuals within these ranks with good skills who are looking for an opportunity to prove themselves.

Avenues for reaching these groups include direct mail, advertisement in publications they read frequently and telemarketing.

Individuals with disabilities

The most underused pool of labor in the United States is working-age adults with disabilities. Even with enforcement of the Americans with Disabilities Act, many still find it difficult to secure employment. Even if you want to employ them, in many cases, individuals with disabilities are difficult to locate. Here are some resources:

> *The most underused pool of labor in the United States is working-age adults with disabilities.*

State agencies: There are 84 state rehabilitation agencies throughout the nation. These organizations provide training to people with disabilities and help with placement into jobs. In some cases, job coaches are available to assist in the first few weeks of employment. A coach stands side-by-side with a worker with severe disabilities and helps that individual adjust to the job.

Most services of these agencies are offered free of charge along with training and equipment to make reasonable accommodation. (Contact the Job Accommodation Network, call 1-800-JAN-7234, or the Council of State Administrators of Vocational Rehabilitation, 1055 Thomas Jefferson St. N.W., Washington, DC 20007.)

Public-private partnerships: The Job Training Partnership Act (JTPA) provides training and placement assistance to workers with disabilities through local Private Industry Councils. These councils assess business needs in the community and identify training programs that can provide the necessary individuals. An arrangement is drawn up so that the firms needing workers hire those who meet their qualifications after they are trained according to the companies' parameters.

Projects with Industry (PWI) is sponsored by the U.S. Department of Education. Industry representatives identify those areas where the greatest job growth is anticipated, and individuals with disabilities are trained to fill those positions. (Contact the U.S. Department of Education, 600 Independence Ave. S.W., Washington, DC 20202.)

Targeted Jobs Tax Credit (TJTC) is a tax incentive for employers who hire workers with disabilities. The program gives employers a credit against first-year's wages paid to the newly hired worker.

Veterans and private placement programs: The Veterans Administration along with some private employment agencies assist with the placement of individuals with disabilities. The local Veterans Administration offices assist employers in locating physically or mentally rehabilitated veterans.

In addition, other organizations throughout the United States offer ways to employ individuals with disabilities. Check with local welfare agencies, colleges and rehabilitation facilities to locate these groups.

Ex-offenders

While the average employer may be hesitant to hire ex-offenders, they are suited for a variety of situations. Although they have been convicted of a felony, they have also paid their debt to society. But this branding tends to make their job search difficult.

In hiring an ex-offender, you will probably obtain a grateful and, therefore, hard-working and loyal employee. In addition, the Targeted Jobs Tax Credit Act provides private employers with wage incentives during the employee's first year. Understandably, an individual of this background should be carefully screened prior to making an offer.

> *"A man can fail many times, but he's not a failure until he begins to blame somebody else."*
>
> John F. Kennedy

> *"A great pleasure in life is doing what people say you cannot do."*
>
> Walter Gagehot

Chapter 4   Recruiting the Best

Locating pools of ex-offenders can best be accomplished through state and local rehabilitation programs, job service offices and agencies within local justice departments. In many cases, these organizations provide job training in addition to placement services.

Economically disadvantaged

A large, and mostly untapped, source of labor is what the government has defined as the "working poor." These individuals, on welfare programs such as Aid to Families with Dependent Children, choose not to work since they lose health care benefits when employed. However, if your organization provides benefits to its employees, these individuals may be an excellent source of labor.

While you may have some legitimate concerns about training, attendance and work ethic, most social services agencies test and train these individuals before they are placed in the job market. In some cases, receipt of benefits is contingent upon the completion of certain programs. While an investment in job training and coping skills may be necessary up front, you will usually be rewarded by loyal employees.

What's in the future

The future labor force will be significantly different from today. In addition to a new focus on the groups discussed above, more global considerations are on the horizon.

Traditionally, white, non-Hispanic males have been regarded as the prime group within the labor force because they tend to be more highly educated than minority men and more closely attached to the labor force than women. But according to the Bureau of Labor Statistics, this group will make up less than 10 percent of the 20 million people expected to be added to the labor force by the year 2000. This will reduce their share of the nation's total workforce to less than 40 percent.

So-called minority populations have begun to outnumber the majority in certain parts of the country. This is resulting in value changes along with the necessity of being bilingual.

As technology continues to absorb the menial jobs, workers will find knowledge-based positions the only ones available. Since it is becoming apparent that many younger workers lack basic skills and older workers lack computer skills, employers will be forced to assume a much greater role in employee training.

The future labor force will be significantly different from today. More global considerations are on the horizon.

"A ballplayer's got to be kept hungry to become a big-leaguer. That's why no boy from a rich family ever made the big leagues."

Joe DiMaggio

These changes are happening now and will continue into the next century. The organizations that adapt their recruiting to address these changes will be the ones that thrive.

VIII. Locating External Applicants

With changes in the workforce, locating and attracting applicants has become increasingly difficult. As a result, employers are developing more innovative and aggressive strategies to reach sources of labor.

External applicants can be recruited through a variety of sources. These break into five categories:
- Recruitment advertising agencies
- Recruiting services
- College placement centers
- Public job services
- Newspaper advertising

> *"Thunder is good, thunder is impressive; but it is the lightning that does the work."*
>
> Mark Twain

Prior to considering these approaches, determine your criteria for the successful candidate. If a job description has been developed for the position, this is an easy first step.

Once you have determined the criteria, look back to other times when you have hired for that and similar positions. Determine where the successful candidates have come from. This should provide a solid picture of how to recruit for the present vacancy.

Available applicants come from different labor pools for different positions. Skilled labor, for instance, can best be located through classified advertising while executive level applicants normally come through referrals and headhunters. It is extremely important that you maintain up-to-date information on the labor pools in your area. An informal list of possible applicants as you discover them can be helpful in an emergency when a vacancy needs to be filled immediately.

It is never a good idea to hire in a panic. But sometimes you are left with no other choice. Your informal list and perhaps the collection of resumes and applications received in the past 90 days will ease the burden of otherwise having to screen all new candidates.

> *"Nothing in the world can take the place of persistence. Talent will not; nothing is more common than unsuccessful men with talent. Genius will not; unrewarded genius is almost a proverb. Education will not; the world is full of educated derelicts. Persistence and determination alone are omnipotent."*
>
> Calvin Coolidge

For the most part, the abundance of applicants many companies are used to receiving has subsided. While this relieves the burden of paperwork, it also requires more diligence when recruiting. Applicants have to be convinced that working for your company can be a secure and rewarding experience. With the low unemployment in many states, applicants have to be lured and convinced that the best opportunity is with you.

Recruitment advertising agencies

Recruitment advertising agencies specialize in assisting organizations to attract qualified candidates. These companies offer expertise and creativity normally not available within your own organization. In addition, they concentrate on this area alone and therefore are more attuned to what strategies work. This is generally not an expensive service since the agencies receive their commission from the media in which they place ads.

Before proceeding with one of these organizations, however, it is best to investigate what each one can do for you. You might ask the following:

- How large is the agency? Does it have multiple offices? If your organization has several sites, can any of these be used?
- What do other clients say about this agency? Ask for and check references.
- How much lead time does the agency need to prepare your campaign?
- What services are offered and which will be charged for? Some agencies offer extensive administrative services such as tracking advertising and results of campaigns. Will the company be charged for these extras? How much?
- How aggressive is the agency? In a tight labor market, more creative techniques must be used to attract candidates. Can this agency demonstrate a track record of innovative and unusual advertising that works?
- Does the agency demand a contract? If so, negotiate a trial period.

Recruiting services

Results from working with services can range from fruitful to disastrous depending on the relationship you have developed. Remember that these organizations are in the business to make money. Therefore, the faster a vacancy is filled, the more they profit. Unfortunately, the emphasis on speed can impair the quality of service. It is your responsibility as a client to define the parameters of the relationship and enforce quality control.

If, for instance, you have posted a managerial position, it is your responsibility to provide a definitive job description. In addition, you should list other critical qualities the successful applicant will have. This information enables the service to tailor its search and increase accuracy along with speed.

> *Mistakes due to impatience, panic or even undue pressure can be costly at a later time.*

If the candidates being referred do not fit the position, turn them away. Agencies, at times, will try to give the "hard sell" to a candidate they think is a match. Mistakes due to impatience, panic or even undue pressure can be costly at a later time.

Recruiting service organizations may be separated into four categories: employment agencies, temporary agencies, executive recruiters and executive search firms (also called "headhunters"). Now let's examine the four recruiting sources:

> **Employment agencies:** These organizations generally serve as a clearinghouse for clerical and staff support positions. They can exact their fee from the employee, the client company or both. A good agency can save you time and money by screening applicants and providing only those who are qualified. It is important, however, to check the references of these organizations before you do business. The ones that have been in business the longest are usually the best. Review your budget before committing to these services. While it takes more time to recruit yourself, those on a tight budget will save money by doing so.
>
> These agencies are typically found in the local phone directory. However, you might ask colleagues for references too.

> *"The big shots are only the little shots who keep shooting."*
>
> Charles Morley

Chapter 4   Recruiting the Best

> *"You can't build a reputation on what you are going to do."*
>
> Henry Ford

Temporary agencies: These organizations are different from employment agencies in that they, rather than the client company, pay the employee. Most enforce a monetary penalty on workers who accept a full-time position with a client. Increasing numbers of people are working on a temporary basis, so these agencies are enjoying a surge in popularity. These agencies can also be found in the phone directory, but it is best to get referrals.

Executive recruiters: These firms will assist you in hiring entry-level and mid-level managers. Their clients are primarily current job seekers. If you were to post your opening in the classifieds, you might come across many of the same names in the resulting stack of resumes.

Executive recruiters base their income on successful matches between company and applicant. They work on either a retainer or contingency basis. Many specialize in a particular industry and can be most helpful provided they have developed the necessary expertise. Working with an effective executive recruiter can save valuable time in locating and screening likely applicants.

The cost of this service averages 30 percent of the new employee's first-year salary. This can be an expensive option, so look closely before committing to this service.

Executive recruiters can be located through phone directories, the classified ads section of the local paper, business directories and referrals. The referral option is probably the best choice.

Professional/executive search firms (headhunters): The colloquial term refers to the fact that these individuals "headhunt" for corporate professionals or executives to fill senior positions in a client company. While the applicant finds the executive recruiter, the headhunter works exclusively for the company.

The process for this type of search is complex. The headhunter will begin by interviewing the company's management and fully investigating its organization. As with executive recruiters, these professionals usually specialize in one industry. Targeted professionals sought by headhunters are usually working managers in the field, who can be lured away to a more challenging and lucrative position.

The compensation for these services averages 30 percent of first-year compensation. For most companies, the use of a headhunter should be confined strictly to filling senior-level positions. Interview these agencies carefully before securing their services. This should be done in your office. Ask for references from current and previous clients.

College placement centers

College placement centers offer a wealth of qualified candidates to fill many needs. Yet, it is primarily the larger companies that take the most advantage of what these centers have to offer.

New graduating students are an excellent source of state-of-the-art information. Student interns can work and learn in your company at the same time. While these individuals may take time to train, an internship provides you with an excellent opportunity to determine whether they would make good full-time employees.

It is important to develop a relationship with colleges from which you intend to recruit. Your presence on campus will have a positive impact on students and faculty, but only if it is nurtured.

Just as you would conduct an advertising campaign to attract applicants to production jobs, you must publicize your existence to students. This includes posters around campus, articles and advertisements in the school paper along with scheduling on-campus recruiting times with the placement office. This nurturing process can also be accomplished by getting involved in campus activities. Sponsor events such as lectures, sports and entertainment. Serve in the visiting executive program if there is one. Participate in job and career fairs.

Visiting with faculty and administrators is of primary importance. Many students rely on the advice of these professionals for guidance in deciding where to work. This is an especially helpful strategy in fields like engineering where demand for graduating students is high.

> *Just as you would conduct an advertising campaign to attract applicants to production jobs, you must publicize your existence to students.*

> *"Far and away the best prize that life offers is the chance to work hard at work worth doing."*
>
> Theodore Roosevelt

Chapter 4   Recruiting the Best

How to approach part-time assistance

A college can also provide part-time help at less expense than the average employment agency. While college students must be paid, they are willing to work for less compensation in order to gain the practical experience and contacts. Call the placement office at your nearby college for additional information.

Public job services

There are a wide variety of public job services in your community that maintain lists of candidates from which to choose. Many times these organizations are unjustly maligned. Some are state and federally supported while others are sponsored by professional associations and civic groups.

The most effective strategy for locating the best applicants is to develop a relationship with the counselors or coordinators of these organizations. They will help you select individuals to address your needs.

IX. Creating an Attractive Job Vacancy Notice

Newspaper advertising is the most common means for announcing a vacancy. Unfortunately, it does not yield the desired results in many cases. The ad must be attractive and specific. Even then, there is a good chance of receiving a number of unwanted resumes.

With the tightening of labor pools across the United States, brief ads don't have the effect they used to. What is put into a small space like this has to compete with hundreds of other openings.

Before advertising in the local papers, peruse the classifieds. Observe their layout and where the type of job you want to fill is placed. If your type of opening cannot be found easily, you should look for another medium. Most cities have two or three papers. Many times the so-called blue collar jobs are listed in one paper while white collar jobs are listed in another. Placement tends to correlate with reader preference.

Besides the classifieds, you also have the option of placing a display ad. Much more can be done with a quarter, half or full page of a newspaper. The special effects unavailable in the classified ad can be used here to attract greater attention.

"When you hire people who are smarter than you are, you prove you are smarter than they are."

R.H. Grant

"Opportunity is missed by most people because it is dressed in overalls and looks like work."

Thomas Edison

But advertising studies have shown that small space ads will draw 75 to 80 percent of the response of a full page for much less cost. While classifieds do not stand out as much as a display ad, it is wise to refrain from inserting more than a quarter-page ad at any one time.

Avoid running a four-line ad in major newspapers that is swallowed up by the ads surrounding it. Instead, place a display ad in a few local papers where your information will get more play. The extra space also allows the opportunity to add work-life issues to the job description and qualifications.

Consider advertising in other areas of the paper besides the employment section. Some companies have had success attracting older individuals, for instance, by placing ads on the obituary page.

In addition to local papers, there are regional and national publications that cater to a specific industry or profession. Unfortunately, these tend to be issued monthly or quarterly, and are not timely enough for the average opening. The one exception would be the large-scale campaign to recruit a sizable number of employees. But this takes substantial advance planning.

> *"Genius is 1% inspiration and 99% perspiration."*
> Thomas Edison

> *Avoid running a four-line ad in major newspapers that is swallowed up by the ads surrounding it.*

Chapter 4 Recruiting the Best

What's Wrong with These Ads?

CUSTODIAN - for a large apartment complex. Experienced and sober. Will be on call every fourth weekend. Knowledge of A/C and plumbing repair helpful. Apply in person: Forest Green Apartment Homes, 34 O'Toole Avenue, Markham, MA.

SERVICE REPRESENTATIVE

To handle service calls for local distributor of electrical appliances. Will train. Reliable transportation a must. Mature man preferred. Call or apply in person: Health Appliances, Inc., 344 Broad Street, Emerson, NJ 07665, 456-6368.

WHAT A GREAT JOB!

ADMINISTRATIVE ASSISTANT to handle bookkeeping, reception and other duties. Permanent opening immediately available. Good writing and typing skills. Sense of humor. Able to work under pressure. Stable woman preferred. Apply to Mr. Storm, P.O. Box 3333, Lewiston, AL 98876.

ANSWER KEY

#1 - May not use the word "sober" or imply abuse. "Every fourth weekend" you may have to make reasonable accommodation.

#2 - "Mature man" infers discrimination. "Reliable transportation" — employer is responsible for providing transportation or reimbursement.

#3 - "Stable woman" infers discrimination. Some courts have held that referring to a job as "permanent" means for the life of the employee.

Writing a job notice

Writing a job notice is like writing an advertisement. The description must sell the job in the best light possible. At the same time, it must be honest and accurate. More than one company has lost a lawsuit over the wording in an ad that hid or exaggerated the true nature of a job.

Recognize that selling the position will also generate a number of unqualified applicants. If you have other positions to fill, this strategy might be a good way to collect resumes for those openings. Follow these guidelines for writing the notice:

- Start the ad with an attractive and descriptive title. Be sure the title you use is an accurate representation of the job and something that those you want to attract will understand.
- Write a brief description of the duties. Be sure to include what makes this job attractive. Do not include the obvious. Listing duties such as "development of software" in a job description for a computer programmer is redundant. Instead, include the uses of the software proposed and in which language. Providing information about the role of the position in the company also helps to sell the job.
- List required experience and education.
- Ask for a salary history. This will help you screen candidates who may be applying for a position for which they are either over- or underqualified.
- Sell the benefits of the job. How will the applicant benefit by holding this position? What's unique? The "Lab Supervisor" example on page 96 illustrates the value of selling benefits.
- Stress quality of work life issues in the ad. Values such as ethics, reward for hard work, personal and professional growth are experiencing a resurgence of priority in candidates' minds.
- Avoid adjectives that do not demonstrate the specific job characteristics. "Exciting, challenging and rewarding," etc., are relative to the individual.
- Personalize the ad. Talking to the applicant instead of just listing duties and qualifications will make the reader stop and think.

> *"The man who wins may have been counted out several times, but he didn't hear the referee."*
>
> H.E. Jansen

> *"We cannot do everything at once, but we can do something at once."*
>
> Calvin Coolidge

Personalized Recruitment Ad

Classified Advertising
"The Right Way"

WE'LL MISS YOU, JACKIE

Jackie is our staff assistant and she's leaving. We're looking for someone to take her place. She can type 90 words a minute (we'll take 65), has flawless English skills and can handle our seven phone lines with ease.

If you think you can fill Jackie's shoes and would like to join a fast-paced, results-oriented company, call Susan Hobbs at 444-3987 right away!

A WORLD-CLASS COMPANY

DIGI-LECTRONICS is a fast-growing subcontractor to the defense and computer industries. Our local plant is one of the most automated in the United States. We offer excellent benefits and training with an opportunity for advancement. We seek a:

LAB SUPERVISOR

Successful individual will supervise 8-10 technicians and must have experience in a printed circuit board environment combined with 3-5 years' supervisory experience in a nonunion environment. A degree in chemistry or chemical engineering required. We offer overtime and a 10% shift differential for 2nd and 3rd shifts. Send resume, letter of interest and salary history to: DIGI-LECTRONICS P.O. Box 13263, Fort Hassle, KY 77876.

KITCHEN AND SERVICE PERSONNEL

We're looking for high-energy individuals who enjoy challenges in a fast-paced environment to join our team. Experience is not necessary as we offer a complete training program. Apply in person between 2-4 pm weekdays to Cuisine Unique, 3404 S. Hempstead Blvd., Chicago, IL.

RETAIL MANAGER

National card, gift and sundry chain has an opening for store manager in a downtown location. No nights or Sundays. Two years of retail management experience or equivalent college training and customer service background preferred. Interested individuals should apply in person or call:

The Sundry Shop
2200 E. Kalamath Street
Littleton, CO
548-3759

- The examples on page 96 attempt to convince the reader to apply. Notice the persuasive language in the job summary. Edit closely. Eliminate unnecessary words and phrases. Assume potential applicants will be able to follow the flow of the ad. Be careful of abbreviations, however. These can be easily misunderstood or indecipherable.
- Answer the questions the candidate is most likely to ask. Put yourself in the reader's position. If you were reading one of the examples on page 96 as a job searcher, what questions would you have? Does this posting answer these questions? What would improve it?
- Listing salary is up to you. Some employers do not want their competitors to know how much they are paying. On the other hand, good candidates may not want to apply unless they know the nature of the compensation.
- The identity of the company can also be omitted at your discretion. Many larger companies do this to reduce the number of unqualified applicants who are simply attracted to the name. Other employers do not provide their name because they do not want competitors to know they are hiring. Not listing the company name also releases you from having to respond to rejected candidates without losing good will in the job market. This can be advantageous when there is a large number of submissions. On the other hand, good candidates may fail to apply simply because they fear the employer they are presently working for may be the advertiser. Some simply want to know where they are sending their credentials.
- How candidates may respond is up to you. For immediate hires such as staff and semiskilled positions, it is best to have the applicants call for an appointment. In many cases, these individuals will not have resumes and will have to come in to complete an application.

If they do apply in person, be sure someone is available to spend a couple of minutes interviewing them. The public relations benefit of this is tremendous.

When you are hiring for a professional or executive position, however, ask for application by resume.

Chapter 4   Recruiting the Best

X. Developing Labor Pools for the Future

Organizations that will thrive in the future must be proactive in their development of consistent labor pools. This development must be implemented now and take place continually.

Here are a few key strategies for ensuring your workforce of the future:

- Make sure recruiting awareness is a way of life for all employees. This will ensure a constant stream of referrals—reward those who do refer.
- Maintain positive employee relations both inside and outside the organization.
- Continue to build corporate image at every opportunity. Maintain a constant flow of information about programs and special events taking place in the company.
- Anticipate changes in the community's demographics and therefore its labor force. Don't follow what the media are saying. Find out before they do!
- Closely monitor applications. Look for patterns in response from certain labor groups. This will provide keys to where you should concentrate your advertising.
- Maintain your aggressiveness in the pursuit of applicants. Be creative and try the unusual to attract attention.
- Hire the best when they appear. Even if you don't have an exact spot, do what you can to get them on board and take advantage of their enthusiasm and skills.
- Get rid of employees who don't produce. These individuals have a negative impact on the teamwork and energy of those who do. Consequently, applicants and new hires will develop the wrong impression of organizational culture.
- Know your organization's strategic plan and where you'll have openings in the next 12 months. Anticipation of need eliminates panic.

"Before everything else, getting ready is the secret of success."

Henry Ford

A Checklist for Recruiting Basics

☐ 1. Have you developed a set of procedures and contingencies for recruiting within your company?
☐ 2. Have you included the cost of recruiting in your budget?
☐ 3. Have you developed a system for recruiting internally?
☐ 4. Have you developed a system for tracking referrals?
☐ 5. Do you provide an incentive program for referrals?
☐ 6. Have you developed a relationship with a reliable employment agency to serve your staffing needs?
☐ 7. Are you consistently checking your recruitment literature and advertisements for potentially discriminatory statements or inferences?
☐ 8. Once again, do you really need to fill the position? (See Chapter Three.)
☐ 9. And again. Do you have a well-defined description for the job to be filled? (See Chapter Three.)
☐ 10. Have you developed a profile for each of the applicant groups from which you recruit?
☐ 11. Have you begun to include senior workers in your recruiting plans for all levels of work?
☐ 12. Have you examined the feasibility of including individuals with disabilities in your staffing plans?
☐ 13. Have you examined the feasibility of including temporaries in your staffing plans?
☐ 14. Have you considered using contract managers and professionals in certain positions?
☐ 15. Have you developed a recruiting plan taking into consideration changes in your staffing needs and labor pools over the next five years?
☐ 16. Have you communicated the importance of recruiting and provided employees with the information necessary to "sell" the company?
☐ 17. Are you taking steps to get involved with local schools to foster relationships for recruiting students and graduates?
☐ 18. Do you regularly evaluate your organization's image?
☐ 19. Have you examined the variety of alternative work plans available, such as flexible scheduling and telecommuting, for their suitability in your organization?
☐ 20. Have you organized and implemented an internship program with local schools?
☐ 21. Have you examined the way you are recruiting professionals to ensure you are addressing their needs?
☐ 22. Have you developed an aggressive stance toward recruiting employees?

Chapter 4   Recruiting the Best

Questions for Personal Development

1. What is the major emphasis of this chapter?

2. What are the most important things you learned from this chapter?

3. How can you apply what you learned to your current job?

4. How will you go about making these changes?

5. How can you monitor improvement?

6. Summarize the changes you expect to see in yourself one year from now.

CHAPTER 5

Family and Friends — Dealing with Nepotism

The production manager was irritated. "I know he's your son and I know he's qualified," he said to the owner, "but I feel like I'm competing to keep my job. I can't use my discretion knowing that anything he questions is going to end up in your ear."
"Be patient with him," replied the owner. "He's learning the ropes."
"Let him learn someplace else," retorted the manager. "I'll be honest with you, Jack. If this continues, I'm going to start looking for a better situation."

Here's What You'll Learn

   I. Nepotism in Business
  II. The Pros and Cons of Family and Friends
 III. The Legal Aspects of Nepotism
  IV. Devising a Nepotism Policy
   V. Tips on Screening Family and Friends
  VI. The Nepotism Checklist

> *"Business, you know, may bring money, but friendship hardly ever does."*
>
> Jane Austen

Chapter 5 Family and Friends — Dealing with Nepotism

I. Nepotism in Business

> *"The haves and the have-nots can often be traced back to the dids and the did-nots."*
>
> D.O. Flynn

Hiring family and friends is a common practice in many companies. In fact, some of the nation's largest enterprises are family-owned. At its inception, a company may consist of a spouse, two or three good friends and a couple of long-time business associates who believed in the idea.

The Small Business Administration has estimated there are 13 million family-owned businesses in the United States. These range in size from the nation's largest corporations to "mom and pop" companies that have been around for years.

Employers tend to rely more on referrals for their recruiting needs than any other source. It can be comforting to know that someone else you trust within the organization has known this individual and can attest to his character and work ethic.

Generally, family members or friends have a larger psychological investment in the future of the organization. They know people in the firm, and this makes it easier for them to adapt. They might work harder knowing whose livelihoods are depending on it.

II. The Pros and Cons of Family and Friends

There are a number of pros and cons to the hiring of family and friends. You must be careful to deal with these applicants the same way you would deal with an outsider. But while there can be unfortunate situations, there can also be substantial benefits.

Most research in the area of nepotism has revealed that even though it is prevalent throughout American business, there is not a lot of support for this practice. Following are some arguments for and against nepotism. Decide for yourself whether this practice should be allowed.

> *Generally, family members or friends have a larger psychological investment in the future of the organization.*

Arguments for nepotism

- Family members generally have a bigger psychological investment in you and the organization. If you started the company, they have probably heard you talk about it for a long time. It might feel as if the company is part of the family.

- Relatives of executives will feel a greater pressure to perform well because they are relatives. Where nonrelatives might "punch the clock," family members will try harder due to the nature of the relationship.

- It takes less time to train and indoctrinate relatives.

- Relatives working together share common goals and values.

- Salespeople bearing the name of the company are more likely to impress clients.

- Family members and friends might be willing to forego a certain amount of compensation and throw in extra time knowing they will reap the rewards later.

Chapter 5 Family and Friends — Dealing with Nepotism

Arguments against nepotism

- Supervisors are intimidated by subordinates who are related to executives.
- Relatives who are not successful within the company are difficult to discipline or fire.
- Relatives tend to be pushed up the ladder within the company, preventing other more competent individuals from advancing.
- Employees are afraid of talking about business around relatives because they fear that these individuals are acting as spies.
- Related employees are frustrated because they are never sure whether they made it on their own or because of family influences.
- Family members can rarely meet the expectations of other employees.
- Many times, there is an assumption on the part of relatives or friends that they are a "shoo-in" for a job, simply because of their relationship with you or someone else within the company. If these people are not qualified for the job, it is not always easy to reject their application.
- If friends or relatives are qualified for the position, it may be very difficult to select someone else without insulting a number of friends or relatives. Further still, these applicants never quite know whether they were hired for competence or because they are members of the family. Other employees are never sure about this either, which can cause some friction.
- Termination of friends or relatives, if they do not work out, is difficult, if not impossible. You may be viewed as persecuting that individual and creating a difficult situation within the entire family.
- There are also issues of leadership transition. Will the son automatically follow in the father's footsteps? Does this practice send a message to the rest of the employees that there is little chance for advancement into the executive ranks?
- Can these individuals be placed in sensitive positions, such as payroll, assistant to other executives, or areas where they would have access to confidential information about the future of the company? If you do not do this, is this a form of discrimination?
- Finally, the hiring of relatives and friends has an influence on the morale of other employees. Questions of favoritism come into play. While these issues may not surface, assume they are being noted and discussed throughout the company.

III. The Legal Aspects of Nepotism

In addition to issues revolving around personal relationships, you must be cognizant of the legal implications of recruiting friends and relatives with regard to antidiscrimination legislation. While it is permissible to hire anyone you wish, the company must also meet equal employment/affirmative action standards if you have 15 or more employees.

The practice of hiring on referral must be watched carefully to ensure proper hiring procedures. Family and friends should be hired in the same manner as any other applicant. Consistency is a key factor.

A number of states have passed legislation prohibiting discrimination on the basis of nepotism. This means that spouses cannot be denied employment because they are married to someone in the company. You may still prohibit that person, however, from working under the direct supervision of a spouse or other relative.

In asking about possible relations within the organization, be aware of possible discriminatory practices. It is perfectly acceptable, for example, to ask if the applicant has relatives working for the company. However, selection decisions should not be based on this information.

Nepotism should not officially be encouraged. A statement in the nepotism policy or elsewhere that encourages the hiring of family and friends could be seen as having an adverse impact.

An example of this would be a firm that has a predominantly white labor force and issues a policy encouraging nepotism. In this case, even requesting information about friends and relatives could be construed as discrimination in certain situations. The only defense for this is job relatedness or business necessity.

> *"I am amazed that anyone who has made a fortune should send for his friends."*
> Aristophanes

> *"Give the best you have to the highest you know — and do it now."*
> Ralph Sockman

> *"Many receive advice, only the wise profit from it."*
> Syrus

IV. Devising a Nepotism Policy

Regardless of whether you support the practice of nepotism, you should develop a nepotism policy to define the hiring practices within your organization. This policy does not have to be complicated, but the following constituencies should be considered:
- Spouses
- Immediate family of employees (i.e., sons, daughters, brothers, sisters, parents and grandparents)
- Extended family (i.e., cousins, nephews, nieces, aunts, uncles, etc.)
- Friends
- Employees who marry each other

Developing the policy

When writing a policy on nepotism, include the following:
- Definition of nepotism
- Hiring policy regarding the hiring of relatives and friends compared with other candidates
- Employees who marry another employee
- Investigation of possible nepotism during the pre-employment process
- Penalties for misrepresenting relationships
- Hiring of temporary employees as it relates to the nepotism policy
- Supervisory relationships between related employees

Word the policy carefully to avoid the implication of discrimination. Refusal to hire wives of employees, for instance, may be regarded as discrimination against women. The appearance of favoritism may attract the attention of the Equal Employment Opportunity Commission.

Recognize that seemingly neutral policies may have an adverse impact and create problems for the company. Consult your attorney prior to implementation.

Recognize that seemingly neutral policies may have an adverse impact and create problems for the company.

"Our belief at the beginning of a doubtful undertaking is the one thing that ensures the successful outcome of our venture."

William James

V. Tips on Screening Family and Friends

Deal with the hiring of family, friends and referrals in a fair and consistent manner. Consider the following hints:

Don't assume too much. Just because candidates come "highly recommended" from a relative or friend, don't assume they will fulfill your every want and need. The offer "Send him over and I'll give him a job" has turned into disaster more than once. Interview the person thoroughly. Ask the same questions you would of a candidate you have never met before. Judge this person on the same criteria.

Interview the contact who referred the applicant. Determine whether the contact knows the candidate well enough to recommend him in good faith. Ask the reference some of the same questions you would ask the candidate.

Don't ignore references. Just because the candidate is being referred by someone you know, check his references. Chances are the person who made the initial referral knows the candidate personally, not professionally.

Exercise extreme fairness. Always err on the side of fairness when hiring family and friends. You are under no obligation to hire anyone, but a little extra care in this process could go a long way.

Don't hesitate to investigate questionable situations. While you should be fair at all times, investigate what doesn't feel right. If you are not sure, for instance, why a particular person was referred, ask the person who made the referral. There may be a specific situation he is trying to hide.

"All work, even cotton spinning, is noble; work is alone noble. A life of ease is not for any man, nor for any god."

Thomas Carlyle

"I think and think for months and years; 99 times the conclusion is false. The 100th time I'm right."

Albert Einstein

> *"You will become as small as your controlling desire; as great as your dominant aspiration."*
>
> James Allen

Don't be influenced by outside sources. Be careful in allowing friends and family to influence your decisions. You know your needs better than anyone else. Friends and family probably have their own agendas. Family pressure may not have the company's best interests in mind.

Take existing employee relationships into consideration. Review the environment where a family member or friend will be placed. Will that person fit in? Is he going to feel comfortable working with these individuals? Also, examine, if possible, the ramifications of placing family members and friends into certain work environments. Placing a good friend of yours directly under a new manager, for example, may be perceived as a strategy to check up on the manager's performance.

Be prepared to address questions about your decision. Once again, you are under no obligation to do so. But a few well-explained answers can smooth ruffled feathers when someone does not understand the circumstances and facts.

Make your expectations perfectly clear to the friend or relative if selected. While these individuals already understand the situation, make sure that they understand the expectations you have for the position. These criteria should not differ from those for any other person who would enter the job. Your selection does not allow them to work by a different set of standards.

If necessary, also address the situation with existing employees. If you suspect there are uncertainties or grumblings about your selection, address the situation. Ask the parties concerned if they would like to air their feelings. Such goodwill can go a long way toward building healthy communication.

> *Favoritism, especially when it comes to compensation, will be your undoing.*

Family members and friends should get "market salary" for the position they hold. Favoritism, especially when it comes to compensation, will be your undoing.

Family members should not participate in the hiring of relatives. Regardless of how competent these individuals may be, this practice leaves the management staff open to charges of conflict of interest and a host of other issues.

Family members should not supervise other family members. Once again, this practice leads to charges of conflict of interest and diminishing influence.

The Nepotism Checklist

☐ 1. Have you reviewed your company's hiring practices to determine the number of family members and friends employed?

☐ 2. Has your company developed a nepotism policy?

☐ 3. Are the employees in your company encouraged to refer candidates for positions within the company?

☐ 4. Are all those who hire within the company aware of the nepotism policy and its practices?

☐ 5. Does your nepotism policy take antidiscrimination legislation into consideration?

Chapter 5   Family and Friends — Dealing with Nepotism

Questions for Personal Development

1. What is the major emphasis of this chapter?
   _____
   _____
   _____
   _____

2. What are the most important things you learned from this chapter?
   _____
   _____
   _____
   _____

3. How can you apply what you learned to your current job?
   _____
   _____
   _____
   _____

4. How will you go about making these changes?
   _____
   _____
   _____
   _____

5. How can you monitor improvement?
   _____
   _____
   _____
   _____

6. Summarize the changes you expect to see in yourself one year from now.
   _____
   _____
   _____
   _____

Evaluating Resumes and Applications

"I've never really done this before," he said. "We were always assigned receptionists from the pool. To be honest, I've never really hired anybody."

"I don't know what to tell you," she agreed. "All the resumes look the same and the only information I can get out of the references are job titles and dates of employment."

> *"I share no man's opinion. I have my own."*
>
> Ivan Turgenev

Here's What You'll Learn

I. Resumes and Applications: Where Should They Be Used?
II. Evaluating a Resume Effectively
III. Evaluating Cover Letters
IV. Development and Review of Applications
V. Evaluating the Resume/Application/Reference Package
VI. The Resume/Application Checklist

Resumes have become the "business card" of a job search. Every day millions are mailed or submitted in person to companies across the United States. An entire industry has grown up around the science of resume development and application completion. Hundreds of companies, colleges and counselors stake their reputation on "how to get inside the employer's head."

Chapter 6 Evaluating Resumes and Applications

What should you be looking for in one of these documents? Most applications and resumes provide a summary of experience, education, high school and college activities. They might begin with an objective that reads "a challenging and responsible career in the field of ..."

Unfortunately, this information can provide only a history of accomplishments (or lack thereof) and fails to inform the reader of what the applicant would do if given a position. This is not to say these documents are not somewhat helpful. By asking the right questions and looking for specific criteria, you may gain important information about their owner from both an application and a resume.

I. Resumes and Applications: Where Should They Be Used?

"The only fool bigger than the person who knows it all is the person who argues with him."

Thomas Foller

While some companies use resumes and applications interchangeably, resumes have been traditionally used for professional-level positions. Applications have been commonly relegated to the areas of skilled, semiskilled and nonskilled labor. In a few cases, larger companies have been using both.

While the application provides the same basic information as a resume, it does so in a more rigid manner. Everyone completes the same information, in the same order, and gaps in information are immediately apparent by blank space.

Resumes, on the other hand, allow the author to express creativity when relating background. This is an opportunity to present the information in the priority which the applicant thinks is important. Resumes have been compared to advertisements in newspapers or magazines. Where do the eyes go? How is the information written to grab the most attention? Studies by job search experts indicate the average evaluator spends no more than 45 seconds reviewing a resume before deciding the fate of its owner.

Both documents have their strengths and weaknesses. While resumes allow for creativity, one has to examine each resume more closely for the information needed to make a decision. The fact that a particular applicant lacks experience or training in a skill can be hidden in a morass of college activities, completed coursework and personal interests. Comparing resumes can be like comparing apples and oranges. They're both fruit but that's where the similarities end.

On the other hand, an application generally allows for no creativity whatsoever. While the information is listed, there is little opportunity for the applicant to demonstrate how much care went into preparation. With labor-oriented positions, a reflection of such caring may not be crucial. By contrast, for positions where many forms of creativity are essential, the resume may serve as a harbinger of things to come.

> *Many owners have experienced the consequences of ignoring their business sense in favor of a political situation.*

II. Evaluating a Resume Effectively

What do you look for in a resume? This depends upon criteria determined ahead of time. Too often, evaluators look at a resume and discover an item they like: "Hey, they went to the same college and held a job as a waiter in high school just like me." There is an obvious empathy with someone who shares your experience, and it can be tempting to include this person in the hiring process simply because of these extraneous facts. While a person's ability to fit into the new environment is important, sometimes too much emphasis is placed on irrelevant details.

On the other hand, the resume may contain some details that the evaluator finds disheartening or inappropriate: "An English major! Why would anyone apply for a job as a processing manager if they were an English major?" This person may be rejected simply due to lack of identification with the applicant, only based on the applicant's resume. Don't jump to conclusions.

Occasionally, you may be reviewing the resume of an acquaintance. This resume may have come from a referral or through an off-chance mention that the company was searching to fill a position. The temptation is to overlook certain shortcomings or mismatches for political reasons. The applicant may be a personal friend, or a friend of the boss. The evaluator may not want to face the possibility of having to reject that person and ruin a relationship.

> *"Thinking is the hardest work there is, which is probably the reason why so few engage in it."*
>
> Henry Ford

The evaluation of these resumes should be made with particular care. Many owners have experienced the consequences of ignoring their business sense in favor of a political situation.

The key to evaluating a resume is to remain impartial. This may be easier said than done, but the attempt must be made. Not only might you mis-hire, but the legal ramifications of off-handed decisions may prove extremely expensive.

Chapter 6 Evaluating Resumes and Applications

Robert B. Roberts
231 Hacker Way
Minneapolis, MN 23254
(555) 848-4832

PROFESSIONAL OBJECTIVE: Semi-conductor research and new product development

[Clear objective with definite goal]

RELATED EXPERIENCE:

Senior Engineer, Key Technologies, Crabtree, MN (1982-present)
  Duties included:
  - Design of semi-conductor products
  - Supervision of five engineers and staff
  - Overseeing projected budgets of up to $1,000,000
  - Selection of professional staff members
  - Supervised design of product that realized $2,000,000 in revenue in the first nine months

[Listed, easy-to-read description]

[Numbers define parameters of responsibility]

[Demonstrated value to firm]

Engineer, Apple Computer, Cupertino, CA (1980-82)
  Duties included: Research and design of software applications for the Macintosh project. Extensive training in software development.

[Points out recognizable product]

Engineering Intern, Lockheed Aerospace, Santa Clara, CA (1979)
  Duties included: Testing of software design and cataloging of projects. Received secret clearance.

[Knows a secret clearance may be an asset]

Other employment has included: computer lab assistant, waiter, cook.

EDUCATION:
  Bachelor of Science, Electrical Engineering, University of California, Santa Clara. Graduation: December 1979 GPA: 3.2/4.0

LICENSES:
  Professional Engineer, May 1985
  Engineer in Training, June, 1980

[Continuing education]

COMPUTER EXPERIENCE:
  Hardware: VAX, IBM, Apple
  Languages: C, Assembly, Cobol, Pascal, Fortran
  Software: Microsoft Word, Lotus 1-2-3, technical packages

[Demonstrates versatility]

OTHER ACTIVITIES:
  President, Computer Systems Club, U.C.S.C. (1978)
  Intramural basketball and softball in college

[Is a leader and team player]

The requirements of the new Immigration Reform and Control Act of 1986 are a good example in this respect. The guidelines for this law specifically state that an applicant may not be turned away simply because of the sound of her name. This, the law says, is clearly discrimination.

Prior to the review of any resume, the evaluator must have a clear picture of the position to be filled. This picture should be provided by a job description and any other information deemed relevant. Place yourself in the successful applicant's position for a moment. What would this person need to know about the job duties, company culture and organizational rules and guidelines to excel in the job? When evaluating a resume, six areas need to be taken into consideration:

- Overall appearance
- Organization
- Educational information
- Experiential information
- Information concerning other relevant activities
- Discriminatory information

Overall appearance

The overall appearance of the resume gives you an indication of the care taken in preparation.

- Are there spelling errors?
- Is everything in the proper tense?
- Is the resume printed on a good quality bond with envelope and cover letter to match?
- Is the printing readable (including style of typeface and clarity of copy)?
- What other criteria do you personally look for when reviewing something of this nature?
- Does it have that "textbook" appearance? Did the applicant write it or was it prepared by a professional?
- What will impress you positively and negatively?

While some of the items above may appear inconsequential, they indicate the level of care put into the resume and therefore the level of interest the applicant may have in doing a good job. When you are reviewing more than a hundred resumes, faded printing, poor quality paper, spelling errors and the like can be distracting.

> *"You don't ever ask a barber if you need a haircut."*
>
> Greenberg

Chapter 6 Evaluating Resumes and Applications

Wayne Nootown
524-A Francine Court
Silver Beach, Utah 89843
(555) 533-4353

CAREER GOAL: Distribution management ⟵ *Vague goal*

EXPERIENCE:
Manager, Topol's Readymart, Manhassett, NY
  Duties: Supervised employees, trained cashiers, responsible for inventory control. (1992)
  ⟵ *Vague duties*
  ⟵ *Misspelling*
  ⟵ *Unspecific date: the whole year?*

Manager, K-Mart Stores, Long Island City, NY
  Duties: Responsible for camera department, hired employees and supervised night shift. (1991)

Distribution supervisor, ABC Store, Long Island City, NY
  Duties: Oversaw all deliveries to 17 stores. Controlled 7 truck drivers. Assisted customers. (1990-91)
  ⟵ *Vague description. Lack of information.*
  ⟵ *Three jobs in three years*
  ⟵ *Why is he helping customers if he's in distribution?*

Waiter: King's Grant Inn, King's Point, NY
  Duties: Table service in 250-seat restaurant. Assisted with scheduling. Trained waitresses. (1980-86)

EDUCATION:
Bachelor of Science in Business Administration, 1986
C.W. Post College, Long Island City, NY

Coursework included: Distribution management, accounting, finance, management, English, economics.
  ⟵ *Lack of specific coursework*

Other activities: Finance club, intramural softball and basketball, Zeta Phi Beta Fraternity, social chairman.

HONORS:
Dean's List, College of Business (1983) ⟵ *How long on the dean's list?*
Scholarship Award, Zeta Phi Beta Fraternity, 1984
Team Captain, Zeta Phi Beta softball, 1984
Resident Assistant, Decker Hall, C.W. Post College, 1983-4

References Available Upon Request

Organization

- Does the resume tell you what you want to know?
- Has care been taken to include information that will help you in the decision-making process?
- Does it ramble with no clear path or direction?
- Are the individual entries consistent and understandable?
- Do you find the information you need when looking under the logical category?

How a person organizes the information on a resume can provide insight into her priorities and her understanding of the position to be filled.

How a person organizes the information on a resume can provide insight into her priorities and her understanding of the position to be filled. It is common sense as an applicant to place yourself in the shoes of the employer and decide how to organize the resume's content to make it most effective. Applicants who do this show a caring and understanding of the process.

Some applicants place education above experience, for example, even though they have several years of related work. These individuals exhibit very little understanding about the importance of practical experience in pursuing a position with a small company.

The organization used in various explanations indicates the person's ability to communicate effectively. The length of explanations can be a reference to how talkative the person is and can also indicate her command of the English language. Make a list of other criteria to judge in the organization of a resume. How can these criteria relate to an applicant's ability to excel in the position?

Education

The evaluation of education is usually fairly straightforward. It is important, however, to determine the educational requirements of the position in advance. While a college degree may be helpful in many cases, it is certainly not mandatory.

An evaluator needs to look at the motivations of an applicant who possesses more education than the position requires. With the number of college graduates each year, it is conceivable that no other work could be found. On the other hand, it is also quite possible that this same applicant will grow bored and unproductive in a short period of time in a nonstimulating job.

More than one company, large and small, has hired on the basis of most education, and has later been hurt by the turnover of that same employee. Matching education to job requirements can be a difficult issue, but one that needs attention.

"Success is getting what you want; happiness is wanting what you get."

Dale Carnegie

Chapter 6   Evaluating Resumes and Applications

Define what level of education is required for the job. Check the resume to ascertain the applicant's educational qualifications. Be flexible in this area since a particular major is not required in most cases. An applicant with an English degree might very well perform the job as capably as one with a degree in management. There are exceptions to this rule, such as accounting and engineering, but these are rare.

Regardless of qualifications, check all educational credentials with the granting institution if you are serious about the candidate! With the tightening job market, more individuals are claiming degrees and certifications they have not earned. These deceptions can be very damaging.

> *Job searchers are taught to assess their transferable skills so they may be explained on a resume or during an interview.*

Experience

For most companies, an applicant's experience is critical information. While there are exceptions to this, of course, having a skilled applicant certainly eases the situation.

Since it is rare that an applicant will walk through the door with identical experience to what you are seeking, the next best alternative is to compare the experience identified with your requirements. Job searchers are taught to assess their transferable skills so they may be explained on a resume or during an interview. While these may be laid out clearly on the resume, the evaluator should examine this information closely to verify a match.

When examining the experience section, consider the following:
- Do they provide parameters from which to judge responsibility (number supervised, size of budget, amount of sales)?
- Duties vs. responsibility (what did they actually do?).
- Has the applicant thought about how her acquired skills will fit into the position sought? It's possible to be responsible for something and not know a thing about it.
- Do they provide a list of accomplishments that give an indication of work ethic and working knowledge of a discipline
- Tenure in the position. "Manager" does not hold much water if they were in the position for three months.
- Is this the real job title? Applicants can be pretty free with descriptions and fool a lot of people. ("Well, I wasn't really the manager. But I did all the work and he just sat around.")

As with education, checking references is of great importance. More than one applicant has exaggerated her past or completely lied. Some experts estimate that 30 percent of all resumes in the market at any one time contain false information.

When examining the experience section of a resume, the evaluator must at once be fair and strict. Remember that the experience detailed may have been significantly more involved, yet the applicant was too modest to claim it. An example of this might be one who lists a job title such as "documents clerk" when the position involved much more than initially perceived.

On the other hand, some experience claimed might not have happened exactly the way it was described. This would be the person, for instance, who claimed the title "manager" when in reality she was responsible for a small portion of a particular project. Yes, there was management taking place. But then a person who is in charge of anything or anybody might be considered a manager.

This same caveat holds true with other types of positions, especially dealing with technically related matter. It may look the same, but is it?

Determine in advance the personal characteristics of the ideal applicant for the position. A long tenure of employment with one company can have its pros and cons. Long-term may imply company loyalty, ability to get along with others and ability to contribute on a team. On the other hand, some of the energy and risk orientation toward one's job may have diminished along with the development of a certain sedentary quality.

A number of short-term employments can have a variety of meanings. The applicant could be moving quickly due to hard work and assertiveness. This might be just the type of person needed for a small company. But short-term employment could also mean lack of concentration, impatience or other negative characteristics. A company that lands such a new employee might lose her a short time later.

Other activities

This category may carry a wide range of information. Community involvement, college activities, church-related functions, hobbies and special interests all provide a glance into the type of person who is applying.

> *"Experience is the name everyone gives to their mistakes."*
>
> Oscar Wilde

> *Long-term employment may imply company loyalty. On the other hand, it could mean the development of a certain sedentary quality.*

While in many cases this information is not related to the applicant's ability to do the job, it provides an opportunity to see potential for other possibilities in the future. Leadership positions in college activities usually provide at least some training, as does involvement in professional associations. These experiences, although not formally compensated, translate well into strong skills.

Discriminatory information

The appearance of discriminatory information on a resume is usually little cause for concern. However, all individuals involved with the selection process should be aware that this type of information may not be included in the consideration of a candidate (no matter how helpful it may be).

Your company should develop a simple policy regarding this information if found on a resume. While the chances of a visit by the Equal Employment Opportunity Commission is remote, the burden of proof that you are not discriminating is sometimes left to the company. This can be an expensive legal nightmare. Some companies have a receptionist cross off the offending material with a felt-tip marker before it reaches the evaluator.

III. Evaluating Cover Letters

Included with most resumes and applications is a cover letter from the job seeker. This document can provide a variety of clues about its author with the help of the following tips.

> *"Most people live ... in a very restricted circle of their potential being."*
> William James

> *"Calvin Coolidge didn't say much, and when he did, he didn't say much."*
> Will Rogers

Tips for review

Ask yourself the following questions when evaluating cover letters:

✔ Is it written in proper business format? Since this is a form of business correspondence, the letter should represent itself as such. Is it clean and crisp, showing that care has been taken in typing it?

✔ Does the letter show care in its preparation? Is it addressed to you or a person within your organization? Does the salutation read "Dear Sir" or "Dear Madam"?

✔ Is it an original letter or are you one of 467 recipients? The best way to detect this is to look for referrals to your organization other than the canned phrases found in junk mail. If there is evidence to this effect, you can assume the applicant has researched your organization to some degree. This is a very positive sign since so few applicants choose to do so.

✔ How correct are the spelling and grammar? Is the letter written concisely?

✔ Does the letter achieve its objective? Does it impress you with the applicant's focus and reasons for wanting the job? Is it well organized?

✔ Finally, does it have that marketing quality that sells you on how the applicant can contribute to your organization?

Every evaluator has her own peculiarities when reviewing correspondence. The best policy is to go with your tendencies since you know the organization better than anyone else. (This, of course, has to be kept within reason. One employer will not review resumes and correspondence unless they are printed on white paper, period!)

> *"Genius does what it must, and talent does what it can."*
>
> Edward Bulwer-Lytton

Chapter 6 Evaluating Resumes and Applications

December 13, 19XX

Mr. Frank Zeppo, President
Liteworks, Inc.
123 Earnest Avenue
Little Rock, AR 66578

Dear Mr. Zeppo:

[She called to develop rapport] Thank you for the information you provided yesterday on the position of controller now open in Liteworks, Inc. The duties sound like a perfect match for my experience and education. As promised, I have enclosed a copy of my resume for your review. [Confident statement]

[She reviews discussion of the day before] As we discussed, I have a significant amount of experience in accounting along with work on a variety of spreadsheet programs. I feel very comfortable in a manufacturing setting since I am in that type of environment presently.

In addition to my technical skills, I have proven management and communications expertise, having supervised other employees in two different settings. Working in a small company is stimulating and I thrive in such an atmosphere. [Good selling point]

[Specifying her value to a small company] Since you are anxious to hire someone, I will contact you later this week to set a time when we can meet. Thank you for your interest in my services. [She is anticipating the person's needs]

Sincerely,

Sharon Grant

[Correct business form] enclosure

IV. Development and Review of Applications

Every company has developed an application of some sort to organize the hiring process. A person enters the office and is handed an application which she completes and returns to the receptionist, and then waits for an interview.

This process has encouraged the creation of hundreds of application forms that are sold over the counter in much the same way as a "boilerplate" apartment lease. While these generic documents can save time in the short run, they may mean trouble. Most companies distributing this type of information do so nationally. Many organizations using these forms fail to realize that state and local labor laws do vary. Therefore, what can be legally asked in one jurisdiction may be prohibited in another.

> *"Every man loves what he is good at."*
>
> Thomas Shadwell

Developing an application

The most efficient strategy for developing your company's application is to first assemble a collection of samples from other organizations. A number of manuals and companies can also be used as sources. Review the application example on the following page.

As you review the various forms, make note of questions that would be appropriate for your purposes. While the samples will resemble each other in many ways, compare the different wordings and choose the best for your firm. Remember — each question needs to be checked for its legality within your locale! (If, in the future, you begin operations in other states, the application will need to be checked against the laws of each state in which you operate.)

If your company has exceeded 14 employees, it falls within the jurisdiction of federal antidiscrimination laws. (See Chapter Two.) In fulfilling these requirements, the organization may need to comply with affirmative action record-keeping. Note that questions related to these areas (sex, marital status, national origin, religion) may be asked on the application but cannot be used in the consideration of candidates. You might develop a system for preventing the evaluator from incorporating this information. A detachable section for these questions on the application is one alternative.

Chapter 6 Evaluating Resumes and Applications

Digi-Lectronics
Employment Application

** Read the statement below *before* completing this application. Complete the entire application.

Position desired_____

NAME Last	First	Middle	Social Security No.

Street Address	City	State	ZIP

Home Phone: Business Phone:	Referred by: (if applicable)
Relatives employed by Digi-Lectronics?	Military Service? When?

* Do you have any physical handicaps that may hinder you from performing the job you have applied for?

EDUCATION

School	City	State	Dates Attended	Course of Study	Grad?

List professional licenses and associations:

** Discrimination because of age, sex, race, color, religious creed, national origin, ancestry, physical or mental handicap, or military status is prohibited by federal and state law. Please exclude any information that indicates the above characteristics. If you are hired, you will be required to provide verification of any information reported on this application.

*Equal Opportunity Employer

If you have a handicap and would like to be considered under our affirmative action program, please inform us. Relevant information provided will not subject you to discriminatory treatment. Digi-Lectronics is a government contractor subject to Section 503 of the Rehabilitation Act of 1973 and is required to take affirmative action to employ qualified handicapped individuals.

EMPLOYMENT (this section abbreviated for example)

Employer name and address	Your position & duties	Dates of employ	Wages (40 hrs)
Supervisor's name and position		Reason for leaving	
Employer name and address	Your position & duties	Dates of employ	Wages (40 hrs)
Supervisor's name and position		Reason for leaving	

Additional remarks:

REFERENCES

Name	Name	Name
Address	Address	Address
Phone	Phone	Phone

Read Before Signing

I hereby certify that all information contained on this application is true and complete. I authorize Digi-Lectronics to contact all sources necessary to verify this information. I understand that any misstatement or omission is sufficient grounds for immediate discharge.

Signature_____ Date_____

Failure to comply with these laws can be costly, and they are sometimes easily overlooked. State authorities could also enter the case. It is best to be very careful.

Review of applications

The advantages of having every applicant complete the same form is ease of comparison along with ensuring that every candidate is treated consistently. This saves time and increases accuracy. However, it is difficult to read anything into the preparation of the form.

The evaluator should have a clear picture of minimum requirements for the position. There will always be exceptional applicants and those who fall within the gray areas of being marginally qualified. Having these requirements in writing discourages mistakes and confusions. Consider education and experience, for example. A candidate with two years' experience submitting an application for a job that requires three might still be included if she also has one year of college coursework in that field. A well-written job description (such as explained in Chapter Three) that identifies education as a viable alternative eases the job of the evaluator.

The following are some key points to be considered when reviewing applications.

Clarity: Cleanliness, legibility and organization are factors influencing an evaluator's opinion of a candidate. A large number of corrected mistakes, for example, can be an indication of an applicant's level of care when working. The applicant may also be adjusting the information to make it more attractive.

Ability to follow directions: Check to see if the information provided answers the question. Does it make sense? Is it logical? Anyone who has dealt with employment applications can tell story after story of illogical answers, some rather humorous:

Q: Length of residence?
A: 75 feet.
Q: Have you ever been convicted of a crime?
A: Never been caught.
Q: Size of previous company?
A: 23 floors.

> "The measure of a man's character is what he would do if he knew he would never be found out."
>
> Thomas Macaulay

Accuracy of information:
- Does the information check out?
- Are there numerous spelling and grammatical errors?
- Do you have to work at deciphering the information offered?

As you might imagine, there are also numerous services on the market to analyze handwriting color of ink, and the psychological implications of written responses. These will be discussed in Chapter Ten.

Remember that only those facts that are job related may be evaluated! A completed application, for example, may contain a number of spelling errors. However, this reason may not be used to disqualify the candidate unless it can be shown that an ability to spell accurately is essential to the performance of the job.

V. Evaluating the Resume/ Application/Reference Package

Once all information has been gathered on the applicants for a position, a decision must be made on who will be interviewed to receive closer scrutiny. The key to this process is organization and documentation.

Tips for decision-making

The best way to handle decisions of this nature is to create a simple form with the pertinent criteria listed. This type of organization maintains fairness in the selection process and also provides clear evidence in discrimination litigation. If this is a position that will be filled repeatedly, it pays to formalize the document and include it in procedural training. The form does not have to be complicated and should resemble the sample on page 127.

Decisions should be made with impartiality. Of course, there are exceptions. But these should be rare. Many smaller companies develop a practice of hiring friends, relatives and other trusted associates in order to save money or to provide peace of mind. Time and time again, these hires turn into difficult and expensive situations. (See Chapter Five.)

"Genius is the ability to reduce the complicated to the simple."

C.W. Ceran

"There will always be someone who will oppose every decision you make."

Anonymous

Hand-Picked: The Complete Guide to Finding and Hiring the Best Employees

In the rush to hire new employees, the best-laid plans can be overlooked. Documentation, organization and consistency are essential to smart hiring.

Record-Keeping

It is essential to maintain accurate records on the application process to ensure compliance with laws and to serve as a paper trail for future planning and recruitment. Because of the large numbers of resumes that pervade the workplace, there is a tendency among employers to discard resumes and applications of individuals who are not hired. Unfortunately, some excellent candidates for the next job are lost in the trash.

Rather than review them here, a table of federal record-keeping requirements for the hiring process is provided in Appendix B. It is best to consult your state's labor department for any additional laws.

Applicant Screening Form

Position to fill_____ Supervisor_____

As you review each application/resume, rate each of the characteristics below according to the following scale:

1 = does not meet expectations
2 = meets expectations
3 = exceeds expectations
4 = outstanding

Decide on a cut-off point depending upon your hiring goals.

Applicant	Educat.	Experien.	Appear.	Readable	Activities		Total

Note: It is strongly recommended that all <u>written</u> notes be destroyed after the selection has been made. More than one employer has gotten in trouble by writing down something that might appear to be discriminatory, such as "black woman," simply to help keep the applicants straight in her mind. While an innocent comment, it can be costly to defend.

Chapter 6   Evaluating Resumes and Applications

The Resume/Application Checklist

☐ 1. Have you examined the options of accepting resumes vs. applications? Which have you chosen and why?

☐ 2. Have you determined your selection criteria for reviewing resumes and applications? Be careful to make your selections based on these criteria. Be wary of letting non-job-related factors influence you.

☐ 3. When reviewing a resume, are you taking the six key areas into account: overall appearance, organization, education, experience, other relevant activities and other discriminating information?

☐ 4. When reviewing applications, and especially resumes, be diligent about checking facts. There is a great tendency among candidates to exaggerate qualifications.

☐ 5. Have you devised a system for screening out discriminatory information (age, sex, marital status, national origin, religion)?

☐ 6. In reviewing cover letters, are you looking for the following qualities?
- Written in proper business format?
- Care shown in the preparation of the letter?
- Original letter or one of 1,000?
- Spelling, grammar, conciseness?
- Is it written with focus?

☐ 7. In developing an application, are you assembling a collection of others, reviewing them for good questions, designing your own and then having it reviewed for legality (especially concerning state laws)?

☐ 8. In reviewing applications, are you looking for the following qualities?
- Overall cleanliness, legibility and organization?
- Did the applicant follow instructions?
- Do the responses answer the questions?
- Spelling and grammar?
- Does the information check out (dates add up, information consistent question to question, etc.)?

☐ 9. When all the information has been gathered, are you handling the decision-making process with fairness and consistency?

☐ 10. Are you maintaining accurate records on the entire application process? A simple checklist might be designed to ease this task.

Questions for Personal Development

1. What is the major emphasis of this chapter?

2. What are the most important things you learned from this chapter?

3. How can you apply what you learned to your current job?

4. How will you go about making these changes?

5. How can you monitor improvement?

6. Summarize the changes you expect to see in yourself one year from now.

CHAPTER 7

Screening Applicants by Telephone

"I'm calling about the job you have in the Post *this week,"
the caller said.
"Oh yeah," responded the manager,
"you mean that mechanic's job."
"Well, it says diesel technician in the paper," said the caller.
"Right," retorted the manager. "So tell me about yourself."
"What do you want to know about?" asked the caller.
"The usual stuff," responded the manager.*

Here's What You'll Learn

I. The Value of Telephone Screening
II. Preparing to Screen by Telephone
III. Reception of Call-In Applicants
IV. Conducting Telephone Screening
V. Evaluating Callers
VI. The Telephone Screening Checklist

I. The Value of Telephone Screening

Other than resumes and applications, the initial telephone call to or from an applicant is the first real contact we have with an applicant. While the amount of information we might obtain through a phone call

Chapter 7   Screening Applicants by Telephone

is limited, there is a tremendous amount we can gather about a person's background, level of confidence, communication skills and a host of other things. Listening for the subtleties that applicants reveal about themselves as they talk begins to paint the picture you need for your evaluation.

But just as we are evaluating applicants, they are evaluating us. How was the phone answered? How long were they put on hold? Was the person they called prepared to answer their questions? Was the interviewer professional and courteous? Did the person seem rushed and harried?

As with any part of the applicant selection process, we are developing a relationship. Therefore, you must determine whether telephone screening will be a part of the selection process. To begin, let's look at the advantages and disadvantages of screening applicants via the telephone:

Advantages

- Screening over the phone is a faster process since each conversation tends to be shorter.
- It eliminates the hassles of scheduling, reserving rooms and the other tasks associated with formal interviews.
- Applicants can be screened as they call in, eliminating follow-up calls.
- Phone interviews are viewed as less formal and therefore are more relaxed.
- The interviewer is not distracted by irrelevant factors such as appearance, nervous habits, age, race and other discriminatory features.

Disadvantages

- Many of the nonverbal elements are lost, thus diminishing your ability to make an accurate judgment.
- While phone-voice quality is excellent in most cases, static and extraneous noise can distract both the interviewer and the applicant.
- Some people, by nature, do not communicate well over the phone. An interviewer or applicant who feels uncomfortable or is more visually oriented may feel inhibited.
- Unless the interviewer has received an application or resume in advance, his ability to ask specific questions about an applicant's background and training can be difficult.
- It is easy for an applicant to avoid certain situations since the interviewer cannot see nonverbal responses.

Screening over the phone is a faster process since each conversation tends to be shorter.

"He that would the daughter win must with the mother first begin."

Old English proverb

- Difficulty in reaching an applicant can create disfavor with the interviewer, perhaps diminishing an applicant's prospects of making a good impression.

These factors and others more specific to your organization must be considered when deciding whether to screen applicants over the phone. A practical suggestion is to attempt it with one opening and then evaluate the results.

> *"Always do what you say you are going to do. It is the glue and fiber that binds relationships."*
>
> Jeffrey A. Timmons

II. Preparing to Screen by Telephone

As you prepare for screening applicants, consider how they will apply. Will they submit resumes? Will they come in person to complete an application? Will they call upon seeing the job advertisement?

Having applicants call in may appear to be difficult and time-consuming. But proper organization will enable you to shorten the actual screening process considerably.

Rather than sorting through resumes, applicants who call directly from the advertisement or posting can be screened immediately. Recognizing that 50 percent or more of applicants will be eliminated upon submission, taking five to 10 minutes to screen each person as he calls may eliminate a good deal of effort later on. The form on page 135 can be used as a format for preparing for phone-in applicants.

Here are a few suggestions if you choose to screen applicants over the phone after accepting applications:

> **Know the job.** If you supervise the position, this is taken for granted. If, on the other hand, you screen for a number of positions, you may want to reacquaint yourself with the job's current duties and responsibilities.
>
> **Develop clearly worded questions and outline what you expect for answers.** Try the questions on a few people inside the company to make sure they are understood and elicit the type of answers you seek.

> *"The difference between a successful person and others is not a lack of strength, not a lack of knowledge, but rather in a lack of will."*
>
> Vince Lombardi

> *"Most of the trouble in the world is caused by people wanting to be important."*
>
> T.S. Eliot

Obtain input from those who will work with the new person. Even if you supervise the position being filled, you will not be the only person to work with the new hire. Soliciting suggestions and input from others will yield some good ideas and build their investment in hiring the right person for the job.

Prepare an evaluation form that will be used for all applicants. Notes on a legal pad do not provide the same clarity as a form that gives a summary of experience in the same place for each applicant.

Prepare what you will say about the job and the organization when screening applicants. The best applicants for any position are talking with more than one employer. How well you represent the job and your organization may determine the quality of the applicants who show sincere interest in working for you.

Prepare for the common questions. Brainstorm a list of questions that applicants are most likely to ask. Your preparation will put them at ease and demonstrate that you are truly concerned about hiring the right match for the job.

Rehearse the screening process. Take the time to call a couple of co-workers and go through the process to iron out glitches. Appearing well prepared will make a positive impression on the best candidates.

Block out a time to screen applicants so you will not be interrupted. Nothing can be more infuriating to an applicant than to be continually put on hold so the interviewer can handle other details. What's worse is to have someone conducting other business or completing paperwork while attempting to conduct the interview. Respect shown to applicants will help lure the best to your business.

Digi-Lectronics, Inc.

Telephone Screening Form
for assembly and QC technicians

Remember:
- This call will be their first contact with Digi-Lectronics.
- Just as they want to make a good impression, so do we!
- Always keep a copy of the Screening Evaluation with this form.
- Take your time and listen closely to the caller's answers.
- Listen to what the applicant says and how it is said.
- Be sure to get a correct name, address and phone number, even if you don't think this person will be passed on to interviews.
- Be careful not to make commitments you can't keep.
- Do not invite callers in for an interview.
- State that you will make a decision within 48 hours and be in touch if interested.

"The assembler's position involves putting together and soldering printed circuit boards that go into large electronic machinery. We have an opening on the _____ shift, which runs from _____ to _____. The Quality Control technician inspects the work of the assemblers; you need at least one year of electronic assembly experience to qualify."

Let me ask you a few questions about your qualifications:

Tell me about your work experience.

Where do you work now?

Where are your duties?

How long have you worked there?

Why do you want to make a change?

Do you have any experience in working with electronics?

How much are you making right now? How much is wages and how much is incentive? (*Do not* discuss Digi-Lectronics' compensation at this point.)

What questions do you have about the job or Digi-Lectronics?

We will be making a decision in the next two days and will be back in touch if we would like to interview you further. Thank you for your interest.

COMPLETE THE EVALUATION FORM IMMEDIATELY

III. Reception of Call-In Applicants

The reception applicants receive when they first respond to a job notice is critical to beginning the process on the right foot. A person answering the phone who does not appear to know anything about the job can greatly harm the way the company is perceived by those applying. Here are a few tips for ensuring that applicants are accorded the proper attention:

Prepare the receptionist. With all the distractions a receptionist deals with during a normal day, it is easy to understand how fielding calls from applicants may not seem important. Take the time to explain how critical first impressions are when attracting new employees.

Provide a prompt sheet for the receptionist. Give the person clear instructions on what to say and how to refer applicants to the proper person. A sample prompt sheet is provided on page 139.

Obtain name, address and telephone number of every applicant. Regardless of whether the person is hired, the vital information on every person who applies should be recorded. In some cases, that may be a legal requirement, such as maintaining affirmative action logs. In other cases, there may be additional openings in which previous applicants may have an interest.

Make sure each call is handled professionally. Reinforce the receptionist's skill at answering the phone. By receiving some positive feedback, that person is more likely to treat those calling you with more respect and friendliness.

Walk through the process with the receptionist. If you're still not sure that your receptionist understands, try giving a couple of sample situations just to see how they are handled. In some cases, you may have a couple of friends call in as applicants to see how they are received.

"Well, if I called the wrong number, why did you answer the phone?"

James Thurber
caption for cartoon in
The New Yorker

IV. Conducting Telephone Screening

We hope that hiring somebody is going to be the beginning of a long-term relationship. Both the organization and the applicant are making a big commitment. It is critical, therefore, that you make the most of every screening situation. Here are some tips for maximizing the way you screen applicants on the telephone:

Develop rapport. Just as you would in a formal interview, take a minute to put applicants at ease when you call. You might begin by asking how they found out about the job. If it was a referral, you might get into a short chat about that person.

Explain the position's duties up front. Begin the interview by telling the applicant about the position and how it fits within the organization. Ask applicants to comment on ways their background fits the job as you ask some questions.

Take notes. Do not rely on your memory to recall all the information the applicant gives you. Jotting down a few key words here and there will help you complete the evaluation form at the end of the interview. You might also jot down follow-up questions as they come up during the conversation.

Listen to what the applicant says and how it is said. While you listen to the words, look for level of confidence, organization of thought, consistency of focus. Even though the person is not sitting in front of you, there are still many ways you can pick up on communication signals.

Treat everyone the same. While you will identify with some applicants more than others, all applicants should receive the same level of attention and consistent message. Simply because you went to the same high school does not mean applicants should get special treatment, especially if they're not right for the job.

Chapter 7   Screening Applicants by Telephone

> *"Be kind. Remember, everyone you meet is fighting a hard battle."*
> Thompson

Ask everyone the same questions. It is easy to wander off the mark, especially if you get engrossed in a particular topic. It will become difficult, however, to make clear comparisons if you have gathered only partial information on some applicants. Take the time to pursue items you think are important, but be sure to cover all the topics you need to.

Take your time. Applicants can detect whether or not you're in a rush. While you may have a million things on your mind, taking the time to concentrate on the applicant will produce a better interview and demonstrate that you really do care about who you hire.

Question inconsistencies in what the applicant says. Do not hesitate to ask about comments that appear inconsistent. Those who shy away from potentially uncomfortable situations lose the opportunity to truly screen the best people into the rest of the process.

Use silence as a tool. One of the most powerful strategies any interviewer has is silence. Since most people are uncomfortable with a long silence, they tend to reveal more than they had planned. Sometimes the answer after the silence is more to the point.

> *"When you have nothing to say, say nothing."*
> Charles Caleb Colton

Take time to answer the applicant's questions. While there will be more time to answer questions if they make it in to the formal interview stage, it is still important to answer the concerns of all applicants. In a few cases nervous applicants have changed the opinion of an interviewer because they made such penetrating inquiries.

Don't make commitments you can't keep. Be careful not to promise an interview as a way of getting off the phone or avoiding a pestering question. You must remain in control of the interview. More than one employer has gotten in trouble by making a promise that was undeliverable.

Explain the rest of the selection process. Before closing the conversation, be sure the applicant understands what's next. One of the greatest sources of irritation for applicants is not knowing when or how a decision will be made. Remember, applicants are also customers.

How to Handle Incoming Callers
for Digi-Lectronics job openings

Remember that this call will be their first contact with Digi-Lectronics. Just as they want to make a good impression, so do we!

- Ask for what position they are applying.
- Ask for name, address and telephone number
- Ask for the best time for an interviewer to reach them.
- Ask where they heard about the job.
- If a referral, get the referral's name.
- Tell them that an interviewer will return the call within 48 hours.

Refer any questions they may have to the interviewer.

V. Evaluating Callers

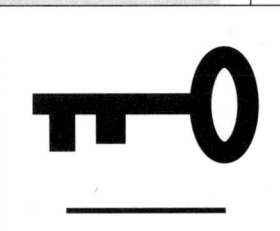

The quality of your interviewing notes will have a direct impact on your ability to make an accurate decision.

Once each screening call has been completed, it is essential that the information be recorded immediately. The hustle of most businesses combined with constant distractions makes us forget most of what we hear within a couple of hours. Here are some quick tips for making the most of the information you gather:

Complete the evaluation immediately. Remain seated and fill out the form as best you can. Waiting to fill out two or three applicants' information at the same time will make the information run together.

Be consistent in evaluating. While there may be a tendency to be more generous with those applicants you liked, this has to remain a business decision. Their ability to get along well with others should be noted, for instance, but not given undue weight. On the other hand, a person with excellent qualifications should not be penalized if he appeared nervous on the phone if dealing with people is not a significant portion of the job.

Write complete thoughts. A jotted note here and there cannot be easily recalled two or three days later. The quality of your notes will have a direct impact on your ability to make an accurate decision.

Confine your comments to business necessity. Remain focused on how well the applicant matches the job requirements. The fact that he would make a great shortstop for the company team is irrelevant. Besides being inappropriate information to record, it could also be questioned should your notes be reviewed during a discrimination complaint.

Be careful what you write. In addition to irrelevant material, take care to avoid comments that would infer discrimination. The words "elderly woman" written on an evaluation simply to help you keep the many applicants apart could be questioned as biased against those covered by the Age Discrimination in Employment Act.

Follow through on commitments you made to the applicant. Once the evaluation has been completed, make sure to send any information you promised the applicant along with investigating questions he asked for which you had no immediate answer. Your prompt follow-up demonstrates your commitment to hiring the best.

> *"Yesterday is a canceled check; tomorrow is a promissory note; today is the only cash you have — so spend it wisely."*
>
> Kay Lyons

Telephone Screening Evaluation

Name of applicant _____
Address _____
Applying for _____ Phone _____
Interviewer _____ Date _____

Place your ratings for this candidate in the categories indicated. (Rating: 1 = Unacceptable, 5 = Exceeds expectations)

	Comments	Rating
Work Experience		
Skills		
Education/ Training		
Electronics Experience		
Present Wages		
Other		
	Total Score =	

The Telephone Screening Checklist

☐ 1. Do you have a clear understanding of the job for which you are screening?

☐ 2. Have you developed a set of questions that reflect what you need to know?

☐ 3. Have you developed an evaluation form for screening applicants?

☐ 4. Have you reserved a block of time for screening applicants without interruption?

☐ 5. Have you prepared what you will say about the company?

☐ 6. Are you prepared for the common questions most applicants will ask?

☐ 7. Have you prepared the receptionist to receive applicants' incoming phone calls?

☐ 8. Do you question inconsistencies during the interview?

☐ 9. Do you ask each applicant the same questions?

☐ 10. Do you refrain from making commitments?

☐ 11. Do you complete the evaluation form for each applicant immediately after the screening?

Questions for Personal Development

1. What is the major emphasis of this chapter?
   _____
   _____
   _____
   _____

2. What are the most important things you learned from this chapter?
   _____
   _____
   _____
   _____

3. How can you apply what you learned to your current job?
   _____
   _____
   _____
   _____

4. How will you go about making these changes?
   _____
   _____
   _____
   _____

5. How can you monitor improvement?
   _____
   _____
   _____
   _____

6. Summarize the changes you expect to see in yourself one year from now.
   _____
   _____
   _____
   _____

CHAPTER 8

Take-Charge Interviewing

"But what is it about this person that makes you so sure we should offer her a job?" asked Frank.
"It's a feeling in my gut," said Steve. "I've never interviewed such a fantastic candidate before."
"Who was interviewing whom?" asked Frank. "I can't go upstairs and say, 'Let's hire Susan because Steve's got a fantastic feeling in his gut.'"

Here's What You'll Learn

I. Detecting the Winners
II. Establishing the Process
III. Developing Questions
IV. Conducting the Interview
V. Alternative Interview Strategies
VI. The Interview Checklist

What is it about interviews that makes us think we can "wing it"? Maybe it's the chemistry we feel with applicants. Maybe it's their appearance. Perhaps we're overwhelmed by their insight and maturity.

On the other hand, maybe we just don't have time to really prepare. Maybe we're distracted with 10 other tasks. Maybe we just don't care enough.

Chapter 8 Take-Charge Interviewing

Interviews must be conducted with care and diligence. Often we rely too heavily on the results of interviews and mistakes are made in the final employment decision.

I. Detecting the Winners

Essentially, there are three goals when conducting an employment interview:
1. To develop an accurate picture of the job for which you are hiring and communicate that to each applicant.
2. To collect enough information on the applicant to make an informed decision.
3. To produce a positive and accurate picture of the company — one that will impress applicants and help them decide to work for you.

But how do you detect the winners among those who apply? Collecting information on an applicant is a complex task. It must be done methodically and with premeditation. Even experienced interviewers find it easy to get caught up in the charisma of some individuals. While chemistry plays a role in this process, a good interviewer will stick to the plan, however.

Just as some applicants will impress you, others may turn you off. Be careful not to judge too soon. If you have conducted employment interviews, you've probably followed the traditional method of asking questions and receiving answers for 30 to 60 minutes and then asked if the candidate had any questions. Much of your evaluation was probably based on emotion and impressions developed in the first five minutes.

While this is the primary method used in business, that doesn't necessarily make it the most effective. A good number of candidates feel comfortable in this format and prepare well for the expected questions. In fact, the most slick among these candidates don't necessarily prepare. But they can impress you with their answers even if they don't have the necessary qualifications for the job.

Other candidates might be excellent possibilities for the opening but they just don't interview well. You may be one of these individuals. How do you feel in these situations?

Ability to "perform" in an interview should be only one consideration in employee selection. Part V of this chapter introduces some effective alternatives to the simple question-and-answer session.

"There is nothing wrong with being a self-made man if you don't consider the job finished too soon."

John Mooney

Just as some applicants will impress you, others may turn you off. Be careful not to judge too soon.

II. Establishing the Process

The first step in developing an interview process is to evaluate the position you are filling and determine the information needed to make an accurate decision. You then tailor the questions to address those needs.

If you are hiring a salesperson, for example, you will need to know that the successful candidate is persuasive, self-motivated, well-organized and affable. If you are hiring an assembly technician, you will look for someone with an orientation to detail, good levels of concentration and an ability to follow instructions.

You personally may have an orientation toward good communicators and will therefore look for those candidates who are conversationalists. But if you're hiring a production worker, a good conversationalist is apt to get less accomplished. However, you would not hire a shy individual to represent the company in sales.

Recognize that the best person to hire is someone who finds the job challenging and is able to do the majority of it upon entering the company. A good rule of thumb is to select someone who can do 80 percent of the job when first hired. This person has room to grow, yet is not starting from the beginning.

Be careful not to hire individuals who are too much like yourself. While the two of you may get along very well, there is the potential for ensuing power struggles and group think. Hire someone who will challenge you in the position, but from a standpoint of growth. This way the person complements your strengths with hers. If you are a pragmatic person, for instance, hiring someone with creativity is a nice complement.

Review the job description before developing the list of criteria. Observe the successful individuals who currently hold the position and others like it in your organization. What makes those people excellent employees? How have they developed? What were they like when first hired? You might even ask them what they would look for in a good candidate for a position like theirs.

Another strategy is to bring together those who are working in the department and ask them, "Now that Richard has left, what qualities would you like to see in the new person that Richard did not have?" Then ask, "What qualities would you like to see in the new person that Richard did have?" Finally ask, "What qualities did Richard have that you would not like to see in the new person?"

> *"Small opportunities are often the beginning of great enterprises."*
>
> Demosthenes

This strategy provides you with valuable input and gives those in the department an opportunity to contribute to the new person's selection.

Rarely will you be able to find a candidate who has the training, maturity and natural smarts to become productive immediately. If you do, she may not be affordable. Everyone has to be trained. Set your criteria for individuals who will grow into the job.

This holds true for every position, from production to customer service to executive levels. Hire totally trained specialists only when absolutely warranted. These individuals tend to be expensive, may have their own agenda and can be difficult to work with. A person who matures into a job has more investment in the outcome.

Interview Priority Checklist

Position_____ Dept. _____

In developing an effective interview process for this position, list the skills and characteristics you feel are most important for a successful candidate. Make sure all are job-related. When this form is complete, use the information to develop the questions and the structure of the interview. Weigh each skill or characteristic according to its level of importance: 1=low, 5=critical.

Priority	Skill/Characteristic	Weight
	Total Weight	

Taking diversity into account

As the labor force continues to change, employers are facing new challenges and opportunities. For example, the stereotypes about hiring only white males under 40 are disappearing due to that group diminishing in size. Forward-looking employers are taking advantage of these changes by targeting the new diverse groups in the workforce.

Women have been a major factor for years in the labor force, and their role has expanded dramatically as they assume more responsibility. While discrimination and bias are widely prohibited, it is still very much in practice throughout the nation. Employers who are continually successful in hiring and retaining make members of diversities work to their advantage rather than discriminating against them. These other diversities include people of color, immigrants, senior workers and individuals with disabilities. Your ability as an employer to adjust to these groups and to take advantage of their interests, experience and work ethic will serve to strengthen your standing within the industry and community.

The greatest challenge facing some employers is the growing number of applicants unable to speak English. While some argue that English should be the only language spoken on the work site, reality indicates that you, the employer, must be able to communicate clearly with all employees, if for no other reason than safety. An employer's willingness to work toward a common solution not only increases communication but demonstrates flexibility and an orientation toward teamwork.

In addition to language barriers, other challenges include differences in cultural heritage, levels and types of education, experience and balance of life issues. When interviewing candidates, all of these factors enter in whether or not the employer is aware of it. Applicants are hiring you as much as you are hiring them. Therefore, your ability to communicate care and sincerity about their welfare is of paramount importance. If you are dealing with applicants of diverse backgrounds, consider what you are doing to accommodate them during the interview process. Place yourself in their shoes and consider their concerns and apprehensions about your hiring process. Keep a list of factors such as language barriers, cultural concerns, reading levels, understanding of language nuances and social norms, appearance, dress and the like. Then strive to address each of these issues.

> *"After 12 years of therapy, my psychiatrist said something that brought tears to my eyes. He said, 'No hablo inglés.'"*
>
> Ronnie Shakes

Chapter 8   Take-Charge Interviewing

> "I want workers to go home at night and say, 'I built that car.'"
>
> Pahr G. Gyllenhammer
> Chairman, Volvo

> "The years teach what the days never know."
>
> Ralph Waldo Emerson

Process factors

A smooth-flowing process is essential to making each interview effective. Here are a few factors to consider:

Urgency of the need. How fast does the position need to be filled? The more urgent, the less care can be allowed in the selection.

Level of the position. You will obviously spend more time in selecting supervisors than receptionists. However, the latter should still be accorded proper attention. Rushing them through an interview says "You're not that important." Front-line people can make or break an organization.

Industry trends. While some industries attempt to reduce turnover, others accept it as a fact of doing business. Food service and retailing are good examples of the latter attitude. Examine your level of turnover. Is it worth reducing? When deciding, balance recruiting costs with training costs.

Taking great care in the selection process only to have employees leave after three to five months is probably not the best use of your time. If you are expecting high turnover, your questions are going to be based more on attendance, punctuality and work ethic than on why candidates are interested in the position and their five-year goals.

Available labor pool. Economic conditions, along with the demographics in your area, may determine the type of interviewing you can conduct. In a tight labor market, for instance, you may find that you're forced to ease some criteria just to fill certain positions.

If the area's demographics indicate a high level of education and you're running an assembly plant, you may either hire locally and expect turnover (due to lack of challenge) or recruit from several towns away in a labor-oriented community. While turnover may decrease in the latter case, you may have to pay a travel differential.

These four factors, in conjunction with established job criteria, dictate the design of the interview process.

Make them work

Most candidates are not made to work in the interview. They arrive expecting the obvious questions and are usually right on target: "Why do you want this job? Tell me about your experience. Why did you leave your last job?" And so on.

Richard Bolles, author of the job-search best-seller, *What Color Is Your Parachute?*, compares this technique to reading tea leaves, trying to tell the future from the past. Unfortunately, the level of accuracy is dismally low.

Allowing candidates to slide through on the expected procedure works against you. The best candidates will enjoy the challenge. Ask tough questions. It shows you care about who fills the position.

> *"Knowing what's right doesn't mean much unless you do what's right."*
>
> Theodore Roosevelt

Defining the process

Design an interview process that is easy to follow and does not include too many steps. Too much information can be just as damaging as too little.

Interview only the best and limit the number. Meeting with 20 candidates because you cannot decide between resumes exacerbates the problem. The first round should not include more than six people. The second round should be limited to three, and the third round (if absolutely necessary) should be limited to two. More than three rounds of interviews become counterproductive.

Stay on time and follow through. A normal selection process should consume no more than three weeks from the deadline for applications. Clerical positions should take much less. Applicants stew over the selection decisions a company makes. In waiting too long, you may lose the best candidates.

> *Ask tough questions. The best candidates will enjoy the challenge.*

No more than three individuals should interview candidates. In many cases one is sufficient. Don't hesitate to make a decision.

Each candidate should receive the same treatment. Questions, exercises and tasks should not vary and all should be job-related.

Be careful not to build marathon schedules. Candidates interviewed late in the afternoon tend to suffer in evaluations. This helps neither them nor you. Try to schedule interviews in the morning when everyone is fresh.

Give candidates a chance to catch their breath. Three hour-long sessions back to back would exhaust anyone.

Think back about the last interview you conducted. Did you prepare as if your livelihood depended on it? In some ways, it does!

> *Be sure questions are job-related and nondiscriminatory. Innocent mistakes can be costly.*

How to notify candidates

Every step in the selection procedure should be uniform. This eliminates the appearance of bias or favoritism. Applicant notification is no different.

All candidates should be called since this speeds the process. It is better to schedule interviews in a block than to stretch them out over a week. This makes for better comparisons. But don't overload yourself. Three 60-minute interviews per day is more than enough.

When contacted for an interview, each candidate should be given the same information. Other than directions, nothing further should be added. Applicants' questions about what to expect should be politely refused. Giving one candidate an edge over another may come back to haunt you. To eliminate temptation, a receptionist or someone not affiliated with the process should do the calling.

III. Developing Questions

The questions selected and how they are formed are the most important elements of an interview. Each question must address defined criteria for the job. Simply asking random questions to "get to know the person" will not suffice.

The inquiry should be understandable and specific, while leaving the candidate an opportunity to elaborate. Each question should be tested before being used. Ask a sampling of employees if they understand it. Is it clear? Is it too long? Should it be broken into two pieces?

Emphasis should be placed in various areas depending upon the position available. Questions about education should take a back seat to skills and abilities when interviewing laborers. Asking a carpenter about college education is irrelevant and may be discriminatory.

When developing questions, be sure they are job-related and nondiscriminatory. Innocent mistakes can be costly.

> *"He who thinks he has no faults — has one."*
> Sheetz

Categories of questions

What questions can you ask in an interview? Questions fall into five categories:
- Career goals/occupational objectives
- Education

- Work experience
- General skills and aptitudes related to job criteria
- Attitudes and personality characteristics

Career goals/occupational objectives

The purpose here is to determine candidates' focus and determination. Why do they want the job? What makes it so special? Ask for specifics. What is their philosophy?

This category is relative, however. Asking a fry cook for goals and objectives may not yield as much valuable information as facts about work history and skills.

Education

Education should not play a large role in the interview unless there is little job-related work experience to discuss. You may still be able to gain some insight by examining extracurricular activities in addition to academics.

Work experience

The majority of time should be spent on the applicant's previous experience, especially that which is directly related to the new position. Look for specifics. Simply having a candidate outline what she did may not be enough. Examine how well she performed the job, how much training was involved and why she left.

Look beyond the job title. Many titles can be misleading. What is it that the applicant actually did?

Ask what improvements she made on the job. What made her stand out? Ask about her boss and colleagues. How did they get along?

General skills and aptitudes related to job criteria

Learn what actual skills an applicant will contribute to the job. How skilled is this person? Has she worked with your materials and/or machinery before? Is she familiar with procedures? Can she demonstrate these skills?

Ask applicants to read aloud during the job interview. By doing so, they will demonstrate two things: (1) their actual ability to read and (2) their level of confidence. Be careful, however, to ask them to read only materials required on the job. A good example of this would be asking a housekeeper to read the safety labels on cans of cleaning fluid.

> *"In spite of everything, I still believe that people are really good at heart."*
>
> Anne Frank

Chapter 8 Take-Charge Interviewing

Once again, you have to be specific in your questions. The fact that an applicant says she can do something is not always exactly correct. She may be exaggerating. Check everything out.

Attitudes and personality characteristics

How well does this person get along with others? Will she fit into your working environment? You can pick up a great deal of information about these characteristics by just listening to her answers to other questions.

Is she stubborn? Does she get angry? Does she like her current occupation? Is she satisfied? Did she leave her last employer under difficult circumstances? All of these considerations and others will give you a better idea of whether this person will fit into your organization.

NOTE: A collection of 500 sample questions for all five categories can be found in Appendix A.

Targeted selection systems

For an improved approach to the traditional interview, a targeted selection process can be very effective. Instead of asking questions such as "Tell me about yourself," the targeted question asks for information on a particular skill or experience. For example: "This job involves a good deal of customer service problem-solving. Please tell me about an experience you've had where you dealt successfully with an angry customer. Tell me about the situation, the strategies you considered and how you resolved the situation."

A variation of this approach is to pick up on claims made by the candidate. In asking a candidate about strengths, for example, that person might have said, "I was the inspirational leader of my team at my last job." You might then ask, "You said you were the inspirational leader at your last job. Give me an example of how you applied this ability. Tell me the situation, what you did and how you knew you were inspiring others."

IV. Conducting the Interview

An employment interview should be a well-planned exercise. The interviewer should prepare by ensuring that proper attention is accorded the meeting. If conducted as an afterthought in a busy day, the results of an interview will most likely be dismal. Care and time must be invested to make the session a success.

Interview Evaluation

Applicant_____ Phone_____

Applying for_____ Supervisor_____

Interviewer_____ Date_____

Instructions: List in priority order the required and preferred skills and characteristics for the job based on the Interview Priority Checklist. When this has been accomplished, make a copy of the completed form for each candidate to be interviewed.

Indicate only numerical ratings on this form when evaluating a candidate. Arrange the interview questions so that all areas listed on this form are addressed. The questions do not have to be asked in order.

Ratings: 1= Unacceptable for this position   5= Exceeds requirements

Required Skills/Characteristics	Weight
Total Weight	

Preferred Skills/Characteristics	Weight
Total Weight	

Chapter 8   Take-Charge Interviewing

"Check the neighbors before you buy the house."

-Ralph Waldo Emerson

Prepare the work site

An interview involves more than just the prepared questions. It also includes the environment in which the person will work. Take a walk around your work site. Examine the general appearance. Are there overflowing trash cans, lights out or a general look of disorganization? Is there a separation between executive and staff washrooms, executive parking spaces and other signs of class distinctions? Look at the bulletin boards. What messages stand out? Are there signs for employee get-togethers and information or are they filled with corporate directives? Does anyone read them?

Fourteen tips to successful screening

Review the candidate's application materials. You have already seen it once, but review it again. Having to repeatedly refer to these papers during the interview is distracting and demonstrates a lack of preparation.

1. **Prepare the location.** Be sure your office is in order. There should be no interruptions during the interview. If a plant or office tour will take place, make sure it has been properly arranged.
2. **Put the candidate at ease.** Seemingly insignificant gestures can go a long way toward setting the right tone for an interview. Meet the applicant on time. Don't make her wait. When opening the interview, make the candidate feel comfortable. Offer a cup of coffee. A little small talk never hurts.
3. **Outline the interview.** Explain the sequence of events and what will happen. Resist the urge, however, to identify a time frame. For example, a defined 45-minute interview may be difficult to end after 15 minutes if things are not going well.
4. **Keep an open mind.** First impressions of a candidate are usually lasting. Try not to prejudge the candidate based on the first 30 seconds of contact. Nervousness and other factors may be obscuring the better qualities.
5. **Let the candidate do the talking.** Ask questions and wait for answers. Interviewer silence can be a powerful tool for eliciting additional information.
6. **Be attentive.** When conducting a series of interviews, boredom can overtake you, along with distractions about

more pressing problems. However, concentrate on what is being said. This may be the only opportunity you have to evaluate this candidate.

7. **Observe body language.** Watch and listen to how things are being said. Is there a level of enthusiasm? Does the person sound confident? Does she make eye contact?
8. **Take notes.** During the interview, record responses and impressions for later reference. When interviewing more than one candidate, information will blur together. These notes will help sort it out.
9. **Maintain control.** Be careful not to let the interviewee take over. An aggressive candidate may attempt to get the better of you by making comments or asking questions, rather than answering them.
10. **Probe incomplete answers.** There may be a reason why answers are incomplete. Ask for clarification, even if it is difficult or embarrassing. You need to know.
11. **Test for character.** After a person has given the answer to a question, ask about her approach and reasoning. Ask how much she would be willing to bet if she thinks she is correct. Testing a person's confidence can be very revealing.
12. **Keep reactions to yourself.** The so-called "poker face" is useful in an interview. Be careful not to display your emotions, regardless of how pleased, shocked, disappointed or frustrated you may be. Signals such as these give candidates an impression, perhaps wrong, of how they're doing.
13. **Take lunch in a comfortable setting.** Take the applicant to a place where the employees usually go for lunch. A more relaxed restaurant results in a more relaxed candidate.
14. **Close the interview on a positive note.** Refrain from announcing a decision. Assure the candidate that you will be in touch within a short period of time and thank her for her time.

Immediately after the interview, write down your general impressions and review your notes. Waiting even one hour will greatly reduce your memory of what took place.

> *There may be a reason why answers are incomplete. Ask for clarification, even if it is difficult or embarrassing.*

> *"To be humble to superiors is duty, to equals, courtesy, to inferiors, nobleness."*
>
> Benjamin Franklin

Interviewer's Self-Rating Sheet

Applicant Interviewed_____ Date_____

Evaluation: 5 = Handled smoothly
4 = Handled well, but needs refining
3 = Has a grasp but needs improvement
2 = Needs significant work
1 = Found this difficult

Rapport with the Applicant

Opened the interview and made the applicant feel at ease _____

Avoided direct criticism of the applicant _____

Listened sympathetically _____

Put applicant at ease in awkward situations _____

Control of Interview

Developed questions in advance of the interview _____

Maintained the focus of the interview _____

Made smooth transition from one topic to another _____

Allocated time appropriately _____

Returned to the original question when answer was evasive _____

Paced interview well _____

Persuaded applicant to elaborate on responses using:

Follow-up questions _____

Silence _____

Paraphrasing of applicant's initial response _____

Note-Taking

Took notes discreetly during interview _____

Did not allow note-taking to interfere with interview _____

Noted dress and appearance if relevant _____

V. Alternative Interview Strategies

There are a number of alternatives to the standard question-and-answer session. These make the candidate work harder for the position. The work the applicant produces in these exercises is a much better indicator of success on the job. Different strategies work for different needs. Consider the following:

> *"Good is not good where better is expected."*
>
> Thomas Fuller

Interview project

Ask the candidates to complete a project during the interview to get a sampling of their work. Evaluation of this work would include organization, cleanliness and written skills in addition to content. You might ask a sales management applicant, for instance, to develop a short marketing plan based on your criteria.

Homework assignment

An expanded variation would ask applicants to take the assignment home, develop the necessary material and return it within two or three days. You could then review it with them.

Make a presentation

After a candidate has completed either of the above, you might ask for a presentation on the material completed. If the position requires the person to make presentations as a normal duty, this will serve as an excellent means for evaluating those skills. Candidates might also make presentations on their goals, how they would attack the job, how their background would enhance the position or a host of other topics.

Provide typical situations

Candidates can be asked to respond to a variety of daily occurrences. To solve these situations, they might have to write a memo, conduct research, interview others, hold a meeting or perform a combination thereof. While this exercise is probably not appropriate for clerical positions, it can clearly demonstrate the skills and abilities of managerial candidates.

This type of assessment takes time and preparation. But if you are interested in hiring the best candidates for your organization, the investment is well worth it.

Chapter 8 Take-Charge Interviewing

> *"To love what you do and feel that it matters — how could anything be more fun?"*
>
> Katharine Graham

Interview minutes

Have each candidate write up minutes of the interview after it has taken place. These minutes can indicate how much interest the candidate has in the position by the care taken in their preparation. On the other hand, minutes dashed off in 15 minutes may indicate that the person is a producer. Candidates who do not fare well in a face-to-face interview may demonstrate their skills in the minutes they write.

Internships

For candidates still in college, an internship in your company benefits all. The student gains practical experience and skills and you have the opportunity to take a long look at a potential employee. The only caveat is that hosting an intern takes some time and preparation. Interns are not simply warm bodies to do the filing.

Assessment centers

An assessment center consists of a series of exercises performed over a day-long period to measure a person's ability to perform specific tasks. The evaluation is conducted by experienced managers. For managerial applicants, the center might consist of an in-basket exercise, a group project involving all of your top candidates and a presentation to other managers. For a non-managerial position, the center might consist of a project involving organization of materials, a report to be developed and a series of letters to be written or typed. While more time-consuming, the accuracy of this process has been proven time and again.

> *"The greatest use of life is to spend it for something that will outlast it."*
>
> William James

Full- or half-day trials

Bring in your final candidates for a paid trial and put them through a designed series of tasks. In addition, give them the opportunity to get to know the members of the team with whom they will be working. Look for chemistry, ability to communicate, personal organization and other factors essential to the position they would be filling. If specific skills are necessary, be sure candidates are required to demonstrate these skills some time during the day.

Videotape interviews

Prepare a list of questions in advance and have the interviewer ask each of your top candidates the questions on tape. This method allows for direct comparisons between applicants.

Computer-assisted interviews

A few companies have developed computer-driven interviews in which each candidate answers questions asked by a computer. The computer asks questions based on the candidate's previous answers, and the candidate may also be asked to type in a response to a particular situation. Companies using this process have found a higher level of motivation in candidates. The system allows employers more consistency in obtaining information and remaining unbiased.

> "Things may come to those who wait, but only the things left by those who hustle."
>
> Abraham Lincoln

Stress interviews

This approach is particularly helpful when hiring for positions that involve significant stress. Applicants are asked questions and then challenged about their answers. The interviewer might also ask the questions in rapid succession to hinder the person's ability to respond. Finally, the interviewer might fake a disagreement with the candidate to see how she responds. Stress interviews should be used only in specific situations when the job involves high emotional stress.

Clerical and staff positions

Most of the alternatives discussed above are not applicable to clerical and staff positions. This does not mean, however, that you should follow only the traditional methods of interviewing for these candidates. Consider the following:

> "I had a monumental idea this morning, but I didn't like it."
>
> Samuel Goldwyn

Two-day trial

Ask final candidates to work for two days on a trial basis to see how both parties like the situation. This will give you a chance to see them in action. Do they dive in? Do they stand around? Do they catch on quickly? Do they get along with others?

Are they willing to take a couple of vacation days, if currently employed, to see if they like the job? Even their reaction to this suggestion might indicate the type of employee they would be.

Give a situation

While candidates are present for the interview, you might ask them to perform a short task selected at random from the daily workload. How well is it completed? How fast? How much instruction was necessary? Even something this simple can provide significantly more data for evaluation than questions such as, "Are you a hard worker?"

Test clerical skills

As the clerical world becomes increasingly complex, it is critical that you ascertain candidates' actual skills. Too many organizations have been burned by individuals claiming certain expertise when, in fact, those skills were minimal at best. A typing test, phone handling, word processing and database management all fall into this category. Don't ask! Test!

It is imperative that new employees fit in. Suggest to final candidates that they stop by and introduce themselves to a selection of individuals with whom they would be working. Provide the names and locations, but let them go by themselves. These visits do not have to take more than five minutes each. Quick evaluations from the people visited by the candidates will give you one more impression of their probability for success.

Invite final candidates for all positions to unconventional activities. Ask them to join the company softball team for a night. Allow them to sit in on one of your weekly wrap-ups. Invite them to a Friday afternoon gathering with other employees. Ask them out to dinner and include their spouses.

While all of the above must be explained as optional, those who do participate in these opportunities will provide another glimpse at someone who could contribute greatly to your organization over the next several years.

Portraying the company

Throughout the interview process, remember that you need to sell the company as much as each candidate needs to sell you. The candidates you want do their homework, investigate your organization and ask the toughest questions when their turn comes.

You need to be prepared to answer their questions and discuss their concerns. This applies to all candidates, not just those with their eyes on the boardroom. If your assembly workers are not emotionally invested in what they're doing, they will not work effectively.

Your interview process must work correctly. Is it timely? Are your staff members punctual? Are they prepared? Are they excited about the prospect of adding a new member to the team?

> *Remember that you need to sell the company as much as each candidate needs to sell you.*

Interviewing Individuals with Disabilities

With the enactment of the Americans with Disabilities Act of 1990, every employer must become more aware how applicants with disabilities are treated during the interview process. Here are a few tips for making the interview process for applicants with disabilities more comfortable.

1. Keep the interview focused on the applicant's qualifications. Do not ask, "How will you get to work?" Instead, ask job-related questions such as, "How will you perform this task?"

2. Remember to shake hands and make eye contact without staring. Treat the applicant like an adult. It is OK to offer assistance, but don't be offended if it is not accepted.

3. If interviewing a wheelchair-bound applicant, do not push or grasp the chair unless the applicant asks you to do so. Move any furniture that makes it difficult for the person to maneuver. Sit in a chair that allows you to be at the applicant's eye level.

4. If the applicant is deaf or hard of hearing, use a physical signal such as tapping the person's hand if you need to get her attention. Don't shout. If an interpreter is not present, you may have to rely on lip-reading gestures and note-passing. Enunciate clearly and situate yourself so that your face is easily seen.

5. When interviewing someone who is blind, identify yourself and any others present. Cue a handshake by saying, "May we shake hands?" Then touch the person's hand. Be clear when giving directions. Say for example, "The chair is six steps to your left."

6. When speaking with someone with mental retardation, use simple language. Repeat any directions several times and give positive feedback when appropriate.

Chapter 8   Take-Charge Interviewing

All of this makes an impression, positive or negative. Interview applicants as if they were your best customers.

The Interview Checklist

Digi-Lectronics Inc.
Attracting the Best Employees

Use this card with candidates for all positions. It provides facts and tips that can be used to persuade the best candidates to come work for us. While it is important to persuade people, make sure you are persuading the right people. Do not lead individuals on and be extremely careful about making commitments you or the company cannot keep.

In explaining the company to candidates, have you mentioned the following?

- We offer a close-knit atmosphere where the benefits of a small company can be used to advantage.

- We offer cross-training that will broaden their skills and experience.

- We have an educational opportunity program that reimburses for related coursework completed with a grade of "B" or better.

- Our benefits program includes dental and eye coverage as part of the base package.

- We are considered one of the top three manufacturers of digital switch systems in the nation.

- Our revenues have grown a minimum of 15% each year for the past three years.

- We have a stock ownership program for all regular employees.

☐ 1. Do you evaluate every position fully before interviewing to ascertain what information is needed?

☐ 2. Are you certain that all questions are job-related?

☐ 3. Do you design the process to ensure professionalism before proceeding with the interviews?

☐ 4. Have you developed interview report forms to handle the process?

☐ 5. Do you review candidate information, questions to be asked, and the setting before every interview?

☐ 6. Do you rehearse the interview before seeing the first candidate to ensure professionalism?

☐ 7. Do you limit the number of candidates you initially interview to no more than six per position?

☐ 8. Do you outline the interview for the candidate before proceeding?

☐ 9. Do you take nonverbal cues into consideration when interviewing?

☐ 10. Do you take notes during interviews to avoid confusion?

☐ 11. Do you indicate to all interviewed candidates when they can expect to hear a result?

☐ 12. Do you write an interview summary after every candidate?

☐ 13. Do you evaluate interviews after you have conducted them to improve your skills?

☐ 14. Have you considered the alternative interview strategies mentioned in this chapter?

☐ 15. Are you conscious of having to "sell" the company when interviewing candidates?

☐ 16. Do you conduct an evaluation of the interview process after every new hire?

Chapter 8   Take-Charge Interviewing

Questions for Personal Development

1. What is the major emphasis of this chapter?
   _____
   _____
   _____
   _____

2. What are the most important things you learned from this chapter?
   _____
   _____
   _____
   _____

3. How can you apply what you learned to your current job?
   _____
   _____
   _____
   _____

4. How will you go about making these changes?
   _____
   _____
   _____
   _____

5. How can you monitor improvement?
   _____
   _____
   _____
   _____

6. Summarize the changes you expect to see in yourself one year from now.
   _____
   _____
   _____
   _____

CHAPTER 9

Obtaining Reliable References

"Would you hire Jim again?" asked the recruiter.
"Well ... yes," came the manager's reply.
"Are there any reasons why you might be hesitant?"
pressed the recruiter.
"I said I would rehire him," the manager snapped.
"Do you want to know anything else?"
"No," said the recruiter. "I think I've got all I need to know."

Here's What You'll Learn

I. Conducting a Reference Check
II. Checking Credentials
III. The Reference Checklist

Other than the information on a resume or application, an employer has little with which to evaluate various applicants. While references provide data only about past performance, they may still be helpful in ascertaining the competence and value of an applicant.

Whereas traditionally references were provided in written form, most employers have turned to phone inquiries as a more efficient means for obtaining information. In a written reference, the reader is provided with only what the author thinks is important. Thus the reader is unable to draw certain conclusions for lack of information. In calling references, on the other hand, the evaluator has the opportunity to ask questions more directly related to job requirements and specific performances.

Remember that reference checks take time. Unfortunately, many applicants are hired in a rush to fill an immediate vacancy. This often results in overlooking some critical elements.

There is a growing proliferation of resume and credential fakers in the job market. Consequently, employers must be thorough in investigating potential employees.

Conducting reference checks is serious business. Courts have found employers culpable where an incompetent employee was at fault. The decisions have indicated that better care should have been exercised in the hiring process. Other related incidents have cost employers, large and small, millions of dollars in damages and lost revenue.

Unfortunately, employers have become increasingly resistant to providing references on former personnel for fear of litigation. Some companies have gone so far as to provide only the name, position held and work dates of previous employees, regardless of their performance on the job.

But without information from previous employers, the evaluator is left with little more than the applicant's word on all the information sought. In most instances, this works to the applicant's advantage, but can result in disaster for the employer.

I. Conducting a Reference Check

> *"Common sense is not so common."*
> Voltaire

A reference check must be performed in a deliberate fashion. Rushing through questions with a past employer will not achieve the results you need.

Questions should be developed around what you need to know about the applicant's performance. They must be job-related! Fishing for personal information just invites trouble.

The references checked should include people with whom the candidate has worked in the past three years. Character references generally do not yield useful and pertinent information. If applicants do not provide the names of individuals with whom they have worked directly, that should automatically arouse suspicion.

When speaking with a reference, ask if there are other individuals who worked with the applicant and if you may speak with them too. Take for granted that references listed by the candidate have been prepped. Contacting someone who is unsuspecting may provide candid information, positive or negative.

On occasion, you will be referred to personnel, especially if the applicant in question left the referenced company a year or more ago. Unfortunately, personnel specialists are trained to provide only job titles and dates of employment.

If this happens, be creative. Try the department again. You might get a different person who will be more cooperative. Attempt different angles and strategies. Put the person with whom you're speaking at ease. A soothing, friendly voice may catch the person off-guard.

If you're having little success, ask someone else in your organization to give it a try. How the reference taker and reference giver interact with each other plays a significant role in the information obtained.

> *How would you describe his work ethic?*

What to ask

Examine the requirements of the position to be filled and build your questions around this information. The questions should be consistent from reference to reference and candidate to candidate. Developing standardized sets of questions might be appropriate.

Questions asked of business and/or professional references should be related exclusively to past job performance. It is appropriate, of course, to pursue clarification if something arouses your interest, as long as the conversation remains in the proper domain.

> *"The best of prophets of the future is the past."*
>
> Lord Byron

A typical set of questions might be:
- "How long did Carl work for you?"
- "Did he hold other positions within the company?"
- "How would you describe his work ethic?"
- "Given the opportunity, would you hire him again?"
- "What reservations should I have about hiring him?"
- "Who else within your organization would be able to comment on his performance?"
- "What were his reasons for leaving?"

Chapter 9 Obtaining Reliable References

> *"The greatest discovery of my generation is that a human being can alter his life by altering his attitude."*
>
> William James

How to ask

Develop a rapport with references. If you rush into a reference check in a perfunctory way, there is little opportunity to establish a positive relationship. Since you are interested in both facts and impressions, a "just the facts, ma'am" approach will defeat your effort.

References may be reluctant to give information on a candidate if the relationship was not very positive. Their hesitancy can be an indication of areas you might want to pursue with other references or the candidate during an interview. People carrying out reference checks should be trained to hear not only what is said but also what is meant.

One way to obtain information or opinion through a reluctant reference is to rephrase the question:

Q: Could you describe Dave Lee's work habits?
A: Yeah. He worked like everyone else. Got the job done.
Q: So you would describe him as a hard worker with plenty of ambition and enthusiasm for the job?
A: Well ... okay ... I guess so.

> *"Take nothing on its looks; take everything on evidence. There's no better rule."*
>
> Charles Dickens

In the above exchange, the reference is agreeing with what the evaluator is saying. Yet what is being said is not necessarily what is meant. An astute listener should pick up the inference. If the candidate was an excellent worker, chances are the reference would have reinforced his first statement with something like, "Absolutely! When he quit, Dave Lee left a void in the morale and productivity around here. I wish I had him back."

> *In some cases, you have to manipulate references into answering certain questions. Stick strictly to the facts, however.*

In some cases, you have to manipulate references into answering certain questions. Stick strictly to the facts, however. One strategy is to create the impression that the applicant has just about been offered the job, something like, "We're down to three applicants and we're looking for the best match." How references respond verbally or nonverbally to the applicant's success thus far will leave an indication of how they feel about that person.

Another option is the indirect inquiry. You might ask, "Since this person will be going through some training once he's on board, I am wondering if you could tell me where he might need the most training." Since references might draw the conclusion that this man already has been offered the job, they might be more open to discussing individual characteristics and skills.

It is up to the reference checker to provide opportunities where the reference can convey information about a questionable employee without risking litigation. (Remember, it is up to the plaintiff to prove intent in a defamation suit.)

Robert Thornton, author of *The Lexicon of Intentionally Ambiguous Recommendations* (Meadowbrook Press, 1988), has developed a humorous set of responses a reference can give to pan applicants. They include:

"In my opinion, you will be very fortunate to get this person to work for you."

"I can assure you that no person would be better for the job."

"I most enthusiastically recommend this candidate with no qualifications whatsoever."

"I would urge you to waste no time in making this candidate an offer of employment."

Appeal to common sense

Still another alternative for obtaining information from reluctant references is to simply appeal to their common sense. If everyone refuses to give references on former employees, the recruiting system will experience a grave loss. Employers who are careful in what they say and document performance along the way have nothing to fear. Unfortunately, most companies are not known for their diligence in record-keeping and, therefore, leave themselves at risk in giving references.

A final option is to ask candidates to sign a release that allows former employers to speak freely about their performance. It is best to have an attorney review any such release prior to its use.

> *Still another alternative for obtaining information from reluctant references is to simply appeal to their common sense.*

Chapter 9 Obtaining Reliable References

Digi-Lectronics Inc.
Telephone Reference Guide

> **Hints:**
> Be friendly but persistent.
> Listen for what is said and also how it is said.
> If the reference is reluctant to speak, appeal to common sense.
> Ask about others who can comment on the applicant's performance.

Record the information as you conduct the reference check.
Don't wait to write it down later.

Mr./Ms. _____, this is _____ with Digi-Lectronics. We are considering_____ for possible employment, and I would like to ask you a few questions about his/her work history with you.

1. What dates was s/he employed with you?
2. What was _____'s job title?
3. What were _____'s duties?
4. How would you describe _____'s work ethic?
5. What would you consider _____'s strong points?
6. Given the opportunity, would you hire _____ again?
7. What kind of supervision did _____ require?
8. What was the basis of _____'s compensation?
9. What concerns should I have about hiring _____?
10. Who else there might be able to comment on his/her performance?

If you have trouble getting through:
- *Call before or after regular business hours; this avoids the receptionist/ gatekeeper.*
- *If you are referred to personnel, hang up and try back at a different time.*
- *Try to build rapport with the reference giver. If you have difficulty, ask someone else to try.*
- *If all references are hard to reach or reluctant, that in itself might be saying something.*

II. Checking Credentials

Besides checking references, verify all other credentials for authenticity. Employers continually discover applicants who have falsified facts in order to "qualify" for a job. As competition for jobs has increased, so have the mistruths.

While some applicants may use a simple exaggeration, others manufacture entire degree programs to satisfy requirements. Ironically, the largest number of falsifications appear to involve the Ivy League and other well-known schools. While these institutions provide badly needed credibility, they are also the first checked in an investigation.

When checking educational credentials, ask not only if the applicant has attended the institution, but also the dates of attendance, the program or major studied and whether he graduated. Having a degree in social work from Stanford is not the same as having a degree in finance, but no one would know if the resume reads "Bachelor of Science, Stanford University, Graduation, 1982."

> *While some applicants may use a simple exaggeration, others manufacture entire degree programs to satisfy requirements.*

Credit checks

In addition to educational credentials, it is permissible for an employer to conduct a credit check. This is advisable for a position involved with the financial dealings of the company. Credit checks are regulated by the Federal Fair Credit Reporting Act as well as many states' laws. Disclosure to the applicant of such a credit check is required. Failure to do so could leave the company open to civil liability. Consult your attorney on what may be done in your locale. (A sample release is contained on the next page.)

Information from a credit history can provide insight into any financial difficulties applicants may be having and an account of their present financial responsibilities. One might be able to draw conclusions from this information about the likelihood of somebody mishandling funds or taking other indiscreet or illegal actions. Once again, you are protecting yourself not only against in-house loss and theft, but also against actions brought by others if the employee acts on your behalf. (This check doesn't prevent the action. It does, however, mitigate the level of risk.)

> *"One loss is good for the soul. Too many losses are not good for the coach."*
>
> Knute Rockne

Release for Credit Check

I authorize Digi-Lectronics to make whatever inquiries it deems necessary in connection with my application for employment. As part of such inquiries, Digi-Lectronics has my permission to contact persons who may have information relative to my suitability for employment and to secure consumer reports (including investigative consumer reports).

I authorize and instruct any person or agency contacted by Digi-Lectronics to participate or conduct inquiries at its request, to compile information and to furnish Digi-Lectronics with any information obtained as a result of such inquiries.

I further authorize Digi-Lectronics, at its sole discretion, to furnish copies of this authorization and my application to any person(s) and/or consumer reporting agency(ies) in connection with the above purposes.

Name_____

Signature_____ Date_____

Disclosure Statement

Information contained in reports obtained by Digi-Lectronics in accordance with the above authorization may include information pertaining to your character, general reputation, police record, personal characteristics and mode of living. You have the right to request that Digi-Lectronics completely and accurately disclose to you the nature and scope of all investigations requested. Such a request must be made in writing to the office of the company's operations vice president within a reasonable period of time after your application for employment is received.

I hereby acknowledge that I have read the above disclosure statement and have understood it.

Name_____

Signature_____ Date_____

Credential services

A final option, if you want to avoid the hassle of checking credentials altogether, is to employ a credential service. These companies will run a thorough check on an applicant and report back with their evaluation. In some cases, their information will have more depth than anything you could gather, since they have time to persevere and are being paid to do so. But there is a point of diminishing return. In some cases, the amount of data provided may not be warranted. Be judicious in the use of these organizations.

In a 1986 survey by the Society for Human Resource Management, 6 percent of those responding indicated using this type of service. These services are located in most cities and can be found through the local personnel association or chamber of commerce.

The Reference Checklist

☐ 1. Are you taking time with your reference checks and performing them in a thorough and consistent manner? Are you planning your questions ahead of time and keeping them job-related?

☐ 2. When checking a reference, are you asking if there are others within the organization who would be willing to add their thoughts? These individuals might be more candid.

☐ 3. When conducting the check, are you listening to what is said but also to what is meant? The two may not be consistent.

☐ 4. Are you careful to check credentials thoroughly with all institutions listed on the resume or application?

☐ 5. Have you considered the option of having a credit check performed on applicants, especially if they will be involved with the finances of the company?

Chapter 9 Obtaining Reliable References

Questions for Personal Development

1. What is the major emphasis of this chapter?

2. What are the most important things you learned from this chapter?

3. How can you apply what you learned to your current job?

4. How will you go about making these changes?

5. How can you monitor improvement?

6. Summarize the changes you expect to see in yourself one year from now.

CHAPTER 10

Employment Testing — Dos and Don'ts

"I feel really funny requiring these urine tests," commented the manager. "To me, whether they use dope is their business as long as they don't use it on the job."

"All this witness stuff kills morale. They think we don't trust them," agreed her colleague.

"Yeah. But then there was that accident with the packing skids," piped in a third. "If Sammie had come to work in his right mind, those wouldn't have fallen over."

"But is that any reason to test everyone?" asked the first manager. "I had a kid in here the other day and I offered her a job. I told her about the test and she said it was an invasion of privacy."

Here's What You'll Learn

I. Overview of Testing Issues
II. Paper and Pencil Testing
III. Selecting Integrity Tests
IV. Polygraph Screening
V. Genetic Screening
VI. Drug and Alcohol Screening
VII. Performance-Based Testing
VIII. Screening for AIDS
IX. The Testing Checklist

Chapter 10 Employment Testing — Dos and Don'ts

I. Overview of Testing Issues

Preemployment screening has been, and will continue to be, a controversial issue. While testing has become a valid method for ascertaining a candidate's suitability for employment, legal implications including invasion of privacy and discrimination still surround the topic.

In reality, only a minority of businesses in the United States conduct any testing during the preemployment screening process. In a 1990 American Management Association survey of workplace testing, the rate of increase in companies testing for drugs, for instance, slowed considerably in 1989 compared with the previous three years. At the same time, the number of companies that train supervisors to spot behavior that might indicate drug abuse rose 24 percent.

Thirty-six percent of companies in the same survey were testing for basic skills and training in 1990. Job competency testing was performed by 45 percent. Finally, paper and pencil integrity testing was being conducted by only 10.1 percent of firms.

Preemployment screening can be divided into two categories:

> **Psychological screening** to determine levels of skill-based competence, honesty and mental attitudes toward performance.
>
> **Physical screening** to determine fitness to perform the job. This includes drug and alcohol screening, genetic screening and testing for Acquired Immune Deficiency Syndrome (AIDS).

With the exception of the transportation industry, the decision to screen, whether psychologically or physically, is totally up to the individual employer. Surveys show that the business community as a whole is divided on the issue. While testing has proven to be an accurate indicator in certain situations, it is expensive and time-consuming. Further, it opens the door to litigation if not closely monitored.

It should be assumed that little information in any organization remains truly confidential. Therefore, the confidential results of testing, whether for honesty or physical capabilities, should be guarded closely.

Too many people think they are being creative when they are just being different.

Testing can be used as a recruiting device if handled correctly. For example, Hawaiian Electric Co. advertised that it would conduct testing for positions in its organization now and in the future. Applicants who passed the test would be eligible for positions as they came open. Because of its good name within the community, Hawaiian Electric was able to attract well over 4,000 applicants who took the test and became eligible for employment.

Requiring a physician's examination, regardless of whether you are screening for drugs, is sound advice. Some applicants suffer from preexisting conditions such as back and head injury, due to previous accidents on or off the job. Few companies can afford to absorb the additional costs of caring for an employee who walked in the door with a preexisting ailment. Have your company physician examine all new employees. The cost of exams should not be a consideration, since the long-term effects of not doing so can be devastating. All job offers should be made with the contingency that the candidate passes the physical.

This chapter will cover the major areas where testing has been implemented in the preemployment process. Each section provides information on the purpose and use of the tests along with a discussion of the arguments surrounding their value. It closes with recommendations on the issue.

> *"The time to repair the roof is when the sun is shining."*
>
> John F. Kennedy

II. Paper and Pencil Testing

So-called paper and pencil testing may be divided into two categories:
- Written honesty and personality tests
- Skills and aptitude testing

The honesty and personality tests are used to determine an applicant's tendency toward honesty and psychological indicators of how she will perform on the job. These characteristics can include truthfulness, tendency toward depression, hysteria, anger, etc.

Skills and aptitude testing, on the other hand, is used to assess the candidate's ability to perform required tasks. These might include typing and mathematical skills, along with verbal and written communication.

> *The cost of physical exams should not be a consideration, since the long-term effects of not doing so can be devastating.*

Chapter 10 Employment Testing — Dos and Don'ts

> *"Nothing astonishes men so much as common sense and plain dealing."*
>
> Ralph Waldo Emerson

The main controversy over paper and pencil tests is accuracy. Applicants who answer "too honestly" may be disqualified, while less honest applicants who manipulate the test may be accepted.

Further, applicants who do not generally "test well" may do poorly on an examination even though they have the required skills or aptitudes.

Tests that fail a higher than normal number of individuals in protected classes have an adverse impact and are considered to be discriminatory.

Finally, opponents of preemployment testing maintain that it violates an individual's right to privacy. These critics point to employers' less intrusive means for gathering information such as the interview, resume, application and reference checks.

In 1990, the U.S. Office of Technology Assessment concluded that existing research does not clearly confirm or refute the assertion that paper and pencil integrity testing accurately predicts dishonest behavior in the workplace. While firms producing these products refute these findings, the report still calls into question the overall validity of integrity testing.

Written honesty and personality testing

With the passage of the Employee Polygraph Protection Act of 1988 (EPPA), an increasing number of employers have turned to these tests for the screening of applicants. Their major aim is to establish an applicant's propensity to be honest. It is difficult to assess an applicant's tendency toward telling the truth, but research indicates some strong correlations between those candidates considered "high risk" and those who were found likely to steal on the job.

These examinations are generally a series of multiple-choice, true/false- or yes/no-based questions or a combination thereof. Packages come with an examination booklet and answer sheets and can be scored quickly by the employer or test vendor. They range in price from $5-14.

Some of these tests contain questions that measure the applicant's truthfulness while taking the test. These questions are interspersed throughout and ask about emotions such as "Sometimes I get frustrated on the job." Since it can be easily assumed that everyone experiences frustration, an applicant who answers "false" would automatically be suspect. This series of questions is tallied during scoring and a "lie scale" is established to reference how truthful the applicant is being.

Information on honesty screening tests is contained in Appendix E.

Skills and aptitude testing

Employers must be careful in the use of skills and aptitude testing. As indicated earlier, the possibility of adverse impact, and therefore discrimination, exists unless the results of these tests are closely monitored.

Honesty and personality testing generally uses standardized instruments. Skill and aptitude tests, on the other hand, may be published examinations that attempt to measure verbal intelligence, or tests created by the employer to assess capabilities in a certain area. The latter group includes physical measures such as coordination and lifting as well as tests of typing, letter writing and organization of paperwork.

Some testing has become rather creative. Japanese automobile firms, for instance, employ assessment centers involving in-basket exercises and production line testing, including team games requiring applicants to assemble a certain number of flashlights in a given period of time. The purpose behind these tests is to discover who may fit best in which position.

Dependability testing

Dependability tests are used to forecast an applicant's likelihood of success on the job. These tests are adaptations of what industrial psychologists have termed "trait testing." As such, they evaluate an applicant's attitudes, practices and values that are job-related, as compared with a so-called cognitive test that attempts to measure reasoning and learning.

A dependability test that is specially designed for a company is validated to show that there is a clear relationship between a particular test result and job performance. These tests vary from an integrity test in that they evaluate a variety of values instead of honesty alone. Developers of dependability tests maintain that integrity tests do little more than predict how applicants will do on a polygraph examination.

Each company must score its own tests since the test is developed specifically for that organization. Some have a pass/fail

> *"The farther backward you can look, the farther forward you are likely to see."*
>
> Winston Churchill

Chapter 10 Employment Testing — Dos and Don'ts

> *Employers can use any test they wish, but must be able to prove, if challenged, that the test does not discriminate against protected classes.*

cut-off, others have a system allowing for a range of scores. Subjective judgments and other factors are usually incorporated into the hiring process as well. Developers' experiences to date have shown that these tests work best with businesses that have many employees and experience a high turnover rate of non-management personnel.

The cost of developing these tests is generally $20-30,000. But each company owns the test developed for it and the cost of each administration declines with use. For a firm with about 3,000 employees, for example, the average cost of the test can be approximately 30 cents per applicant.

Validation

The Equal Employment Opportunity Commission (EEOC) allows employers to use skill and aptitude testing as a form of pre-employment selection. Employers should be aware, however, that the validity of using a test in one circumstance does not guarantee that it may be used successfully in another.

The EEOC does not require that these tests be validated unless it can be shown that they produce an adverse impact. In other words, employers can use any test they wish, but must be able to prove, if challenged, that the test does not discriminate against protected classes.

To ensure that the testing has no adverse effect, most employers "validate" their tests through one of three methods approved by the commission:

- Content validity studies
- Criterion validity studies
- Construct validity studies

Content validity studies establish that the content of the test is consistent with the duties and responsibilities of the job. For instance, a test that questions an applicant's ability to perform basic mathematics for a bank teller's position has content validity.

Criterion validity studies measure the predictability of the test-taker to succeed on the job. If there is a significant statistical correlation between the test results and subjects' performance on the job, then the test is considered valid.

Construct validity studies are the least used of the three because of their complex nature. These studies measure evidence of the extent to which a subject's individual characteristics match identifiable characteristics of the job. Because of the amount of empirical data required to establish validity, these studies have been declared invalid numerous times.

The most convincing proof that a test is valid is found in a predictive validity study. This is a study in which the test is administered to job applicants, their attitudes are recorded and their behavior on the job is tracked. When deciding which test to use, consider practical testing features such as the test's required reading level, ease of administration and scoring, computer scoring technology, clarity of test output, pass rate, satisfied client references and the test's business history. Finally, evaluate the test publisher's ability to provide thorough training to your test administrators.

Handwriting analysis

Another means for assessing individuals is analysis of their handwriting. While this method has been popular in Europe for years, it is relatively new to our employment system.

Handwriting analysis involves a review of the physical characteristics of a person's handwriting such as size and slant of the letters, pressure on the paper and the rhythm with which the writing was produced. In some cases, handwriting analysis can provide selection officials with a new perspective on job candidates who otherwise might be overlooked because of difficulty with another part of the selection process.

A number of employers have expressed a high degree of satisfaction with the results of handwriting analysis. They claim it is a simpler and less expensive system to administer than psychological tests.

While some companies have given this technique high ratings, critics charge that there is no scientific basis for the conclusions drawn. Analysis of this type ranges from $25-$400 per person.

> "A man's character is his fate."
>
> Heraclitus

Chapter 10 Employment Testing — Dos and Don'ts

Consider the impact of employee testing on employee morale. Trust is delicate in any organization.

Recommendations for paper and pencil testing
- Know why you are testing. What information do you expect a paper and pencil test to provide that will assist you in hiring more accurately?
- Consider also the impact of employee testing on employee morale. Trust is delicate in any organization. Many employees view testing as a statement of distrust. Consult with employees about problems related to theft. They might have a better solution.
- In addition to federal statutes, check state regulations on pre-employment testing. In many cases, these requirements are more stringent or totally prohibit certain forms of testing.
- When using preemployment testing, make sure it is not having an adverse impact on protected classes of applicants. Record-keeping is essential in addition to confidentiality.
- Examine the cost/benefit ratio of using tests in the pre-employment process. While these instruments can provide an indication of a person's honesty and capabilities, the annual expense for this information might better be spent elsewhere.

"Character is power."
Booker T. Washington

Check references and reputations of testing services and products
- Be sure the test you are considering is measuring what you want it to measure. Researching a test before using it is critical. Will it give you the information you seek? Look past the fancy product packaging.
- Be sure all testing is validated. All instruments, published and employer-created, should be checked for relatedness to the job duties. This needs to be done for each type of position. There is no such thing as a blanket test.
- If you have created your own tests for certain positions, have them validated by an outside source following the *Guidelines for Employee Selection Procedures* available from the Equal Employment Opportunity Commission.

III. Selecting Integrity Tests

Employee theft has become a national problem. According to the National Business Crime Information Network, American businesses lost more than $200 billion in 1988 to cash and merchandise thefts committed by employees. The Department of Justice estimates that insider theft is growing at 15 percent annually.

One possible solution is to administer integrity tests to all candidates you plan to hire. Paper and pencil integrity testing has been in use for more than 40 years and has evolved into a multimillion dollar industry. Testing firms have developed a host of honesty tests that can be taken in five to 30 minutes and claim to reveal whether the applicant is likely to steal or otherwise act dishonestly on the job.

> *"If you don't know where you're going, you'll probably end up somewhere else."*
>
> Lawrence J. Peter

A debate about the reliability of these tests has raged for years and no clear anwer is in sight. Many of the firms that use them swear by their accuracy. They maintain that since polygraph testing is no longer an option, these tests provide a reasonable alternative. They argue that if administered properly and tracked closely, these tests will provide a reliable predictor of applicant honesty. Yet in a 1990 survey by the American Management Association, only 6.2 percent of businesses responding indicated that they use integrity tests as part of their applicant screening process.

If you do decide to investigate the testing option, here are seven quick tips for making the job effective:

1. Know why you are testing. What is being stolen? Is it concentrated in one department? Does one site have more theft than others? What other options for reducing theft might you have? What information do you expect an integrity test to provide that will help you hire more accurately? Have plenty of questions for every testing firm you approach.
2. Consider the impact of testing on employee morale. Trust in any organization is a delicate balance. Many employees view integrity testing as a statement of distrust. Consult with employees about problems related to theft. Ask for their input since company losses have an effect on everyone. Active employee participation in theft prevention might have more of an impact than any integrity test.

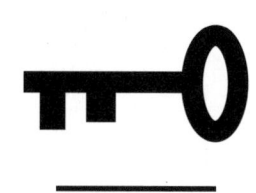

Chapter 10 Employment Testing — Dos and Don'ts

> *"As I grow older, I pay less attention to what men say. I just watch what they do."*
>
> Andrew Carnegie

3. Check federal, state and local regulations for testing prohibitions. Before approaching testing firms, consult with your attorney about state and local laws regarding preemployment testing.
4. Be sure the test you choose is validated. While there are no federal laws banning tests, the test you give must fall within the validity guidelines of the Equal Employment Opportunity Commission. These guidelines ensure that the test is reliably measuring what it is supposed to measure.
5. Make sure the test is not going to have an adverse impact on those groups from which you hire. In addition to being reliable, the test should not discriminate against protected classes of people.
6. Thoroughly check the references of the testing firm you plan to use. Ask for the names and contacts of at least three other comparable firms that are using the test with success. Then ask lots of questions, especially about the test's reliability in distinguishing between honest and dishonest applicants.
7. Finally, recognize that there is no such thing as the perfect test. While everyone has a desire to have a "black and white" answer about applicant honesty, these tests, no matter how reliable, are only one part of the equation in hiring honest people for the job.

IV. Polygraph Screening

The purpose of the polygraph or lie detector is to determine whether an applicant is telling the truth. Proponents claim that on this basis it can be projected whether a candidate will be honest on the job.

One of the major pieces of federal legislation passed in 1988 was the Employee Polygraph Protection Act. Having taken effect December 27, 1988, it effectively prohibits private sector use of polygraphs, voice print devices and related technology for screening applicants. There are exceptions to this, but they are limited to certain jobs involving defense and national security, pharmaceuticals and private security firms.

> *"The real problem is not whether machines think but whether men do."*
>
> B.F. Skinner

Overall considerations

The polygraph has been the source of controversy for a number of years. As with other forms of testing, the major issue is accuracy.

The basic logic behind the polygraph is that lying creates stress and that this stress can be measured mechanically. The mechanically measured stress can then be used to determine whether the candidate tends to be dishonest based on whether she lied during the examination.

The most common form of polygraph testing is the Relevant Control Method, where the subject is asked a series of questions, some related to the job and others irrelevant. For instance, irrelevant questions might ask applicants if they have ever shopped for groceries. The stress associated with the answer is also recorded mechanically. When asked if they have ever stolen anything from an employer, applicants' stress related to this answer is also recorded. The levels of stress recorded for both should be relatively the same. If the stress is significantly higher on the question regarding theft, it is concluded that the subject is lying.

But there are ways to manipulate the test. Use of muscle tension, drugs or physical stress such as pinching oneself can alter the outcome of data.

The location in which a test is taken may also be a biasing factor, along with the training of the polygraph operator. Finally, honest subjects who are nervous about taking the test may fail because of apprehension. Error rates in the polygraph have been estimated as high as 50 percent.

Legal ramifications

Practically speaking, it is not wise to even contemplate the use of a polygraph in your business. While employers are still allowed to use this equipment to investigate theft and employee misconduct, the guidelines are so complicated that it could prove to be more harmful than helpful.

> *"There is the greatest practical benefit in making a few failures early in life."*
>
> Thomas Huxley

> *It is not wise to even contemplate the use of a polygraph in your business.*

Chapter 10 Employment Testing — Dos and Don'ts

Recommendations

If you are eligible to administer polygraph tests, be extremely careful in your interpretation of the guidelines. The act is enforced by the Wage and Hour Division of the Department of Labor. Check any procedures with them before proceeding. If you are a defense contractor, check to make sure use of the polygraph is necessary under your agreement.

If you do choose to use this technology, here are a few recommendations:

- Make sure the purpose falls within the guidelines of the EPPA. Simple lack of trust is not an acceptable reason for administering the polygraph. You must be able to defend your use in court.
- Select your polygraph examiner carefully. Ask for references. In states where a license or certification is required, ask to see it. The examining firm should also be a member of the American Polygraph Association. Ask if the firm has ever been named as a defendant in a lawsuit concerning its polygraph examinations.
- Know exactly what you're testing for. Review with the examiner what questions will be asked and have your attorney check these questions for acceptability. Polygraph examiners are considered agents of the employer.
- Be honest with all applicants. If applicants will be rejected after failing the polygraph, tell them ahead of time. Leading them on with promises of possible exceptions can only damage your selection process and leave you open to litigation.
- Have all applicants sign a consent form. This procedure eliminates claims that the polygraph was conducted under duress or that permission was never given.
- Keep all records absolutely confidential. Under no circumstances should anyone have access to these files unless authorized to do so.
- Consider the "second chance." It is very possible for honest individuals to fail the polygraph for the reasons given earlier. If there is a reasonable doubt, always give the applicant the opportunity to take the polygraph a second time to verify results.

Have all applicants sign a consent form. This procedure eliminates claims that the polygraph was conducted under duress.

Much has been written on the subject of polygraph screening. See the bibliography in Appendix E for additional sources.

Acknowledgment of Polygraph Testing

I acknowledge that Digi-Lectronics Inc. will be administering polygraph examinations to employees whenever the company believes that such an examination is warranted. I understand that the company will make every effort to schedule such an examination at a mutually agreeable time and that refusal to submit to a polygraph examination is grounds for termination of employment.

_____

Employers: *This type of clause is included in the application forms of companies where security is extremely important. With few exceptions, federal law now prohibits the use of polygraphs in the screening of applicants. Be sure to check federal regulations before administering such a test.*

V. Genetic Screening

On the horizon of preemployment testing is the area of genetic screening. While the courts have made no definitive statements regarding its use, you should be familiar with its purposes and procedures. Employers using any chemicals within the workplace on a large-scale basis should pay special attention to this information.

Genetic screening involves testing for certain human characteristics, most commonly through blood samples. With the proliferation of chemicals entering the workplace in the past 50 years, scientists are discovering that certain individuals react differently to certain substances than others do. In some cases, these reactions can be harmful. The purpose of genetic screening should be to ascertain whether an applicant will experience an adverse reaction to chemicals found within a workplace. The Toxic Substances Act requires all employers to post notice of any toxic chemicals or compounds being used on the premises.

The arguments

Genetic screening was introduced with the best of intentions. Employers using certain substances within the workplace became concerned with the possible side effects employees were having to these compounds. In an effort to maintain a safe work environment, therefore, they began testing employees and applicants to determine why such reactions were taking place. Out of this sprang a practice of screening all employees. While opponents of genetic screening acknowledge the good intentions, they also raise concerns about these issues:

- Because certain races are more likely to have certain genetic characteristics, is this another way to block the hiring of these groups?
- If certain chemicals can react dangerously when in contact with employees, why are they being used in the workplace? If they are a necessity, why isn't more care taken with their handling?

Little has been done at this time to answer these concerns. The U.S. Office of Technology Assessment, while studying the subject extensively, has not approved any of the screening technology for routine use in the workplace. At the same time, it has not been prohibited.

"You must pay the price if you wish to secure the blessings."

Andrew Jackson

Opponents have argued that discrimination by genetic characteristics falls under Title VII of the Civil Rights Act of 1964. But according to this legislation, genetic characteristics are not a protected class.

Finally, the Occupational Safety and Health Administration makes no mention of genetic screening in the workplace. However, this legislation does mandate that in a preemployment physical examination, the physician must take into consideration a wide range of physical conditions.

What does this mean for the employer? While this is not a large issue at the present time, attention to it could have an impact on organizations using any of the 35,000 chemicals currently in use in business. This situation could range from toner in the photocopier on one extreme to hazardous toxins on the other. The bottom line is to remain informed.

> *"Laws too gentle are seldom obeyed; too severe, seldom executed."*
>
> Benjamin Franklin

Recommendations

- Perform a thorough analysis of your workplace if you are considering genetic screening. This situation will not apply to most companies. If you are considering this type of selection, be extremely aware of its ramifications.
- Genetic screening, if implemented, should be part of an overall physical. It should not be used simply to reject applicants. If certain traits are revealed, you might consider offering the applicant a less hazardous placement within the firm.
- Take care in selecting the testing service. As with other testing services, referrals and reliable information should be sought to establish credibility.

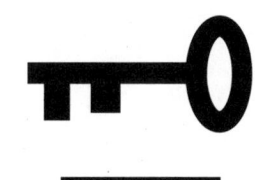

VI. Drug and Alcohol Screening

With the proliferation of drug and alcohol abuse in the United States, worker productivity has been increasingly affected. The work ethic has decreased dramatically while absenteeism has increased.

In addition, impaired employees can present a safety hazard within the work environment. With the advance in technology and the addition of thousands of dangerous chemicals and machines to the workplace, attentiveness is mandatory at all times.

As companies are becoming more cost conscious, each person's attendance and productivity have a greater impact. If your only lathe operator is absent, a number of employees might have to adjust their schedules and tasks. A missing receptionist can cause havoc with the phones. Each person is critical and if drugs are a problem, the normal flow of daily work can be disrupted.

The controversy

As with any controversy, there are legitimate arguments on both sides. Regardless of your feelings toward the use and abuse of drugs and alcohol, you have a responsibility as an employer to provide a safe, profitable workplace while still staying within the law.

Proponents of testing for drugs point out that the workplace becomes safer when testing is performed and therefore demonstrates the employer's concern for the health and well-being of the employees. In addition, the rate of productivity rises, which has a positive effect on morale. Further, if applicants know when they apply for a job that they will be screened for drugs, you may well save substantial money simply because some who may present problems later on will not apply and be tested. Proponents add that many of the drugs are controlled substances; therefore, employees possessing them are breaking the law.

Critics of testing for drugs maintain that potential employees' rights to privacy are being violated since what they do on their own time is their business. They also complain about the poor levels of accuracy for many of the testing techniques, in some cases as low as 50 percent. Many false positives are also reported because of medication the applicant may be taking at the time.

> *Each person is critical and if drugs are a problem, the normal flow of daily work can be disrupted.*

> *Many false positives are reported because of medication the applicant may be taking at the time.*

Additionally, opponents maintain that abusers who have completed a treatment program are considered disabled under the Americans with Disabilities Act. Current abusers could be classified as handicapped under the Rehabilitation Act of 1973 and are a protected class. This second law covers employers with federal contracts and/or funding.

Finally, critics point out that the testing could have a disparate impact on protected classes under Title VII of the Civil Rights Act of 1964. This means, for instance, that drug testing of certain groups for which a higher incidence of substance abuse has been established, will be faced with discrimination.

General worker attitudes may have an influence on drug testing. Seventy percent of 1,000 workers polled by the Gallup Organization said that employers should have the right to test employees suspected of drug use. More than 50 percent supported random drug testing.

The legalities of testing

At this point, the federal government has not acted directly to regulate drug and alcohol testing in the workplace. As mentioned above, the Rehabilitation Act of 1973 might be used by some applicants to avoid the testing issue. This may be done only if applicants are willing to admit that they have abused the substance and then claim the handicap. Most are not willing to do so. The law has been interpreted to mean that an employer can refuse to hire only when the handicap of alcoholism or drug addiction would make the applicant unable or unqualified to perform in the position.

Another consideration would be disparate impact under the Civil Rights Act of 1964. Currently, however, there have been no federal court decisions regarding this issue.

Finally, the National Labor Relations Board has taken the position that testing for drugs should be a mandatory subject of collective bargaining and that these negotiations should take place prior to the implementation of a program.

On the state level, some action has been taken to address applicants' rights of privacy concerning alcohol and drug testing. While no state has passed legislation specifically prohibiting drug testing, Alaska and California have specific privacy guarantees covering private employment.

> *"Progress always involves risk; you can't steal second base and keep your foot on first."*
> Frederick Wilcox

> *"Well done is better than well said."*
> Benjamin Franklin

Chapter 10 Employment Testing — Dos and Don'ts

Legal Considerations of Drug Screening

- There are no federal guidelines regulating drug screening.

- Applicants who have abused drugs in the past are considered disabled under the Americans with Disabilities Act provided they completed or are in the process of completing a treatment program. Those currently abusing drugs are not protected.

- Applicants may invoke the Rehabilitation Act of 1973 if:
  1. The employer is within the act's jurisdiction.
  2. The applicant is willing to admit to drug abuse.

- Employers within the jurisdiction of Title VII may risk disparate impact.

- While prescreening applicants for drugs has become a generally accepted practice, random screening of current employees is still being debated due to privacy considerations.

- Unionized employers should assume that drug screening will be a part of the collective bargaining agreement.

- No state has specifically prohibited drug screening. Applicants' right of privacy is a current issue.

Confirming screenings should always be performed.

Procedures for testing

While it is not the author's intent to provide a full-scale explanation of drug testing, familiarity with the concepts is helpful.

Most employers who are currently screening for substance abuse use a urine testing procedure. Other more sophisticated methods are available involving blood, breath, skin, hair and saliva.

The most common test used by laboratories that provide such services is "enzyme multiplied immunoassay," which measures the reaction of the urine specimen to radioactive animal antibodies. This reaction indicates the presence of drugs. The "gas chromatography mass spectrometry" (GC-MS) test is considered the most accurate and is used to confirm the presence of drugs since the initial screening has a higher error rate.

Confirming screenings should always be performed. Tests can produce a "false positive" reaction because some bodily chemicals may be detected as illegal drugs. Some over-the-counter pain relievers and prescription drugs produce the same effect.

In the course of a drug screening, any legitimate drugs the applicant is using will also be identified. These, however, may indicate conditions of an emotional or physical nature such as depression or epilepsy. You should be careful to judge applicants on the hiring criteria for the job, not on your emotional reaction to one of the conditions. Some conditions may also be protected under handicap legislation.

If you have chosen to implement a screening program, selection of a laboratory service is critical. Check references thoroughly. Ask to see facilities and what procedures are used. Ask why the laboratory considers its testing methods to be accurate.

Tests should be conducted out of a genuine concern for the organization and the applicant.

Your organization should execute an agreement with the laboratory, reemphasizing the importance of confidentiality that includes a "hold harmless" clause making the laboratory, not the company, liable for negligence in the event of litigation. A "chain of custody" should be established for every specimen to ensure proper handling. A careful record should be kept, tracing each specimen. This discourages tampering and the switching of samples.

Any applicant who does test positively should be given the opportunity for a confirming test to ensure accuracy, even if this is at the applicant's expense.

Screening Checklist

✔ Be careful to define why screening for alcohol and drugs is important to your organization. Don't be caught in the periodic waves of publicity surrounding this topic. Testing can be much more trouble than it is worth.

✔ Drug screenings should be conducted as part of an overall physical, not as an isolated preemployment criterion. Tests should be conducted out of a genuine concern for the organization and the applicant.

✔ Investigate laboratories thoroughly before proceeding. Check references, methods, accuracy and "chain of custody."

✔ Have applicants sign a release, if at all possible, before conducting a screening for substance abuse. Make sure the applicants understand that their refusal means automatic elimination from consideration.

✔ Test only those who have reached the final stages of selection. This eliminates additional costs.

✔ Applicants who fail the drug screening should be rejected on the basis of their not passing the physical. This eliminates difficult questions and explanations.

✔ Maintain absolute confidentiality at all times. All records should be locked and marked confidential. Only essential personnel should know the results.

Chapter 10   Employment Testing — Dos and Don'ts

VII. Performance-Based Testing

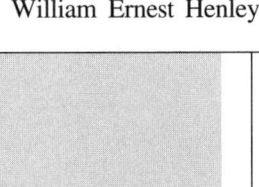

"I am the master of my fate; I am the captain of my soul."

William Ernest Henley

An alternative to drug screening is that of performance-based testing. While generally administered to current employees, it warrants mention in this chapter. This type of testing requires employees on a daily basis to pass a test demonstrating various abilities required for performance on the job. These might include visual acuity, hand-eye coordination, reflex timing and other elements of physical fitness. The technology generally involves a computer-based video game requiring employees to pass a test before going on the job.

Companies using this type of testing presently include trucking firms, taxis and entertainment/tour companies requiring professional drivers. The applications are widespread and provide a viable alternative to drug screening.

Performance testing measures current impairment from a variety of sources including drugs, alcohol, fatigue, stress and emotion. Testing for current impairment provides the employers with an evaluation of the employee's actual physical and mental state at the time of work, as opposed to drug testing, which requires a significant waiting time for results. Performance testing can also be performed every day without raising questions of privacy. Performance-based testing generally costs less than $1 per employee.

Because it measures impairment rather than presence of drugs, performance-based testing challenges the way one can evaluate accuracy in testing. Drug use may not be the only reason employees fail these tests. If an employee cannot reach a level of proficiency previously established, then the employer can surmise that something is wrong. If performance testing catches on, it will provide an extremely viable alternative to the more controversial drug screening.

Recommendations
- Determine what you wish to measure with a performance-based test. What constitutes adequate performance for each position being tested?
- Thoroughly research the various alternatives for performance-based testing. These would include video games, physical performance exercises such as lifting and manual coordination.
- Research federal, state and local regulations to ensure compliance with law.
- Determine start-up costs. Costs may be significant at first but diminish with long-term use of the equipment. Costs include

video hardware, software development and training time. Some firms have found that insurance companies are willing to subsidize these costs due to eventual savings in accident prevention.

VIII. Screening for AIDS

Acquired Immune Deficiency Syndrome (AIDS) has sent shock waves throughout our society. This concern has spread to the business community.

Employers are faced with the difficult choice of whether or not to test for AIDS. Not only do they have to deal with the health concerns related to the disease, they may also be faced with charges of discrimination unless their testing of applicants can be demonstrated to be a business necessity.

While there is still much to be discovered about AIDS and its effects, this section will provide an overview of the disease and its impact on employers, along with recommendations on handling AIDS-related issues in the workplace.

> *"The future belongs to those who believe in the beauty of their dreams."*
>
> Eleanor Roosevelt

Overview of the disease

AIDS is a human immune system dysfunction. Scientists believe it is caused by infection with one or more of the following viruses:
- Human T-lymphotropic virus type III (HTLV-III)
- Human immunodeficiency virus (HIV)
- Lymphadenopathy-associated virus (LAV)
- AIDS-related virus (ARV)

The presence of these viruses depends upon the developmental stages of the disease within the person's body. The result is the disability of the individual's immune system, making the person vulnerable to diseases that do not threaten other members of the population. There is no known cure and current research indicates the disease is eventually fatal.

According to the Centers for Disease Control in Atlanta, AIDS is transmitted through bodily fluids such as blood and semen along with contaminated hypodermic needles or the transfusion of blood and blood products. It is not transmitted through casual contact. Therefore, the Centers for Disease Control does not recommend that employers screen for AIDS in the workplace except for particular occupations, primarily medically related.

> *"He has the right to criticize who has the heart to help."*
>
> Abraham Lincoln

Chapter 10 Employment Testing — Dos and Don'ts

Employer impact and legal overview

How does AIDS impact employers? For the most part, it should not. The information available at the present time is conflicting. While AIDS is a deadly disease, it is not communicable via casual contact. Therefore, screening applicants for AIDS could be considered discriminatory.

A major influence in this, however, could be the requirements by insurance carriers who fear major liability. Regardless of whether you are screening for the disease, it is critical that you check with your insurance carrier and stay as thoroughly informed as possible.

Additionally, employees may protest having to work with individuals carrying AIDS. This will certainly create havoc in the workplace. The best solution to this situation is education. Hold seminars and distribute material explaining the actual implications of the disease as it is presently known.

The Occupational Safety and Health Act (OSHA) mandates that all employers maintain a safe work environment for employees. However, because AIDS is not considered communicable through casual contact, it appears that the disease would not be covered under this legislation since it does not present a workplace hazard.

You, as an employer, must take all factors into consideration. As AIDS is a relatively new development, a great deal of attention is being paid to its effects. It is important to discern the difference between the emotional distress surrounding it and the true long-term impact on your organization.

This is not meant to play down the deadly impact of the disease. It is simply meant to point out that screening for AIDS in your workplace may leave you open to charges of discrimination from those who have contracted the disease but will not communicate it to other employees under normal workplace conditions.

The Americans with Disabilities Act (ADA) is the major federal legislation addressing the needs of individual who have AIDS. In addition, federal contractors are still obligated under the Rehabilitation Act of 1973.

While the ADA prohibits discrimination in the hiring of those with AIDS or the HIV virus, it does not require an employer to include a person with this disease on its insurance coverage if the condition existed prior to the beginning of employment.

Companies will not be able to refuse employment solely because an applicant has AIDS. In addition, reasonable

---

"Happiness lies in the joy of achievement and the thrill of creative effort."

Franklin Roosevelt

"As a rule, men worry more about what they can't see than about what they can."

Julius Caesar

accommodation will have to be made for an employee who progresses into advanced stages of the disease where ability to perform may be impaired.

There is inconsistency at this point, however, since it is very conceivable that an employee who contracts AIDS may never experience physical symptoms while working for your organization. Yet the disability can be extended to mean a psychological disorder such as the trauma a person experiences knowing that she has the disease.

Persons carrying AIDS have not been found to be disabled on the basis of communicability but on the basis of having the disease. On this basis, a person could be refused employment without the employer fearing liability. The burden of proof would be on the AIDS-carrying applicant to show that the rejection was because of the disease.

The best way to approach this issue, however, is to assume AIDS carriers are disabled. Focus on whether the applicant is otherwise qualified for the position. Various states have enacted legislation regulating the screening of diseases by employers. Some of the states prohibit discrimination on the basis of AIDS. A number of major cities have also prohibited discrimination on the basis of AIDS. Consult your attorney for interpretation on the laws of your state.

AIDS' Impact on Employers

- AIDS should not have a significant impact on employee health in the workplace.
- Education about AIDS should significantly reduce employees' anxiety.
- Screening for AIDS is not advisable unless you have a specific job-related reason for doing so.
- Workplace insurance could become an issue if you employ victims of AIDS. Be sure to consult your insurer about coverage.
- Victims of AIDS are considered disabled under the Rehabilitation Act of 1973 (federal contractors).
- Victims of AIDS and those carrying the AIDS virus are considered disabled under the Americans with Disabilities Act.

Chapter 10   Employment Testing — Dos and Don'ts

Testing for AIDS

While every employer has the right to require a preemployment physical examination, a specific type of testing cannot be singled out. Therefore, if you screen for AIDS, the applicant must submit to a total physical.

The results of these examinations must remain confidential. Dissemination of this information without proper authority violates an applicant's rights to privacy. As with drug and alcohol screening, a chain of custody should be established for all specimens. This cannot be emphasized enough.

It is important to understand that the tests presently in use cannot detect whether a person will actually acquire the disease. They can only indicate whether the person's body is producing antibodies to combat the AIDS virus.

Testing for presence of the AIDS antibody can be performed in several ways:

- Enzyme-Linked Immunosorbent Assay (ELISA)
- Radio Immuno Precipitation Assay (RIPA)
- Western Blot Test

The ELISA is currently in use for screening of blood donors, but is the least accurate (cost = $2-$3). The latter two tests are more accurate but also significantly more expensive. Common procedure is to begin with the ELISA test. If the individual tests positive, the more extensive testing should be completed.

Testing positive to the presence of the AIDS antibody may mean one of four things:
1. The individual is carrying the AIDS virus.
2. The individual may develop AIDS in the future.
3. The individual is immune to the effects of AIDS.
4. The individual tested "false positive" because of a reaction to another chemical in the system.

Once again, there is no absolute way to know if the person has AIDS. Therefore, you should be extremely cautious when drawing conclusions about test results.

> *A specific type of testing cannot be singled out. Therefore, if you screen for AIDS, the applicant must submit to a total physical.*

> *There is no absolute way to know if a person has AIDS.*

What can be done?

What can be done concerning applicants who have tested positive for AIDS?

Unless the individual is unable to perform the required duties of the position, you may be exposing yourself to liability by refusing this person employment. Even if the person is experiencing overt physical symptoms such as infections, it is best to provide reasonable accommodation if possible.

There are very few occupations where an employer will be able to refuse employment based on an applicant carrying the AIDS virus. Likely exceptions (although these have not been approved by the courts) are professions where the individual would come in contact with bodily fluids such as blood and saliva. Therefore, dentists, dental technicians and other health care workers who deal with certain patients may be excluded from employment.

The Centers for Disease Control has indicated, however, that proper precautions must be taken in situations where health care or food preparation workers have AIDS, but that they should not be denied employment. You may not deny employment on the basis that an AIDS carrier may infect other workers.

> *"It is a funny thing about life; if you refuse to accept anything but the best, you very often get it."*
>
> Somerset Maugham

Recommendations

- Fully acquaint yourself with the ramifications and legalities surrounding AIDS before implementing a policy. Regardless of whether you choose to test for the disease, you should have a working knowledge to share with other employees. A bibliography of sources is provided in Appendix E.
- Be extremely careful in selecting a laboratory to conduct physical examinations. Check references, procedures and litigation history due to negligence, and sign an agreement of confidentiality that contains a "hold harmless" clause.
- Create and maintain confidential files for employees' medical records. This should include a "chain of custody" procedure for all specimens.
- Conduct an educational program for all employees on the effects and conditions of AIDS. This should ease tension in the workplace and discourage inappropriate behavior.
- Be extremely careful in the development and implementation of all hiring procedures to avoid discriminatory practices. Once again, staff needs to be trained thoroughly.

Chapter 10 Employment Testing — Dos and Don'ts

Digi-Lectronics Inc.

Employment of Victims of AIDS

Digi-Lectronics Inc. believes it is our legal and humanitarian obligation to provide equal opportunity to chronically ill and other disabled individuals who are capable of performing their job duties properly and safely. We also believe that in the event that such an individual's capability should be legitimately called into question, a physician's assurance of this individual's capability to work should be sought.

Medical experts have concluded up to this point that AIDS is not communicated through everyday exposure to an AIDS carrier in the workplace. Everyday exposure is defined as shaking hands, eating food or touching objects that have been exposed to the AIDS carrier. In this context, therefore, it can be assumed that co-workers will not develop the disease.

With these conclusions and assurances, Digi-Lectronics Inc. intends to continue to employ victims of AIDS as long as their doctors pronounce them fit to work. Disability coverage will be in force for those employees whose health does not permit them to work, provided they are considered regular employees.

The company will continue to provide educational programs on AIDS periodically. Additional information can be obtained in Alex Raski's office.

Employers: *This type of policy should be enforced only for employers who are legally mandated to give equal employment opportunity to individuals with disabilities. Issuing a policy such as this may create anxiety and controversy within the workplace. Therefore, it is best to wait until AIDS becomes a significant issue to act in this way.*

The Testing Checklist

☐ 1. If you are considering the use of preemployment testing, have you fully investigated the effectiveness of these tests, the legal liabilities involved and the costs per applicant?

☐ 2. Have you checked your paper and pencil test for validity as outlined in the federal *Guidelines for Employee Selection Procedures?*

☐ 3. If you are considering the use of a polygraph, have you checked federal regulations to be sure your use is permitted?

☐ 4. If you are screening for genetic factors, have you investigated all considerations involved such as legal liabilities, procedures, laboratories and costs?

☐ 5. If you are screening for drugs and alcohol, have you considered all aspects of legal liability, procedures, alternatives and costs involved?

☐ 6. Have you put an AIDS education program into effect within your organization?

☐ 7. If you are planning to screen for AIDS, have you investigated all legal liabilities, employee relations factors, procedures and costs involved?

Chapter 10 Employment Testing — Dos and Don'ts

Questions for Personal Development

1. What is the major emphasis of this chapter?

2. What are the most important things you learned from this chapter?

3. How can you apply what you learned to your current job?

4. How will you go about making these changes?

5. How can you monitor improvement?

6. Summarize the changes you expect to see in yourself one year from now.

CHAPTER 11

Landing Performers — Making the Right Offer

"I am making the decision," said the owner as he walked out of the room. "And my decision is Romano. I have seen all the candidates and I know you all like different people. But my choice is the one that stands."

"Why did he ask us to participate if he had already chosen Romano?" complained the marketing manager. "I was shocked when she made it through the first round."

"I can see what you're saying," agreed the controller. "Weaver's always been my top candidate because of his track record."

"Yeah, but we let Weaver slip through our fingers because our leader didn't act in time."

Here's What You'll Learn

I. Final Selection
II. Notifying Candidates
III. Negotiating Offers and Compensation
IV. The Decision-Making Checklist

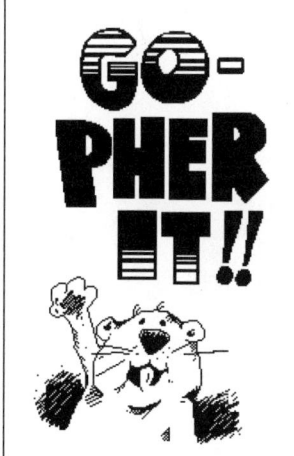

Although it may appear simple on the surface, selection of the final candidate is a difficult task. There are many factors to be considered. Does this person really have the qualifications? Will he fit in? Will he get the job done? Can the organization meet the salary demands?

Chapter 11 Landing Performers — Making the Right Offer

I. Final Selection

Selecting and luring candidates has become much more complicated than in the past. Where once making an offer almost guaranteed the person would come to work with your firm, most organizations now have to be more cognizant of selling the candidate on why he should work for the company. Many factors are considered surrounding applicants' wishes for life balance, compensation and challenging work environment.

In a tight job market, good candidates are in more demand. Therefore, selection needs to be timely. Following through on promises is of paramount importance. Hiring candidates who will remain for a long tenure is critical to hiring success. Writer and consultant Harvey MacKay observes that his "acid test" for hiring is to ask the question, "How would you feel having this person working for the competition?"

The mechanics of final selection should be approached methodically. The number of people involved should be limited to only those necessary. Attempting to reach consensus, unless there is only one truly outstanding candidate, is time-consuming and counterproductive. For labor and clerical positions, one decision maker is optimal. This person should be the position's immediate supervisor since he will have the best working knowledge of job requirements and environment.

For managerial levels, a maximum of three should be involved. These individuals should include the immediate supervisor and perhaps two managers from other departments with which the person will have contact. On occasion, it might be a good idea for final candidates to meet with the president and other executives. This ensures support for the hire. Meeting with the executive staff also tends to impress and lure a particularly strong candidate.

A logical sequence

The selection process must follow a logical sequence. Applicant pools should be narrowed, based on a previously developed list of criteria. Records should be kept concerning the reasons why some candidates were passed on when others weren't. These records are not only necessary for organization of the process, but also to protect the company. If a rejected applicant files suit, you may be formally requested to justify your reasons for refusing that particular person.

It is best to develop a form such as those on pages 209 and 210 to assess various criteria and qualifications. All questions on this form should be job-related. They can include qualifications, evaluation of skills and experience, along with education and training. It is extremely important to remind interviewers that comments made on these forms should be job-related. Biased remarks, certain attitudinal evaluations, even doodles may be interpreted as discriminatory if examined later.

When filling a position, look at the candidates' desire to learn new skills. Filling a position with a candidate who meets 80 percent of the job requirements allows that individual to grow. Filling the position with someone who is totally qualified may result in premature turnover due to lack of challenge.

In making the final selection, you have two options. One is to compare candidate against candidate. The other is to match each candidate against a common standard, namely, the job description. Valid arguments can be made for both practices.

Some maintain that comparing candidates to each other is a more reasonable means for judging available talent since matching them against a standard might very well be unrealistic. Who we have pictured as the perfect candidate does not always exist in real life. This reasoning does not infer you have to compromise. It does mean, however, that your final candidates are probably a good representation of who can fill the position.

Others maintain that comparing candidates can lower the standards originally defined. If none of the candidates meets the standards, are you still going to choose the "best" candidate even though that person does not match the defined characteristics?

These same individuals maintain that it is better to reject all candidates and begin the search again. While this approach is time-consuming, settling for an inferior choice is counterproductive. Before proceeding with a new search, however, review your recruiting and selection techniques to make sure the system is not at fault.

"I want everybody to tell me the truth even if it costs them their jobs."

Samuel Goldwyn

Obviously, there is no correct answer to the dilemma. Consider your need, importance of the position, complexity of duties and normal turnover in deciding which practice to use.

Chapter 11   Landing Performers — Making the Right Offer

Competing for the best

As the competition for skilled employees grows, you will need more effective strategies for securing the people you want. But landing skilled employees is not the only concern. Hiring lower-skilled, enthusiastic workers has become a major concern in many firms, especially due to the high cost of replacement. Where in the past, you may have been accustomed to taking your time in the recruiting process, you now need to move more quickly to sell to your targeted applicants before they take a job with the competition.

Romancing the candidate should begin immediately after the initial screening of resumes. Anticipating the concern your top candidates may have will enable you to treat them with care, helping them to develop a positive perception of your organization. While the little extra touches may be time-consuming, they are valuable in hiring a top candidate with a long tenure.

Here are a few hints to get the job done:

> **Keep the knowledge of who is being interviewed on a need-to-know basis.** Every organization has gossips. Ask candidates if they are aware of anyone who has joined your company recently from their company. Take steps to avoid embarrassing meetings in the hall or word getting back to their current employer.
>
> **Share as much information as you can with your strongest applicants.** The top people will appreciate the opportunity to get to know your company in depth.
>
> **Escort candidates from interview to interview.** This little touch keeps everyone on track and gives the opportunity for a little informal chatting between sessions.
>
> **Have a substitute ready for each scheduled interviewer.** This eliminates delays and disruptions in the selection process. (Be sure to weed out all people who do not sell the company in its best light.)
>
> **Recognize that this is a negotiating process.** Plan for all contingencies before entering into discussions. Consider all factors including salary, benefits, working conditions, location, independence and so on.

Romancing the candidate should begin immediately after the initial screening of resumes.

"Where the determination is, the way can be found."

George S. Clasm,
The Richest Man in Babylon

Candidate Selection Form #1

Position_____
Supervisor_____
Date of Selection_____

Applicants

Priority Rating
1 = Low   5 = Critical

Applicant Rating
1 = Does not meet requirement
5 = Exceeds expectations

Priority	Required Qualifications

Priority	Preferred Characteristics

Priority of Choice

Chapter 11 Landing Performers — Making the Right Offer

Candidate Selection Form #2

Name of applicant_____
Address_____
Applying for _____ Phone_____
Interviewer_____ Date _____

Write required and desired qualifications in order of priority in the spaces provided. Place your ratings for this candidate in the categories indicated. (Rating: 1 = Unacceptable, 5 = Exceeds expectations)

Qualifications required	Rating
	Total Score =

Qualifications desired	Rating
	Total Score =

Establish a common language. Ask for clarification of each applicant's needs, desires and qualities. Misunderstandings can be costly later on.

Look for "hot buttons" during your conversation with the top candidates that will reveal what the person's real priorities are and any concerns about the job. Clues include comments about success, needs for recognition or monetary rewards or challenges. A penetrating sample question would be "What things are important to you in your career development?"

Use your intuition. If something doesn't feel right, investigate. Uncomfortable facts have to be uncovered. But better now than later.

Don't be afraid to sell. Applicants, especially those in high-demand areas, need to be wooed. Ask them directly, "What will it take for you to come to work for us?" Get them to identify all concerns and desires. Then go about addressing each one to mutual satisfaction.

Act quickly. Deliberating for too long a time will result in missed opportunities.

Involve as few people in the process as possible. Even for an executive-level position, the maximum number of decision makers should be three.

Conduct the hiring process as if you are beginning a new working relationship with an applicant. This gets your strong candidates invested from the start.

Limit your finalists to three at the most. Spreading your energy among too many candidates dilutes the emphasis on each one. They need to feel special!

Get on their wavelength. Conduct the interviews in a conversational style. Do what you can to give applicants special attention. Remember you're attempting to answer their needs as well as yours.

> *"I am gradually approaching the period in my life when work comes first. No longer diverted by other emotions, I work the way a cow grazes."*
>
> Kaethe Kollwitz

Striving to be the preferred employer

As our culture's priorities change, employers must be more aware of how to attract the best candidates. Priorities such as balance of life and challenging work are becoming more important than actual income and job security. Look at what you are doing as an employer to foster a work environment that addresses these needs.

Companies on the forefront of employee satisfaction make personal and family matters an integral part of the workplace. They provide scheduling options such as flextime to enable those with children to provide better child care. Some provide on-site or contract child care facilities. These companies also pay more attention to specific groups and their needs. They pay attention to the needs of retirees and single mothers. They address the scheduling needs of students enrolled in classes.

As these issues are addressed and the needs of target groups are taken into consideration, a better perception of the company develops. This results in lower turnover, better productivity and a stimulating work environment. Perks that have been provided include on-site fitness facilities, centers for leadership and management development, opportunities to take elder care or child care leave, and housing assistance in areas of the country where the cost of living is exorbitant.

Regardless of whom you hire and at what level, your organization's ability to attract the best will become more and more dependent on your ability to be perceived as a preferred employer.

Don't misrepresent the company

Trust is the most important element of an employment relationship. While you want to put your best foot forward, you should also be up front about the working conditions, politics, policies, company growth and health. Promising what you can't deliver results in premature turnover. Throwing prospective employees a curve ball will only serve to make them distrustful once they are on board.

For many candidates, hours of work and possibilities for advancement are big issues. A candidate who is told one thing about these issues and then discovers another will be more likely to leave, resulting in thousands of dollars of replacement cost.

Companies on the forefront of employee satisfaction make personal and family matters an integral part of the workplace.

"Wisdom consists in knowing what to do with what you know."

Diogenes

Misrepresentation may also lead to a poor reputation in the community, making it difficult, if not impossible, to reach quality applicants in the future.

Smaller employers may have to overcome candidates' apprehension about working in riskier situations. Rather than avoiding the issue, address the concern up front using the best possible terms. The same strategy holds true in organizations that are experiencing a downturn in business or bad publicity at the time they are hiring. Be prepared to answer questions about information or hearsay the candidates may have picked up from the media.

Make your top candidates understand the working conditions within your organization. This is especially relevant if your company requires heavy or dirty, physical work. Some firms have resorted to developing a videotape of the work environment. While this may scare away some individuals, that is still better than increasing turnover. If you are interviewing on site, a plant tour serves the same purpose.

> *Resist the temptation to be overly impressed by education, training or the institution attended. Having knowledge and being able to use it are two different things.*

Protecting against personal bias

Unfortunately, it is impossible to remain totally unbiased when considering candidates for employment. The culture in which we have grown up has tempered us with a host of stereotypes and prejudices.

Do not be swayed by appearance or a pleasant personality. Resist the temptation to be overly impressed by education, training or the institution attended. Having knowledge and being able to use it are two different things.

If you identify with a candidate because of similar backgrounds, try not to allow this to influence your decision. Peculiar mannerisms can be a distraction. Unless these would have an influence on the person's ability to perform the job, they should not be taken into consideration.

Others who try to sway your decision may also be a consideration. What are their motives? What do they get out of it? Rely on facts only and avoid rumors and innuendo.

> *"A great leader molds public opinion; a wise leader listens to it."*
>
> John F. Kennedy

II. Notifying Candidates

Timing is an important part of the final selection process. Just as much as you are evaluating them, applicants are evaluating you. While you are considering a number of applicants, they are considering a number of companies.

Swift decision-making reduces the loss of excellent candidates and also sends a clear message of corporate decisiveness. The company that waits for an "even better" candidate to come along will probably lose its best choice to a competitor.

The entire selection process for any candidate should take no more than three weeks. Once the procedures are in place and the applications received, those doing the hiring should move along with definiteness of purpose.

An excellent way to keep everyone on target is to announce selection schedules to candidates invited for interviews: "We will be making our second-round decisions by Friday of next week. The final offer will be made three days hence." Committing yourself to this kind of plan keeps everyone motivated and satisfies the applicants' impatience.

A second means for accomplishing prompt decision-making is to sell those involved with the search on how acting swiftly will save them time and increase productivity: "The faster we get someone on board, the sooner we can get on with new projects."

Rejections

Every applicant who has been interviewed should receive a response. When candidates have been eliminated, they should be notified within two to three days. Notification should take the form of a letter such as the one below. You are not obligated to explain your reasons for rejection, and volunteering such information is just asking for trouble.

While you may not hire every candidate, each person rejected may eventually become a customer. It is always in your best interest to treat everyone with concern and courtesy. Applicants who feel dissatisfied with the hiring process pass that feeling along to others. Don't let poorly handled rejections come back to haunt you.

Sample Letter of Offer

Dear . . . . ,

    We at Digi-Lectronics were pleased to meet you on Monday, September 4. We offer you the position of . . . .

    This offer is contingent upon the following:
- A satisfactory physical exam.
- Satisfactory references from your present place of employment.
- Proof of authorization to work in the United States.
(Please bring such proof on your first day of work.)

    Accepting this offer means you will be working as a . . . . and will be responsible for . . . . Your salary will be $ . . . . monthly.

    I hope you will accept this offer. We feel we provide excellent working conditions, opportunities for advancement and a comprehensive benefits package.

    I would like to have your decision by . . . . If you have any questions or concerns about this offer or the position, feel free to call me at . . . . . .

    I look forward to your reply.

                                    Sincerely,

                                    . . . .

enclosures: benefits brochure
                  new employee information packet

Chapter 11 Landing Performers — Making the Right Offer

Sample Rejection Letters

Dear . . . .,

Thank you for applying for the position of . . . . with Digi-Lectronics.

We were fortunate to receive a number of applications from highly qualified individuals. Our decision, which was difficult, has been made.

We will retain your application for six months in the event a similar position becomes available. Please accept our regrets and best wishes for success in your job search.

Sincerely,

. . . .

Dear . . . .,

Thank you for your interest in Digi-Lectronics. We have reviewed your application. While we will continue to hire for the opening of assembler, we have filled the current position with someone who more closely meets our requirements.

As additional assembler positions become available, we will once again review your application with others we have received. If at that time we have an interest in interviewing you, we will be in touch.

Please accept our best wishes for continued success in your job search.

Cordially,

. . . .

III. Negotiating Offers and Compensation

Once the final decision has been made, the chosen candidate should be notified as soon as possible. When the offer has been made verbally, follow with a letter of confirmation stating the starting date and compensation agreed upon. Be careful not to include anything in the letter that would imply permanence. New hires may be full-time, but not forever.

> *Don't include anything in the letter that would imply permanence. New hires may be full-time, but not forever.*

Other sections of the letter may also create concerns. The courts, for instance, have held that if a salary is stated as an annual amount, the employee may not be fired for a one-year period. They have also held that if a letter of offer says that a new employee's performance will be reviewed in six months, then the employee must be retained for at least that long. To avoid these situations, always give salary in monthly or weekly terms and indicate that performance will be reviewed periodically. Always end the letter with the statement, "This letter does not constitute a specific term of employment."

Offering strategies

In some situations, you may have to negotiate with the chosen candidate because the person is in demand. Certain technical specialties continue to command higher salaries because of their lack of availability. Negotiations for executive-level candidates are also more complex. Here are a few tips:

> **Know your parameters before negotiating.** Do your homework. Research salaries and compensation in your area. Prepare a list of what you are willing to offer and stick to the plan. Attempting to wing the negotiations may cost you money and the candidate.
>
> **Get the applicant to commit before the selection is made.** If the applicant has responded to a posting that identified salary range, you can assume he is accepting the salary range. If the candidate is exceptional, consider offering 1 or 2 percent over the advertised salary. This should lock the applicant in since he applied for the position at a set salary range.

> *"Nothing is free, even age. Age is the fee God charges for life."*
>
> Horace Mann

Chapter 11   Landing Performers — Making the Right Offer

Ask candidates about their compensation demands during the interview process: "What do you think you're worth?" This will immediately give you an indication of their expectations.

Offer nonmonetary perks. Make a list of factors that may attract good candidates such as working conditions, an office, a larger operating budget and more influence in decision-making.

Offer moving expenses and mortgage assistance. For candidates in middle management, this can be very helpful. Your company may be able to obtain better rates than an individual. Build incentives and bonuses into compensation. You may also tie performance to compensation. This saves you money and allows candidates the opportunity to increase their income.

A more expensive but very popular strategy is to offer a "signing bonus," where the candidate is offered a flat sum up front.

Offer a contract. Although very few companies offer contracts to new employees, this offer of security may be just the incentive to land an exceptional candidate. Contracts may also be offered after a period of time as an incentive.

Don't oversell the position. While you may think you have the perfect candidate, be careful not to offer so much that the offer is taken on money alone. If the candidate has some misgivings about the position, it is better to address these up front than to allow them to smolder.

A candidate who takes a position simply because of fantastic compensation may leave a short time later if initial difficulties are not resolved. Money is not the answer to every concern. High-demand candidates sometimes take positions where they can be challenged, in spite of less-than-sterling compensation.

"There are people who have money and people who are rich."

Coco Chanel

Refusals

Unfortunately, your first choice may not always accept the offer. Once again, candidates are evaluating you as you are them. If you have not received a reply within a day or two of making the offer, contact the candidate again. Ask if there are any questions or concerns that might be resolved.

There is always the possibility that the candidate will hold out for additional compensation or other considerations. Be careful not to overcommit yourself in this situation. In fields where there is a shortage of well-trained candidates, the individual may just be playing games to see how high you will go. Is this a person you really want on your team?

If more than one candidate is turning down your offer, it is best to reevaluate the company's recruiting techniques. Are you asking for too much? Are you promising too much up front? Are you misrepresenting the position? Before proceeding with another search, perform a reality check on how your process is working.

The Decision-Making Checklist

☐ 1. Have you developed a written procedure for selecting managerial and nonmanagerial employees?

☐ 2. Have you developed candidate evaluation forms for the selection process?

☐ 3. Are you maintaining a file for every search containing the candidate evaluation forms on all rejected applicants?

☐ 4. Do you notify candidates in a timely fashion of both acceptance and rejection?

☐ 5. Have you had all correspondence pertaining to job offers and rejections reviewed by an attorney for inappropriate statements or commitments?

☐ 6. Are you fully prepared when negotiating offers of employment?

Chapter 11 Landing Performers — Making the Right Offer

Questions for Personal Development

1. What is the major emphasis of this chapter?

2. What are the most important things you learned from this chapter?

3. How can you apply what you learned to your current job?

4. How will you go about making these changes?

5. How can you monitor improvement?

6. Summarize the changes you expect to see in yourself one year from now.

Appendix A

Sample Interview Questions

How applicants answer a question can be just as important as what they say. Everything, including eye contact, voice inflection, sincerity, enthusiasm and confidence, plays a role in helping to determine suitability. While most applicants can tell you what you want to hear, they can't hide natural nonverbal traits. Use your intuition. If the words sound OK, but something doesn't feel right, probe deeper. If it still doesn't feel right, there probably isn't a match, no matter what the applicant says!

Take care to make the following questions your own. Tailor them for your use. Experiment with new questions occasionally to see which will work better in your setting. The questions in this appendix are divided into two categories: Questions for nonsupervisory positions and questions for supervisory positions. However, you are encouraged to review both sections before selecting the questions you wish to ask.

Appendix A Sample Interview Questions

Nonsupervisory

The job for which the applicant is applying

How did you find out about our company?

How did you find out about this job?

What do you know about this job?

What do you know about our company?

What do you know about our industry?

Why did you apply for this position?

How does this job fit into your career plans?

Why should I be worried about hiring you?

What would you expect your duties to be for a job as a _____?

What would you expect to do on the first day on the job?

Tell me about your attendance record at your last job.

Is there anything that will prevent you from getting to work on time?

Tell me about your safety record on your last job.

If the employee working next to you had an accident, what would you do? (Why?)

If a fire suddenly broke out in the plant, what would you do?

What questions do you have about the job and/or working for us?

What do you know about the products we offer?

How would you like our company to assist you if you join us?

What would you say are the broad responsibilities of a _____?

What would you say are the major qualities this job demands? or What would you say are the traits a good _____ would possess?

What are you looking for in your next job?

How long will it take you to make a contribution?

Explain your understanding of the job's responsibilities.

What kind of work interests you the most?

Tell me what you think a typical day would be like.

What do you think the position earns?

How will this job help you reach your long-term and career goals?

How do you define a successful career?

Are you willing to relocate for the company?

What other functional, day-to-day activities were you involved with that we haven't discussed?

> *How long will it take you to make a contribution?*

Applicant's work experience

Have you held other positions like the one you are applying for? Tell me about them.

If yes, what is the most important thing you learned that you can bring to this job?

Tell me about your last (or present) job. (Encourage the applicant to discuss details. It will reveal work habits.)

What did you enjoy most about your last (or present) job?

What did you enjoy least about your last (or present) job?

What were the biggest pressures on your last job?

If there were two things you could change in your last (or present) job, what would they be and how would you change them?

Why did you leave your last job? or Why do you wish to leave your present job?

Why do you think you were successful in your last job?

How has your present (or last) job changed while you've held it?

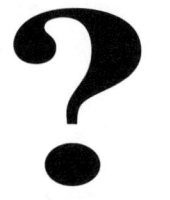

Please describe your last (or present) boss's management style.

If you could make one constructive suggestion to management, what would it be?

What other people do you deal with in your present (or last) job?

If I asked your boss to evaluate your performance, what would he say?

What qualifications do you have that make you successful in this field?

What has been the most interesting job or project so far in your career?

What have you learned from previous jobs?

What is your boss's title and what are your boss's functions?

Please describe for me a typical day on your current job.

How do your previous work experiences prepare you for this position?

What aspects of your work do you consider most crucial?

Of all the work you have done, where have you been most successful?

Describe to me how your job relates to the overall goals of your department and company.

What are the most repetitive tasks in your job?

What special skills or knowledge did you need to perform these duties?

What decisions or judgment calls did you have to make in these areas?

What was the most important project you worked on at that job?

Did you work much alone in your previous job?

Appendix A Sample Interview Questions

Applicant's leadership/management potential

Tell me about a situation where you had to pull a team together successfully.

How effectively did your boss handle evaluations?

Do you set goals for yourself?

What have you done to reach it?

How do you organize yourself for day-to-day activities?

How many hours a week do you find it necessary to work to get your job done?

How do you plan your day?

Tell me about a system of working that you have used and what it was like. What did/didn't you like about it?

Tell me about a method you've developed for accomplishing a job. What were its strengths and weaknesses?

What have you done to become more effective in your position?

In what areas could your boss have done a better job?

Describe the best manager you ever had.

Describe the worst manager you ever had.

Have you ever been placed in charge of the department, store, etc.?

What did you like about being in charge?

What did you not like about being in charge?

If you were placed in charge again, what would you do differently?

How did your peers act toward you when you were in charge?

> *Describe the best manager you ever had.*

Communication skills

When you are assigned to work with new people, how do you go about getting to know them and how they work?

How do you get along with your present boss?

What type of person is the hardest for you to get along with?

Tell me about your experience in working on teams.

What can you contribute to a team?

What do you get out of working on a team?

Do you prefer working alone or with others?

What kind of people annoy you most? (Note: The applicant is probably the opposite of the type of person given as a response.)

How did you get along with your former boss?

What sort of person would you least like to work with? (Note: Again, the candidate is probably the opposite of the kind of person given as a response.)

Tell me about a work situation that required excellent communication skills.

What sort of person do you enjoy working for?

How well/often do you communicate with the person who receives the output of your work?

Define "cooperation."

How important was communication and interaction with others on this job?

What other titles and departments did you have dealings with? What were the difficulties you encountered there?

What was more important on your job, written or oral communication?

How many levels of management did you interact with? What was your communication about?

Do you prefer to speak with someone or send a memo?

When do you have trouble communicating with people?

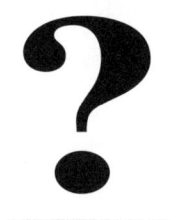

Appendix A Sample Interview Questions

Conflict/persuasion skills

Have you ever been in a dispute with a supervisor? What was it about and how was it resolved?

Have you ever been in a dispute with a co-worker? What was it about and how was it resolved?

Describe the best person who ever worked with you.

How do you handle conflicts?

What are the disadvantages of your chosen field?

Have you ever worked with a group like this before? What was it like? or How did you handle it?

Tell me about a time when you needed to get an understanding of another's situation before you could get your job done. How did you get the understanding, and what problems did you encounter?

Are you able to predict a person's behavior based on your reading of that person?

Tell me about a specific accomplishment you have achieved as a group member.

What difficulties do you have in tolerating people with different backgrounds and interests from yours?

When you joined your last company and met the group for the first time, how did you feel? How did you get on with them?

How would you define a "conducive work atmosphere"?

As a member of a department, how do you see your role as team builder?

Tell me about a time when you came up with a new method or idea. How did you get it approved and implemented?

Can you think of a time when another idea or project was rejected? Why was it rejected and what did you do about it?

I would be interested to hear about an occasion when your work or an idea was criticized.

Tell me about a situation when people were making emotional decisions about your project. What happened and how did you handle it?

Tell me about an occasion when there were objections to your ideas. What did you do to convince management of your point of view?

Have you ever been in a situation where people overruled you or wouldn't let you get a word in edgeways? How did you respond?

Tell me about an occasion when you felt it necessary to convince your department to change a procedure.

What are some of the things about which you and your boss disagreed?

What are some of the things your boss did that you disliked?

Tell me about an occasion when there were objections to your ideas. What did you do to convince management of your point of view?

Education & training

What was your overall grade point average in school?

Do you feel your grades are an accurate reflection of your work? If not, why not?

What subject did you do the best in? Why?

What subject did you have the most trouble with? Why?

What subject did you like the best? Why?

What subject did you dislike the most? Why?

What skills did you learn in school that will help you on this job?

Were you involved in extracurricular activities? If yes, which ones?

What have you learned from your extracurricular activities?

If you could do so, how would you plan your academic studies differently?

What prompted you to choose _____ as your major?

What courses do you think are directly transferable to the job?

What kinds of skills were acquired as a result of your training?

What extracurricular positions have you held?

What have you learned through volunteer leadership?

Do you think that your extracurricular activities were worth the time you devoted to them? Why?

Can you forget your education and start from scratch?

What plans do you have for additional training or education?

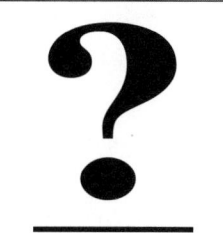

Appendix A Sample Interview Questions

Personal traits

What kind of person do you get along with best?

What do you do when people have different backgrounds and values from yours?

What makes a job enjoyable for you?

What do you want out of a job?

What qualities would you bring to this job that others would not?

Where do you feel you need to improve?

If you worked for the perfect boss, what would this person be like?

What do you consider important in a job?

How do you define "doing a good job"?

What is your greatest strength? Worst deficiency?

What books or magazines do you read?

What do you think are the most serious problems facing business today?

What are you best known for?

From whom have you learned the most?

Tell me about a time when you conformed to a policy with which you disagreed.

Which American businessperson do you admire most and why?

Have you ever taken a public-speaking course?

What do you do to keep in good physical condition?

Tell me about a responsibility you have enjoyed.

Describe a project that required high energy over an extended period of time.

What did you do to keep your enthusiasm up?

Give me an example when your performance didn't live up to your expectations.

How long will you stay with the company?

What books have had the greatest effect on your business life?

How do you define a "successful career"?

Is this the type of career you want for yourself?

How do you take direction?

For what have you been most frequently criticized?

Recall a time when someone was not being honest. What did you do?

Tell me about the last time you felt anger on the job.

In what ways did your manager contribute to your decision to leave your current job?

> *How do you define a "successful career"?*

Problem-solving/decision-making skills

Tell me about a specific situation where you prevented a problem before it occurred.

Explain in detail the most difficult task you have had to complete.

What do you do when you're having trouble solving a problem?

What is the biggest decision you have had to make in the past year?

What kinds of things do you find difficult to do?

What kinds of decisions do you find particularly hard to make?

What problem-solution situation are you most proud of?

Describe a situation that required you to use fact-finding skills.

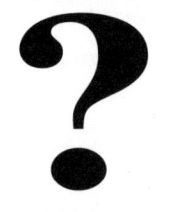

What was the last truly innovative suggestion you made for your firm?

What has been your most important work-related idea?

What kinds of things bother you most about your job?

What was the most complex report you ever had to write?

Who caused you the most problems in executing your tasks?

Tell me about a time when a team fell apart. What did you do?

Have you ever had to build motivation or team spirit with co-workers?

Tell me about a complex problem you had to deal with.

Where/to whom do you turn for help? How do you overcome the problem?

How do you organize and plan for major projects? Recall for me a major project you worked on. How did you organize and plan for it?

Tell me about a time when you failed to reach a goal.

How many projects can you handle at a time?

Describe a typical day for me. What problems do you normally experience in getting things done?

Think of a crisis situation where things got out of control. Why did it happen and what was your role in the chain of events?

What do you do when you have a great deal of work to accomplish in a short time span? How have you reacted?

What do you do when there is a decision to be made and no procedure exists?

Tell me about a time when, rather than following instructions, you went about a task in your own way. What happened?

Appendix A   Sample Interview Questions

> *What motivates you to put forth your greatest effort?*

Money questions

How much money are you making? What I am really looking for is your salary, not the value of your benefit package or other fringes.

How much money do you want?

In your professional opinion, how much do you think a job like this should pay?

If you went to your boss for a raise, why would you be doing it?

Tell me about your salary history.

Personal motivation

What has been your greatest accomplishment at work? Why?

How do you feel about your present workload?

Give me an example of a situation where you had to go above and beyond the call of duty to get something done.

What do you do when things are slow at work?

What have you learned from your mistakes?

What motivates you to put forth your greatest effort?

Describe an accomplishment that's given you the most satisfaction. Why?

How can we best reward you for doing a good job?

Why do you think you'll be successful in this job?

What gives you pride?

Tell me about a time when you went "out on a limb" in a job.

What concerns should I have about hiring you?

What do you think it takes to be successful in this company?

Why should we hire you?

Why are you giving up your current job?

Why did you choose your particular field?

What is more important to you: the salary or the job itself?

What are the disadvantages associated with your chosen field?

What are your goals — both short-term and long-term?

What are your hobbies or pastimes?

Describe your "dream" job.

What motivates you?

Hand-Picked: The Complete Guide to Finding and Hiring the Best Employees

How intuitive are you?

How do you cope with the inevitable stresses and pressures of the job?

Have you ever thought about starting your own company?

What ways have you discovered to improve your productivity?

What did you find most frustrating on your last job?

What do you think has accounted for the success you've had in your career?

What would you say are some of the basic factors that motivate you in your work?

How have you grown in your job over the last few years?

How did you handle your biggest career disappointment?

What job in our company would you choose if you were free to do so?

What job in our company do you want to work toward?

What else should I know about your qualifications for this job?

How did you divide your time among your major areas of responsibility?

In what ways did your boss contribute to your desire to leave?

Why were you fired?

Why have you changed jobs so frequently?

What have you learned from jobs you have held?

What reservations do you have about working here?

What personal qualities do you think are necessary to make succeed?

Give me an example that demonstrates your persistence.

How do you rank among your peers?

What have you done that you are proud of?

Tell me about a project that really got you excited.

What are some of the things you find difficult to do?

When you have a great deal of work to do that requires extra effort and time, where does your energy come from?

How is your approach different from that of others in the same job?

Are you willing to go where the company sends you?

What are your reservations about living/working here?

How would working evenings affect you?

How would travel affect you?

A

231

Appendix A Sample Interview Questions

> *What problems do you experience when working alone?*

How did your boss get the best out of you?

Would you like to have your boss's job?

How do your work habits change when your boss is absent?

What problems do you experience when working alone?

How do the work habits of others change when the boss is absent?

Tell me about a time you felt adequately recognized for your contributions.

What kinds of rewards are most satisfying to you?

What can you do for us that someone else cannot do?

Are you looking for a temporary or a permanent job?

What have you done that shows initiative and willingness to work?

How did you spend your vacations while at school?

Supervisory/management

The job

How did you find out about our company?

How did you find out about this job?

What do you know about this job?

What do you know about our company?

What do you know about the products we offer?

What do you know about our industry?

Why did you apply for this position?

How does this job fit into your career plans?

Why should I be worried about hiring you?

What would you expect your duties to be for a job as a _____?

What would you expect to do on the first day on the job?

What questions do you have about the job and/or working for us?

How would you like our company to assist you if you join us?

What would you say are the broad responsibilities of _____?

What would you say are the major qualities this job demands?

What would you say are the traits a good _____ would possess?

What are you looking for in your next job?

How long will it take you to make a contribution?

Why do you think you might want to live in the community where our company is located?

Are you willing to spend at least six months as a trainee?

Appendix A   Sample Interview Questions

Work experience

Tell me about other positions you've held like the one you are applying for.

Tell me about your last (or present) job. (Encourage the applicant to discuss details. It will reveal work habits.)

What did you enjoy most about your last (or present) job?

What did you enjoy least about your last (or present) job?

What were the biggest pressures on your last job?

If there were two things you could change in your last (or present) job, what would they be and how would you change them?

Why are you leaving your present job?

Why do you think you were successful in your last job?

How has your present job changed while you've held it?

Please describe your last (or present) boss's management style.

What other people do you deal with in your present (or last) job?

If I asked your boss to evaluate you, what would she say?

Where do you think you have been the most successful at work?

How do you feel about your present workload?

What are the most repetitive tasks you do on your present job?

How do you feel your present boss can do a better job?

How will your supervisor react when you resign from your present job?

What qualifications do you have that make you successful in this field?

What has been the most interesting job or project so far in your career?

Describe the most significant report you have prepared.

What have you learned from previous jobs?

Please describe for me a typical day on your current job.

How do your previous work experiences prepare you for this position?

What aspects of your work do you consider most crucial?

Describe to me how your job relates to the overall goals of your company.

What special skills or knowledge did you need to perform these duties?

What decisions or judgment calls did you have to make in these areas?

Did you work much alone in your previous job?

What responsibilities do you hold in relation to other departments?

> *What have you learned from previous jobs?*

Communication skills

When you are assigned to work with new people, how do you go about getting to know them and how they work?

How do you get along with your present boss?

What type of person is the hardest for you to get along with?

Tell me about your experience in working on teams.

What can you contribute to a team?

What do you get out of working on a team?

Do you prefer working alone or with others?

What kind of people annoy you most? (Note: The applicant is probably the opposite of the type of person given as a response.)

How did you get along with your former boss?

What sort of person would you least like to work with? (Note: Again, the candidate is probably the opposite of the kind of person given as a response.)

Tell me about a work situation that required excellent communication skills.

What sort of person do you enjoy working for?

How well/often do you communicate with the person who receives the output of your work?

Define "cooperation."

How important was communication and interaction with others on this job?

What other titles and departments did you have dealings with? What were the difficulties you encountered there?

What was more important on your job, written or oral communication?

How many levels of management did you interact with? What was your communication about?

Do you prefer to speak with someone or send a memo?

When do you have trouble communicating with other people?

Appendix A Sample Interview Questions

Conflict/persuasion skills

Have you ever been in a dispute with a supervisor? What was it about and how was it resolved?

Have you ever been in a dispute with a co-worker? What was it about and how was it resolved?

Have you ever been in a dispute with someone you supervised? What was it about and how was it resolved?

Describe the best person who ever worked for you or with you.

How do you handle conflicts?

Have you ever worked with a group like this before? What was it like? or How did you handle it?

Tell me about a time when you needed to get an understanding of another's situation before you could get your job done. How did you get the understanding, and what problems did you encounter?

Are you able to predict a person's behavior based on your reading of that person?

Tell me about a specific accomplishment you have achieved as a group member.

What difficulties do you have in tolerating people with different backgrounds and interests from yours?

When you joined your last company and met the group for the first time, how did you feel? How did you get on with them?

Define "cooperation."

How would you define a "conducive work atmosphere"?

As a member of a department, how do you see your role as team builder?

Tell me about a time when you came up with a new method or idea. How did you get it approved and implemented?

Can you think of a time when another idea or project was rejected? Why was it rejected and what did you do about it?

I would be interested to hear about an occasion when your work or an idea was criticized.

Tell me about a situation when people were making emotional decisions about your project? What happened and how did you handle it?

Tell me about an occasion when there were objections to your ideas. What did you do to convince management of your point of view?

Have you ever been in a situation where people overrule you or won't let you get a word in edgeways?

Tell me about an occasion when you felt it necessary to convince your department to change a procedure.

> *How would you define "conducive work atmosphere"?*

Education & training

What was your overall grade point average in school?

Do you feel your grades are an accurate reflection of your work? If not, why not?

What subject did you do the best in? Why?

What subject did you have the most trouble with? Why?

What subject did you like the best? Why?

What subject did you dislike the most? Why?

What skills did you learn in school that will help you on this job?

Were you involved in extracurricular activities? If yes, which ones?

What have you learned from your extracurricular activities?

If you could do so, how would you plan your academic studies differently?

What books have had the greatest effect on your business development? Why?

What prompted you to choose _____ as your major?

What courses do you think are directly transferable to the job?

What kinds of skills were acquired as a result of that training?

What extracurricular offices have you held?

Do you think that your extracurricular activities were worth the time you devoted to them? Why?

Can you forget your education and start from scratch?

What additional education or training do you plan to pursue?

Appendix A Sample Interview Questions

Personal traits

What kind of person do you get along with best?

What makes a job enjoyable for you?

What do you want out of a job?

What qualities would you bring to this job that others would not?

Where do you feel you need to improve?

If you worked for the perfect boss, what would this person be like?

What do you consider important in a job?

How do you define "doing a good job"?

In what kind of work environment are you most comfortable?

Under what conditions do you work best?

How have the jobs you have held prepared you for more responsibilities?

What is your greatest strength? Worst deficiency?

Are you willing to relocate for the company?

What books or magazines do you read?

What do you think are the most serious problems facing business?

What are you best known for?

From whom have you learned the most?

Tell me about a time when you conformed to a policy with which you disagreed.

What American businessperson do you most admire and why?

Have you ever taken a public-speaking course?

What do you do to keep in good physical condition?

What are the disadvantages of your chosen field?

Tell me about a responsibility you have enjoyed.

What did you do to keep your enthusiasm up?

How long will you stay with the company?

What books have had the greatest effect on your business life?

How do you define a "successful career"?

Is this the type of career you want for yourself?

How do you take direction?

What are some of the things about which you and your boss disagreed?

What are some of the things your boss did that you disliked?

For what have you been most frequently criticized?

Tell me about the last time you felt anger on the job.

In what ways did your manager contribute to your decision to leave this job?

Problem-solving/decision-making skills

Tell me about a specific situation where you prevented a problem.

What is the most difficult task you have had to complete?

What do you do when you're having trouble solving a problem?

What is the biggest decision you have had to make in the past year?

What kinds of things do you find difficult to do?

What kinds of decisions do you find particularly hard to make?

Tell me about a situation where you had to deal with a grievance.

How do you make important decisions?

Tell me about a situation where you overcame objections of other people and convinced them your plan was best.

Tell me about how you have handled a major problem.

Tell me about a time when you had to make a quick decision.

What problem-solution situation are you most proud of?

Describe a situation that required you to use fact-finding skills.

What was the last truly innovative suggestion you made for your firm?

What has been your most important work-related idea?

What kinds of things bother you most about your job?

What was the most complex report you ever had to write?

Who caused you the most problems in executing your tasks? Why?

Tell me about a time when a team fell apart. What did you do?

Have you ever had to build motivation or team spirit with co-workers?

Tell me about a complex problem you had to deal with.

How did you overcome the problem?

How do you organize and plan for major projects?

Tell me about a time when you failed to reach a goal.

How many projects can you handle at a time?

Describe a typical day for me.

What do you do when you have a great deal of work to accomplish in a short time span? How have you reacted?

What do you do when there is a decision to be made and no procedure exists?

Appendix A Sample Interview Questions

Money questions

What salary do you expect to make in this position? What do you base that figure on?

How can we best reward you?

What is your current salary?

What do you expect to be earning in five years?

How much money are you making? What I am really looking for is your salary, not the value of your benefit package or other fringes.

How much money do you want?

In your professional opinion, how much do you think a job like this should pay?

If you went to your boss for a raise, why would you be doing it?

How would you justify a raise to your boss?

Besides salary, what other benefits are you looking for?

Do you have an interest in owning equity?

Have you ever worked on commission? Tell me about it.

> *In your professional opinion, how much do you think a job like this should pay?*

Personal motivation

What has been your greatest accomplishment in a work environment and why?

How do you feel about your present workload?

Give me an example of a situation where you had to go above and beyond the call of duty to get something done.

What do you do when things are slow at work?

A year from now, what might your boss here say about your work for our company during a performance review?

What have you learned from your mistakes?

What motivates you to put forth your greatest effort?

What two or three accomplishments have given you the most satisfaction? Why?

How can we best reward you for doing a good job?

Why do you think you'll be successful in this job?

What gives you pride?

Tell me about a time when you went "out on a limb" in a job.

What concerns should I have about hiring you?

What do you think it takes to be successful in this company?

What criteria are you using to evaluate the company for which you would like to work?

How do you like to be managed?

How has your boss been able to get the best out of you?

Do you consider yourself successful? Why?

What have you done to become more effective in your present position?

How do you plan to achieve your career goals?

What are the most important rewards you expect from your career?

What kinds of rewards are most satisfying to you?

How do you determine "success"?

Why are you giving up your current job?

Why did you choose your particular field?

What is more important to you: the salary or the job itself?

What are the disadvantages associated with your chosen field?

What do you think determines a person's progress in a firm?

Do you think you would be underemployed if you accepted this position?

What are your goals — both short-term and long-term?

Appendix A Sample Interview Questions

> *How did you handle your biggest career disappointment?*

What are your hobbies or pastimes?

Describe your "dream" job.

What motivates you?

How intuitive are you?

How do you cope with the inevitable stresses and pressures of the job?

If you were me, would you hire you? Why?

Have you ever thought about starting your own company?

What ways have you discovered to improve your productivity?

What did you find most frustrating on your last job?

What kinds of things would you want to avoid in future jobs?

What kinds of developmental experiences might be necessary to reach your goals?

What do you think has accounted for the success you've had so far in your career?

What would you say are some of the basic factors that motivate you in your work?

How have you grown in your job over the last few years?

How did you handle your biggest career disappointment?

What job in our company would you choose if you were free to do so?

What job in our company do you want to work toward?

How necessary is it for you to be creative on your job?

What else should I know about your qualifications for this job?

What else should I know about you?

Is there anything else you want to tell me?

How did you feel about your workload at that company? How did you divide your time among your major areas of responsibility?

Have you discussed your desire to leave with your boss?

In what ways did your boss contribute to your desire to leave?

Why were you fired?

Why have you changed jobs so frequently?

Some people feel that spending so much time on one job demonstrates a lack of initiative. How do you feel about that?

What have you learned from jobs you have held?

What reservations do you have about working here? What would your references say?

What personal qualities do you think are necessary to make a success of this job?

Give me an example from your current job that demonstrates your persistence.

How do you feel about your progress to date?

In hindsight, in what ways could you have improved your progress?

How do you rank among your peers?

What have you done that you are proud of?

Tell me about a project that really got you excited.

What are some of the things you find difficult to do?

When you have a great deal of work to do that requires extra effort and time, where does your energy come from?

Is it ever necessary to go above and beyond the call of duty to get your job done?

How was your approach different from that of others in the same job?

When you have been in difficult and crisis situations, which areas of your professional skills do you vow to work on further?

Can you recall a time when you went back to a failed project to give it another shot? Why did you do it and what happened?

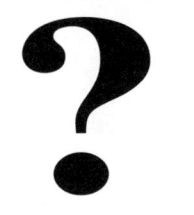

Why aren't you earning more at your age?

What can you do for us that someone else cannot do?

Are you willing to go where the company sends you?

What are your reservations about living/working here?

How would working evenings affect you?

How would travel affect you?

How did your boss get the best out of you?

Would you like to have your boss's job?

How do your work habits change when your boss is absent?

What problems do you experience when working alone?

How do the work habits of others change when the boss is absent?

Tell me about a time when there was a decision to be made and your boss was absent.

Tell me about a time you felt adequately recognized for your contributions.

What kinds of rewards are most satisfying to you?

How does this affect what you do on the job? How does this affect the effort you put into your job?

Appendix A   Sample Interview Questions

Budgetary/fiscal management skills

Do you perform employee salary reviews? If yes, what is your approach?

Are you in charge of the budget for your department?

If yes, tell me about how you budget for the year.

What problems do you have staying within your budget?

Are you involved in the overall budget planning for your organization?

What was your involvement in short-/mid-/long-term planning?

How do you quantify the results of your activities as manager?

Are you competent with electronic spreadsheet programs?

How do you deal with unanticipated expenses?

How do you defend the budget in your present position?

Tell me about a time when you had to ask for additional monies.

Tell me about a time when you had to restructure your budget in the middle of the year. What approach did you take?

How would you create a budget in the position for which you are applying?

> *How do you deal with unanticipated expenses?*

Supervisory/management skills

Tell me about a situation where you had to pull a team together successfully.

How do you define the job of a manager?

Who reports to you and what functions do they perform?

What has the employee turnover in your department been over the past two years?

To what do you attribute this turnover?

What do you actively do to retain employees?

What programs have you put in place to build morale among those reporting to you?

What are the typical problems and grievances your staff bring you?

How do you go about assigning and scheduling projects and assignments?

What other organizational responsibilities do you have besides managing your department?

Describe your management style for me.

How do you measure your success as a manager?

What patterns have you observed in the turnover in your department?

How many people have you hired in the past two years? Into what positions?

What training have you performed of other people? How do you measure its success?

How do you determine which individuals need what training?

How do you plan your daily activities?

If you are hired for this job, how will you approach the first 30 days?

How do you keep your present staff informed of new developments and organizational decisions?

Describe the relationship that you feel should exist among a supervisor and those reporting to him.

What aspects of this job would you consider most crucial?

How have you allocated your time between the duties in your present job?

Tell me about the best manager you have ever had.

Tell me about the worst manager you have ever had.

Describe an innovative change you implemented in your last job.

Give me an example of a problem in which you and your boss disagreed over how to accomplish a goal.

Appendix A Sample Interview Questions

Tell me about a project where you had to interact with people on different levels and how you coordinated that successfully.

Have you ever had to make unpopular management decisions? Tell me about one of these situations and how you handled it.

How long will it take for you to make a contribution in this position?

How do you cope when a decision has to be made and no procedure exists?

How, specifically, do you contribute toward an atmosphere of teamwork?

How would you define "leadership"?

What is your philosophy of business?

What can a department do to build teamwork?

What was the most creative work project you ever completed?

Do you manage your time well? Explain.

What are your views on quality?

Describe a time when you were able to have a positive influence on others.

How flexible are you?

What can be done about employees entering the workforce without the proper skills?

Do you train others well? Please give me an example of your effectiveness.

How well do you think on your feet?

How effectively did your boss handle evaluations?

What level of management are you most comfortable with? What levels are you most uncomfortable with?

Do you set goals for yourself?

What have you done to reach them?

How do you organize yourself for day-to-day activities?

How many hours a week do you find it necessary to work to get your job done?

How do you plan your day?

Tell me about a system of working you have used and what it was like. What did/didn't you like about it?

Tell me about a method you've developed for accomplishing a job. What were its strengths and weaknesses?

> *Tell me about a directive that really challenged you.*

What have you done to become more effective in your position?

Tell me about a directive that really challenged you.

In what areas could your boss have done a better job?

If you could have made one constructive suggestion to management, what would it have been?

How would you define the job of a manager?

Who performed salary reviews on employees?

What method did you use in performing salary reviews?

What type of turnover was most frequent, terminations or resignations?

When were resignations most likely to occur?

How do you analyze the training needs of your department or of specific individuals?

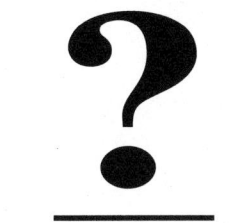

How do you keep your staff aware of information and company activities that might affect them?

Have you ever had an employee suddenly start acting out of character?

Tell me about a program you introduced to improve morale.

How do you motivate staff?

Tell me about how you motivated your staff when faced with a specific tight deadline.

What methods have you found successful in setting job objectives for subordinates?

Have you ever had to make unpopular decisions?

Tell me about a time when an emergency/directive from above caused you to reschedule workload/projects. How did you feel?

How did you schedule projects, assignments and vacations?

How would you characterize your management style?

Tell me about a time when people were making emotional decisions about your projects. What happened and what did you do?

Appendix A Sample Interview Questions

Hiring skills

What do you do to orient new employees to your department?

If you were hiring someone for this job, what qualities would you look for?

How many people have you hired?

How do you plan to interview?

Tell me what questions you would ask or techniques you would use to establish if the person was willing to do the job.

What steps do you normally take to get a new employee oriented?

How would you seek applicants for open positions within your department?

Tell me how you would budget for recruiting.

What do you look for on a resume or application?

Tell me about your biggest hiring success.

Tell me about your biggest hiring mistake.

How do you go about checking references?

On what criteria do you base hiring decisions?

How could we improve the hiring process we are using to select a person for this position?

> *Tell me about your biggest hiring mistake.*

Discipline/termination skills

Do you have the authority to terminate people? If yes, describe your approach.

How do you maintain discipline within your department?

How many employees have you fired in the past year?

Tell me about the last time you fired someone. What were the reasons?

How many people have you fired?

What is the most common cause of termination?

How do you maintain discipline in your department? What special problems do you have with the day-to-day management of your staff?

What are the typical problems and grievances that your staff bring to you? How do you handle them?

In working with others, how do you go about getting an understanding of them?

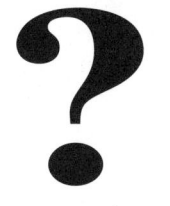

Appendix A Sample Interview Questions

Sales

Telephone skills

How do telephone sales differ from outside sales?

What strategies do you use to get through the secretary or receptionist?

Have you ever sold anything over the telephone?

What special skills or techniques are necessary to be successful over the telephone?

Tell me about a time when you called a complete stranger on the phone. How did you initiate a discussion?

When getting through to a sales prospect for the first time on the phone, what roadblocks can you expect the clerical staff to put in your way and how do you handle them?

How much time do you spend on the telephone in your job?

What services or products have you sold over the phone?

How many phone calls do you make in a day?

Demonstrate your telephone sales technique for me.

Where do you find your telephone leads?

What do you enjoy about telephone sales?

What do you despise about telephone sales?

Tell me about the person who supervised your telephone sales.

What can you do to improve your telephone sales technique?

> *What do you enjoy about phone sales? What do you despise about it?*

Prospecting skills

What are people's reasons for buying a particular product or service?

How do you plan effective use of your day?

Tell me about why you plan your day in that way.

How do you overcome the difficult periods that everyone in sales faces?

What is your ratio of initial contacts to actual sales presentations?

What kinds of people do you like to sell to? Why?

What kinds of people do you not like to sell to? Why?

How do you manage to sell to those people?

How would you go about identifying customers in a new market?

How do you initiate discussion with a complete stranger?

What percentage of your sales calls results in full presentations?

How long does it typically take you from initial contact to close the sale?

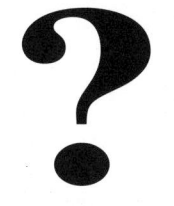

Appendix A   Sample Interview Questions

Closing skills

How would you approach the sales of our products?

Why can you sell for us in a way that no one else can?

Tell me about a time when you almost lost a sale and then fought hard to get it back.

What are the five most common objections you face and how do you deal with them?

What percentage of your sales calls results in sales?

Tell me about your most difficult sale and how you approached it.

What was the most surprising objection you ever received, and how did you handle it?

What are the very toughest objections you have to meet in your job?

Sell me this pen.

Tell me about a time when all seemed lost in an important sale. What did you do to weather the crisis?

Give me an example of a sale that was, for all intents and purposes, lost. How did you turn the situation around and make the sale?

> *Tell me about your most difficult sale and how you approached it.*

Customer service skills

What is your philosophy of customer service?

Tell me about your worst customer service dilemma and how you overcame it.

How do you turn an occasional buyer into a regular buyer? Have you ever taken over an existing territory/desk? What was the volume when you started? What was it when you left?

How involved should a company be with its customers?

I'd be interested to hear about a difficult collection problem you have experienced.

What do you stress to support staff about customer service?

How do you deal with customers who think they are right even when they are wrong?

What is the customer service attitude in your present organization?

Where did you learn your customer sales skills and philosophy?

Tell me about a difficult collection problem you've had and how you dealt with it.

What kinds of people do you like to sell to?

What type of people don't you like to sell to? How do you manage to sell to these people?

How do you cope with customers who ask for unreasonable discounts or service?

How have you handled customers who took advantage of sales support staff?

How do you encourage customers to pay on time?

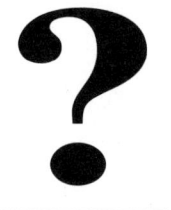

Appendix A   Sample Interview Questions

Sales management skills

By what percentage have you increased the volume in your territory since you took it over?

Describe a typical day.

How do you plan your day?

Why is it important to prioritize?

Give me an example of when it was necessary to reach a goal in a short period of time and how you planned to achieve it.

For what have you been most frequently criticized, and by whom?

How large a client base do you need to maintain to keep sales on an even keel?

Have you ever broken in a new territory/desk for your company? How did you like it? How did you approach the job?

How would you go about identifying customers in a new market?

How do you prefer to go about securing new prospects and clients?

What steps are involved in selling your product?

How much time do you spend doing paperwork and other nonselling activities?

What is the one thing you could do right now to improve your sales management skills?

> *How would you go about identifying customers in a new market?*

Marketing skills

Why do people buy a product or service?

What do you know about our product line?

Tell me how you reach your present customer base.

Tell me how you would reach our customers.

Do you have a marketing budget in your present position? Tell me what it is composed of.

Here is one of our products. How would you go about marketing it?

What media contacts do you have that would help us market our products?

Tell me about your biggest marketing success.

Tell me about your biggest marketing flop. What happened?

Appendix A Sample Interview Questions

Motivation for sales

What do you dislike about most sales?

Why have you chosen to become a salesperson?

What rewards do you find most satisfying?

Compare yourself with your peers.

How do you feel when you don't meet your quota?

What awards have you won as a salesperson?

How do you feel about out-of-town/overnight travel?

What kinds of rewards are most satisfying to you?

How smart are you compared with your peers?

How articulate are you?

How well dressed are you?

How witty are you?

How do you rank professionally?

How tenacious are you?

How well do you accept disappointment?

I'd be interested to hear of a time when you proved yourself to be more tenacious than your peers.

Share with me an example of surpassing what was expected of you from your employer.

I'd be interested to hear about a specific time when you greatly exceeded the norm.

What different types of customers have you called on, and what titles have you sold to in these companies?

Tell me about your most crushing failure.

Give me a specific example of a time you were rejected and how you handled it.

When you don't meet your goals, how do you handle it?

What will you do if I don't hire you?

> *How well do you accept disappointment?*

Appendix B

Federal Record-Keeping Requirements

Appendix B Federal Record-Keeping Requirements

Statute	Employers Affected	Requirements	Period of Retention	When Required	Posting Required
Title VII Civil Rights Act 1964 **Americans with Disabilities Act of 1990**	Employers with 15 or more employees. Employers of 25 or more employees — July 2, 1992. Employers of 15-24 or more employees — July 26, 1994.	Retain all personnel and employee records. Retain records relevant to a charge of discrimination. Maintain records of impact on employment decisions, including hiring, termination, promotion.	Minimum of 6 months or after the last record was made, whichever is longer. Until final disposition of the charge.	Annually by March 31. Do on an annual basis.	Official EEO poster available from any EEO district office. This consolidated poster will also cover ADEA, Executive Order 11246, Rehabilitation Act of 1974 and the ADA. It also covers a portion of FLSA. (See FLSA.)
	Employers with 100 or more employees (except state and local governments, primary and secondary school systems, institutions of higher education, Indian tribes, tax-exempt private membership clubs, other labor organizations, and employers in Puerto Rico, Guam and the Virgin Islands.)	File Employer Information Report EEO-1.			
Title VII Civil Rights Act 1964 (continued)	Employers with 100 or more employees, and government agencies, labor organizations and apprenticeship committees involved in employee selection. Joint labor-management apprenticeship committees with: five or more apprentices enrolled, at least one sponsoring employer who employs 25 or more members and at least one sponsoring union with 25 or more members.	Maintain records of impact on employment decisions and calculate impact under the "4/5 rule" on a job-by-job basis. File Apprenticeship Information Report EEO-2.		Impact should be measured at least annually. Annually by Sept. 30.	
	Banking and financial institutions that serve as depositories of government funds in any amount or as issuing or paying agents for U.S. Savings Bonds. (Except those in Puerto Rico, Guam or the Virgin Islands.)	File Employer Information Report EEO-1.		Annually by March 31.	
	Federal contractors and subcontractors with 50 or more employees and at least $50,000 in contracts. (Except those in Puerto Rico, Guam or the Virgin Islands.)	File Employer Information Report EEO-1.		Within 30 days after contract is awarded and annually by March 31 thereafter.	
Executive Order 11246	Federal government contractors and subcontractors: contractors under federally assisted construction contracts.	Written affirmative action programs and supporting documentation. Other records pertaining to EEO compliance including validation and use of testing. Compliance with construction industry EEO plans and requirements. No particular form of retention specified.			

Hand-Picked: The Complete Guide to Finding and Hiring the Best Employees

Statute	Employers Affected	Requirements	Period of Retention	When Required	Posting Required
Age Discrimination in Employment Act	Employers with more than 20 employees and engaged in interstate commerce.	Retain all payroll records. Personnel records relating to applications, resumes and other responses to job advertising for full-time, part-time and temporary positions including records pertaining to failure or refusal to hire. Promotion, demotion, transfer, selection for training, layoff, recall or discharge records. Record of job orders submitted to employment agencies, unions. Test papers in connection with employer-administered aptitude or other employment test. Physical examination results in connection with a personnel action. Job advertisements to the public or employees regarding openings, promotions, transfers, training programs or opportunities for overtime work. Employee benefit programs, written seniority or merit.	Three years. One year from date of personnel action to which the record relates, except 90 days for applications and other pre-employment records of applicants for temporary jobs. The period the plan is in effect plus one year.		Consolidated EEO poster.
Rehabilitation Act of 1973	Federal government contractors and subcontractors with a contract of $2,500 or more.	Complete and accurate employment records for all handicapped applicants and employees. Department of Labor suggests a notation in each person's application or file to indicate each vacancy, promotion or training program for which he was considered, including a statement of reason as to how that person was compared to others' qualifications as well as special accommodations. Records regarding complaints or action taken under the act.	One year. One year.	No filing required.	Consolidated EEO poster.
Vietnam Era-Veterans Readjustment Assistance Act	Federal government contractors and subcontractors with a contract of $10,000 or more.	Copies of reports made to state employment service regarding number of individuals and veterans of the Vietnam era, both nondisabled and disabled, hired, and related documentation, such as personnel records, respective job openings, recruitment and placement. Records regarding complaints under the act.	One year after final payment under the contract. One year.		Consolidated EEO poster.

B

Appendix B Federal Record-Keeping Requirements

Statute	Employers Affected	Requirements	Period of Retention	When Required	Posting Required
Fair Labor Standards Act	Employers engaged in interstate commerce.	Basic records containing employee information, payroll, individual contracts, or collective bargaining agreements, applicable certificates and notices of Wage-Hour Administrator, sales and purchase records.	Three years.		FLSA notice to employers. Consolidated EEO poster.
		Supplementary basic records including employment and earning and records and wage rate tables. Also work time schedules, including order shipping and billing records. Records of additions to or deductions from wages paid. Documentation for basis of payment of any wage differential to employees of the opposite sex in the same establishment. Certificates of age.	Two years.		
		Written training agreements.	Until termination of employment. Duration of training program.		
Davis Bacon Act	Employers on public construction contracts exceeding $2,000.	Pay minimum wages found by Labor Secretary to be prevailing in the area.	Three years from date of completion of contract.		Notice to employees of wage scale to be paid.
		Payroll records and classification of each laborer and mechanic, rate of pay, daily.			
Walsh-Healy Public Contracts Act	Employers holding federal contracts.	Retain unexpired certificates of age for employed minors. Records including name, address, sex, date of birth and occupation. Also wage and hour records with contract number.	Period of employment. Three years from date of last entry.		No posting required.
		Earnings records, wage rate tables and time schedules. Records and annual summary of illnesses and injuries.	Two years from date of last entry or last effective date. Three years after date of entry.		
Immigration Reform and Control Act of 1986	All employers regardless of size.	All employees must complete INS form I-9 and provide proof of eligibility to work in the United States within 3 days of hire.	Three years after date of hire or one year after employee termination, whichever is later. (Best to maintain records indefinitely.)	No filing required.	No posting required. Consolidated EEO poster.

Appendix C

Sample Compensation Plan

Champion
SOFTWARE CORPORATION
Compensation Plan

I. Introduction

It is important for each employee of Champion Software Corporation (C.S.C.) to understand the company's compensation policies and procedures. The purpose of this document is to provide basic information about job evaluation, the salary structure and the administration of the Compensation Plan.

II. Compensation Objectives

C.S.C. wants each employee to be paid compensation that:
— Rewards good performance.
— Fairly reflects the duties and responsibilities of each position.
— Is competitive in the market.
— Will attract, motivate and retain competent persons.
— Is internally equitable.
— Is cost effective for the company.

Appendix C Sample Compensation Plan

III. Job Description and Position Evaluation

Each employee, with her supervisor, should complete a position information form or a job description, which will be used in the job evaluation process.

Also, each employee is urged to review her job description annually and discuss it with the immediate supervisor. The Human Resources Department should be advised whenever there are significant changes in responsibilities of a position so that a job evaluation review may be completed.

In determining the relative worth of one position compared with another, many factors are considered, such as frequency and types of business decisions made.

— Frequency and types of analytical and creative output expected of the position.
— Independent actions and decisions that directly impact the sales and profitability of the company.
— Frequency and importance of relationships with customers, suppliers, shareholders, the general public, government agencies and other C.S.C. departments.
— Numbers and types of budgetary responsibilities.
— Special skills or knowledge required to perform the job.
— The minimum formal education required to perform a job in a satisfactory manner.
— The minimum experience required to perform a job in a satisfactory manner.

It is important to note that job evaluation is concerned with the content of a job and the translation of the evaluation into a salary grade — not with the performance of an individual in the job.

IV. Salary Ranges

Each job is assigned to a specific salary grade. Frequently, more than one job will be in a particular salary grade. Together, all salary grades comprise the company's salary structure. The salary range represents the "going rate" in the marketplace for trained, experienced persons.

Each salary grade will have a minimum, midpoint and maximum salary for all positions in the grade. The minimum salary is a fair rate for a person who just meets the basic qualifications of a job, with little or no experience. The midpoint of the salary range is considered an appropriate rate of pay for all experienced, fully qualified, competent employees performing all duties and responsibilities of the position in a completely satisfactory manner. The maximum of the salary range is the upper limit of potential dollar value of a position to C.S.C.

Each employee will be informed of her salary grade and the range for the grade.

V. Salary Surveys

To ensure that C.S.C. salary ranges are competitive with companies of comparable size in similar businesses, C.S.C. will participate in periodic salary surveys. The results of the surveys will be reviewed by the Human Resources Department and the officers of C.S.C. Salary ranges will be adjusted when necessary to remain competitive.

VI. Salary Administration

Job evaluation and salary structures deal with positions, their value to C.S.C. and their assignment to a salary grade. Salary administration involves managing and processing employee salaries. The policy of C.S.C. is to base each employee's salary primarily on work performance — the business results that an individual achieves that contribute to the growth and profitability of the company.

Annually, the chief executive officer of C.S.C. will approve a budget for merit salary increases, based on recommendations by the Human Resources Department. Within departments, the size of each employee's merit salary increase will be governed by:
— The employee's performance on the job.
— Elapsed time since the last increase.
— The employee's current quartile in the salary range.
— The employee's recent salary history.
— The relationship of the employee salary to his peer group within a department.

VII. Performance Measurements

Performance Standards

For each major responsibility of a position, performance standards will be established by each employee in cooperation with his supervisor, which describe when a specific position responsibility is being done in a satisfactory manner.

Business Goals

At the start of each business year, incumbents of managerial positions will also develop a few personal business goals, above the basic position responsibilities, which they commit to accomplish in a specified time period.

VIII. Performance Evaluation

At least annually the performance of each employee must be evaluated by the immediate supervisor and reviewed by the department head. Normally, this will be close to the anniversary date of the employee.

Generally, in a business organization, not more than 10 to 15 percent of employees can truly be noticed as outstanding performers and only 20 to 25 percent are really excellent. Usually, a majority of individuals should be classified as good performers in their jobs.

Each employee will be given a performance rating from one of the following:

E. Excellent

This employee frequently exceeds the basic position requirements on some of the most difficult and complex parts of the job. She will also achieve some individual business goals in a timely manner.

This person requires less supervision than a person in the G. (Good) category. The individual frequently contributes a "little extra," anticipates problems and takes appropriate action.

G. Good

This employee is performing all basic position responsibilities in an acceptable manner. The performance is that expected of a qualified trained individual in the assigned position. Most work or projects are completed on schedule.

This person requires normal supervision and direction. However, the work of this individual probably requires more careful and frequent review than a person in a higher category.

M. Marginal

A person in this category is not performing some of the basic responsibilities of the position in a satisfactory manner, and also misses deadlines. This person may lack basic training and/or experience, which must be gained on the job.

Frequent and close supervision from the immediate supervisor is required and regular, careful reviews of the individual's work probably is necessary. With attention and application, the performance of a person in this category should rise to an acceptable level within a reasonable time frame.

A person in this category who does not improve to a G. (Good) level after a reasonable period should be assigned to another less demanding position or terminated by the company.

O. Outstanding

Optimum performance in meeting every basic position responsibility and individual business goals.

A person in this category has comprehensive knowledge about her field and is highly experienced. This person achieves significantly more in quantity and quality than other employees. She may bring exceptional creativity to the job. This person exercises rare business judgment, and the performance usually shows a broad understanding of more than her own work.

An individual in this category represents outstanding worth to Champion Software in her position. This person requires minimal direction.

U. Unsatisfactory

A person in this category is failing to meet many basic position responsibilities and/or is particularly deficient in one or more of them. Frequently, this individual needs a disproportionate amount of guidance and direction from the supervisor.

Usually both the quality and quantity of the work are deficient and/or the person frequently misses deadlines.

A person in this category must be advised that his work is unsatisfactory and given the reasons why. After counseling, a reasonable period should be established for prompt, significant improvement in job performance. If a satisfactory level is not reached after a probation period, the individual should be demoted or terminated.

IX. Salary Administration

Merit Increases

The job performance of an employee should be the primary consideration in making a salary increase decision. However, other factors, such as the total merit budget for a department and the employee's position in the salary range, will also influence the size of the increase.

Usually, an employee's salary will be reviewed once a year on his anniversary date. Normally, retroactive increases will not be granted. Increases will become effective on either the 15th or 31st day of the month following final approval of the increase.

A Personnel Action form must be prepared by the immediate supervisor and approved by the department head. The Human Resources Department must review and approve each proposed increase to ensure consistency and compliance with C.S.C. policies and procedures.

Promotional Increase Guidelines

A promotion is when an employee is given different and significantly larger job responsibilities that cause the position to be moved to a higher salary grade. (Note: An increase in the volume of the same work performed by an individual is not a promotion.) Depending on a variety of factors, a promotional increase may range to up to 20 percent of the salary in the former position. Usually, the increase will become effective when the employee assumes the new responsibilities. However, sometimes he cannot perform the duties in an acceptable manner. In such cases, the promotional increase should be deferred until the orientation and training period are completed. Normally a promotional increase should be large enough so that the new salary is at least at the minimum of the new salary grade.

Merit Progression Guidelines

Some positions are members of job families (e.g., Accountant I, II, III and Programmer I, II, II). Based on preestablished criteria developed by the head of a department and the Human Resources Department (such as education, experience, job skills, job knowledge, tenure in the position and performance), the department head may advance an individual through the job family grade. An employee so advanced may be given a merit progression increase of up to 5 percent.

Special Salary Adjustments

Usually, the salaries of new employees will be reviewed in less than one year:
— Between three and six months for nonexempt employees
— Between six and nine months for exempt personnel

Merit increases may be granted depending on performance and other appropriate factors, e.g., completion of the orientation and training period.

Salary Decreases

It is not the policy of C.S.C. to decrease salaries except in extraordinary circumstances, such as the demotion of an employee to a lower salary grade. However, even after a demotion, the salary will be decreased only if it exceeds the maximum of the new lower salary grade.

Appendix D

Recruiting Strategies

Media for Your Message

The number of ways to reach your target audience is enormous. They range from the conventional to the outrageous. With the tightening of labor pools, organizations are turning to unusual ways to attract attention.

Even conservative firms like banks are finding that aggressive marketing strategies are the keys to recruitment. Here is a selection of proven media for reaching the people you want:

Airplane banners are an effective way to attract attention at large outdoor events and recreational areas like beaches. A short message with a phone number has yielded large numbers of applicants.

Billboards have been used extensively in the Silicon Valley, for instance, to recruit technical professionals for computer firms. This technique works equally as well for other positions.

Bumper stickers with a recruiting slogan and a phone number appeal to people looking for work in an unassertive manner. Catchy phrases also attract those looking for a change of environment.

Career fairs can be used to fill current openings, but more importantly for promoting your organization to various labor pools. Little giveaways in exchange for completing a short application yields a large number of potential applicants to contact in the future.

Cinema billboards and billboards around areas of entertainment get the attention of younger individuals contemplating a summer or part-time job. Such advertisements should be lighthearted and convey the idea of having fun while working.

Direct mail has been used in situations where a large number of employees are needed. While rather involved, this technique reaches hundreds of potential applicants with relatively little expense. Mailing lists can be obtained from specific organizations from whom you would like to recruit and/or from list brokers who can provide names based on demographics, ZIP codes and a host of other variables. You might also include fliers about available job opportunities in any other direct mail you send. Potential customers can be potential employees.

Appendix D   Recruiting Strategies

Door hangers are effective in situations where the geography of potential applicants is limited. This includes retail recruiting around apartment complexes, colleges and military bases.

Envelope stuffers can be inserted into your customers' mail like their bills, newsletters, product information and stockholder reports. Applicants recruited in this way may be some of your best since they already support your products.

Job fairs are an excellent way to showcase opportunities within your organization. They are generally aimed at specific groups such as engineers, technicians and those in demand. In addition to the exposure to applicants, you can observe other companies' tactics for recruiting.

Kiosks offer the opportunity to advertise openings in high-traffic areas. You may obtain space on kiosks in shopping malls, centers of entertainment, college campuses and other public areas. In addition, you might build or purchase mobile kiosks to place in areas your targeted groups frequent. Be careful, however, to obtain necessary permission before doing so.

Leaflet distribution can be another way to attract the attention of those seeking part-time or supplementary income. Quick-reading, aggressively written fliers with simple contact instructions work the best. Once again, obtain appropriate permission before distributing.

Magnetic signs work well in a variety of places, such as the sides of company vans and trailers or on steel warehouses. These messages should be exciting and to the point, with easy contact instructions.

Open houses play to the public's curiosity about your organization. You can take advantage of this by opening your doors and conducting interesting tours. A recruiting booth can be set up at the end to encourage applications.

Point of sale in retail situations. Informative fliers will catch the eye of potential applicants. If they like your store, maybe they would like to work for you or know someone who does.

Posters with tear-off coupons make applying convenient for those who might otherwise hesitate taking the trouble to call or visit your employment office. Returned coupons can be followed with a phone call and application.

Presentations to local groups can serve several purposes, including recruiting. All company representatives should address job opportunities as part of every presentation. You don't know who might be listening.

Radio can be an excellent medium for attracting applicants. Commercials should be tailored to the listening audience. Phrases such as "Call today" or "Stop by right now!" really work.

Telemarketing, like direct mail, is an involved process. But it is also extremely effective if properly conducted. Research your target markets. Develop the "pitch" and train those calling potential employees on how to represent the company. For professional-level positions, you might even involve managers in a phone campaign. Most applicants find "being recruited" an attractive proposition.

Television, though expensive in most cities, can be an effective means for attracting applicants. Daytime and late night are the best times to reach those out of work. The ads should be exciting and convenience-oriented, such as "Call our office right now at 123-4567 and join our team."

Trade shows, while not geared specifically for recruiting, offer you the opportunity to make contact with a large number of people within your industry. Blatant recruiting may be discouraged, but you should always be prepared to discuss opportunities.

Transit advertising is perfect for reaching commuters working in your vicinity. Travel to and from work tends to be a considerable issue.

Developing Innovative Strategies

Now that you are aware of the variety of media available, the next step is to decide how to make best use of them. This section covers 51 strategies that have been used by companies for recruiting the right people. As you might imagine, each theme has many variations. Adapt them to your benefit.

Overall strategies

These strategies take a commitment on the part of the entire organization and are generally long-term projects. The results, however, can be phenomenal if they are executed with enthusiasm and follow-through.

Develop better relations with local schools. The overall goals for doing this are twofold: (1) to improve applicants' skills, and (2) to attract attention to your company. Meet with the local principal or superintendent and discuss ways you can help, such as organizing tutoring programs and sponsoring contests and other events. Arrange presentations by "role model" employees or employees who attended that school. Co-sponsor a "business week" or a booster club for academic achievement. You might also work through business groups that have ongoing programs.

Research and access employee pools from downsizing organizations. Even in a strong economy, there are always companies laying off employees. When these become apparent in your area, approach the management about holding a "job-opportunity meeting" with those being released.

Encourage full-time employees to assume a second, part-time job. Some of your employees may be looking for ways to earn extra cash. This type of program allows them to do so along with solving your recruiting needs. In addition, you are filling traditionally high-turnover jobs with reliable people.

Stay up-to-date on personnel in other organizations who may be available. Massage the network of professionals and executives on a regular basis. Attending association meetings and civic functions will keep you abreast of who's doing what, where.

Appendix D   Recruiting Strategies

Initiate a retiree job bank. Every year, companies lose good employees to retirement. Yet studies indicate that most of these individuals would still like to contribute. Organize a program to incorporate your retirees into part-time, temporary roles. They can also serve in consulting and training positions. Take advantage of this tremendous source of experienced and loyal labor. Give personal attention to those who leave the company by keeping in touch with cards and letters. Check up on how they are doing. Many return.

Invite retirees from other companies to "un-retire." A number of companies have developed programs to recruit retirees from other local companies to work for them. Not only have they found enthusiastic support, they have also been able to locate individuals already skilled in the areas needed.

Conduct programs that shepherd high school students through college and into your company. A number of organizations have implemented programs that assist minorities and the underprivileged through high school programs and college. They also provide summer employment and internships. In return, it is hoped that these individuals will join the company on a full-time basis after graduation.

Initiate a telecommuting program. A number of insurance companies have instituted arrangements whereby the employee works at home four days per week and commutes to the office on the fifth day. The company provides the necessary equipment and materials, such as computer, telephone modem and desk, to allow the employee to function without leaving the home. This has opened up new possibilities for those who are homebound, mothers with small children and individuals who have trouble with transportation. In addition, it allows the company to recruit in a larger geographic area since commuting is not an issue.

Expand your use of temporaries and part-timers. More and more organizations are adapting their personnel needs to fill positions with individuals who work on a non-full-time basis. In addition to saving money on benefits, companies find that these people are more flexible and project-oriented. While temporaries are generally more expensive, this expense is offset by the fact that you are not committed to them on a long-term basis.

Offer job-sharing opportunities. This is not a new concept, but one that has been accepted in relatively few companies. While there are sometimes difficulties with continuity and supervision, your organization's willingness to adapt to this practice can open up a large pool of individuals interested in working only part time. These groups include highly trained women bringing up small children and semi retired professionals with no interest in returning to work full time.

Train supervisors to accept and cope with nontraditional applicants and their issues. As the labor force grows more diverse, supervisors will be faced with a variety of situations and issues. These include child and elder care responsibilities, language differences, transportation problems and cultural conflicts. Their coping with and making the most of these events will result in better employee relations, higher productivity and lower turnover. Do not assume supervisors will automatically adapt to these challenges. Training in cultural and social issues is essential.

Initiate an internship program. Thousands of organizations across the United States conduct internship programs in conjunction with local colleges. Internships give students the opportunity to apply those skills they have learned. The advantages for the organization are manifold, including the training and development of a high-performing employee after graduation. Remember, however, that these individuals should not be hired to perform simple clerical duties. If they do not have the opportunity to practice their interests, they will probably sour on the organization.

Rehire those who have left. While this has been frowned upon in the past, rehiring former employees can save the company significant time and money. This is especially true for those with in-demand skills. Obviously, care should be taken to review the circumstances under which such employees left.

Position the company as an organization that is "committed to the importance of family." As society evolves, family issues appear to be taking on additional importance in the minds of employees. The days of working 60-hour weeks seem to be subsiding. Positioning your company as one that is concerned about the balance between work and family will attract the large group of workers who are mindful of this situation.

Incentives

These features can be used as "come-ons" to attract pools of applicants. Their use in a recruiting campaign should be tailored to the audience.

While some of the following incentives may be used directly in the campaign to attract applicants, others can be used more indirectly to improve employee relations and encourage those already working for the organization to recommend others.

Shared housing for employees can be especially helpful in tight housing markets or recreational locales. Ski resorts, for example, go so far as to build dormitories on their property to house winter workers.

Subsidized housing for employees relieves the strain of having to find affordable accommodations in an expensive locale. In some cases, a housing allowance is provided. In others, the company steps in to negotiate better deals with landlords.

Commuter rail and bus passes are of tremendous assistance to those in areas such as New York and San Francisco where the daily commute can cost more than five dollars. You might be able to purchase these passes at a discount and use them in a variety of ways to attract applicants.

Company-operated van services transport employees from outside the local area to their site. An indirect effect of this is that it forces employees to be on time.

Company-operated escort services transport employees to and from company sites for purposes of security. For plants located in undesirable areas, this may be the best way to overcome applicant hesitation.

Employee parking lots are a great attraction in large cities or other areas where parking is a problem. In some cases, companies provide shuttles to outlying lots.

Full-time benefits for part-time employees is a very attractive come-on, especially for those in single-parent situations. Although this can be an expensive proposition, you must weigh the cost against the opportunity to recruit good people.

Relocation programs for the most part have been confined to professional- and executive-level hiring. In certain cases, however, a superior candidate may be lured with a small stipend to subsidize actual moving expenses.

Sign-on bonuses have traditionally been used to entice executives. But small bonuses, especially in cash, can be very attractive. One company, for instance, went so far as to give out $100 bills to employees on their first day of work. (The taxes for this were accounted for in the first paycheck.)

Sponsored entertainment events, especially for families, can have a very positive impact on how employees perceive the company. Getting as many employees involved as possible also increases morale.

Employee appreciation programs demonstrate your interest in the staff. Ideas such as plaques, flowers, dinners and "employee of the month" parking spaces boost employee interest. This interest can be translated into referrals of applicants.

Meetings with employee groups to air concerns are an excellent means for staying in touch with the company environment and provide the opportunity to encourage recruitment. It is paramount, however, that follow-through take place on commitments. Without this, all credibility is lost.

Creative techniques

The following strategies have been used successfully to recruit employees. While you may find some inappropriate for your organization, most can be adapted to work for you.

Contest featuring substantial cash awards can be implemented to reward employees who actively recruit applicants. This type of program can also be tied to an incentive where the longer the hired recruit stays with the company, the more money the referring employee receives.

Eligibility for drawings to win cash prizes is an alternative to the above and might also be designed to include newly hired applicants.

Successful job applicants becoming eligible for a drawing for an automobile is still another alternative and might also be designed as an incentive for employees.

Brochures promoting job opportunities can be distributed to employees to use when they meet potential applicants. You might also distribute a little "cheat sheet" of benefits to be brought up.

Business card-size applications that employees can give to interested individuals is an attention-getting gimmick. While all applicants will have to complete a full application when they visit the organization, these smaller versions can be used as a prescreening device.

Personalized recruitment advertisements have worked extremely well in hiring for clerical and support staff. They are placed in the classifieds but take a different approach.

Layered information in advertising attracts the attention of applicants through curiosity. The Bank of Boston, for instance, used the words "temporary sanity" at the top of their recruiting advertisements for temporaries.

Print and broadcast ads in languages associated with the community demonstrate your organization's interest in working with those around it. A large number of referrals may also result from this, since these communities tend to be close-knit.

Posters aimed at foreign students printed in their language displayed on college campuses attract the attention of these individuals. Some American electronics firms operating in Japan, for instance, recruit Japanese students to work in their home country when they graduate.

Visiting executives at colleges and high schools, while not a direct recruiting tactic, can produce tremendous goodwill and notoriety. These individuals can teach classes, consult with faculty, sponsor events and execute a host of other ideas.

Promotions with media to attract applicants such as contests, charity events and fun runs can generate awareness of the company and its participation in the community. Not only can public relations benefit, but the organization receives the indirect endorsement of the station or publication.

Celebrity-hosted events attract attention and promote goodwill in the community. Celebrities can be used in programs such as the opening of a new plant, debut of a product or the beginning of a recruiting campaign. Once the celebrity has attracted the crowd, it is up to you to sign up the applicants.

On-site interviews in malls, job service agencies and other public places make the application process convenient for those who might be interested. Some large companies with high turnover have established permanent storefronts in malls to enhance recruiting of students and older individuals who frequent these locations.

A telephone job line with the latest opportunities is a convenient way for those interested in work to discover what positions are available. In a busy company, getting through the receptionist is sometimes difficult. Having a dedicated line for applicants provides an information source while not disrupting other company business.

Toll-free numbers encourage applicants to apply at no cost to them. This holds true especially for graduating college students who are applying out of state.

Return postage guaranteed makes it easier for applicants to reply, especially those who are economically disadvantaged.

Mobile recruiting vans take the recruiting effort to the applicants. These can be parked at shopping malls, sporting events and other large gatherings. Be sure, however, to obey local parking ordinances and to obtain the necessary permits.

Advertising to your customers through direct mail and envelope stuffers can be a great way to obtain referrals. If customers like your product, they'll refer people or perhaps apply themselves.

Local teachers unions and school districts can be tremendous sources of labor during the summer. Approach local schools early in the spring to ask about making presentations at meetings and sending invitations to their faculty.

Revive the dead resume file. While some of these applications may be several months old, there is no guarantee that the applicants have found work. A 10-second phone call will establish this.

Ask applicants being interviewed for the names of two or three other people who might be interested in positions. These off-chance referrals can provide some excellent candidates.

Asking for referrals of other people on applications is a variation of the above. Since some people do not make it to the interview process, asking a question like this on the application garners all referrals possible.

Advertise that a training session will begin in the next week and see who shows up. Some people do not apply for jobs because they think they don't have the training. If you eliminate that obstacle, you may find they are very interested in your organization. After such potential applicants have contacted you about the training session, they can then be screened for suitability.

Develop a slogan specific to recruiting. The Los Angeles Police Department uses "Color Me Blue" and "Be Somebody. Be a Cop" in its recruiting campaigns. Quick and memorable sayings come to applicants' minds and provide a value with which they can identify.

Hot air balloons are great attention-getters and can be used in a variety of ways. The only caution here is to research and observe the laws and ordinances associated with these vehicles.

As you can see, when it comes to recruiting employees, the sky has become the limit! The same rules and techniques used to market your product can be adapted to hiring people.

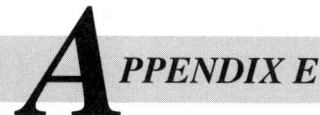

Appendix E

Bibliography and Resources

Books

Robert Half on Hiring
Robert Half, 1986
NAL-Dutton
375 Hudson St.
New York, NY 10014

How to Conduct Win-Win Performance Appraisals
Karen McKirchy, 1994
National Press Publications
6901 W. 63rd St., P.O. Box 2949
Overland Park, KS 66201-1349

Employee Matters
E. Kenneth Snyder, 1991
Probus Publishing Co.
1925 N. Clybourn
Chicago, IL 60614

The Complete Hiring Manual
Joseph D. Levesque, 1991
Prentice Hall, Inc.
113 Sylvan Ave., Rte. 9W
Englewood Cliffs, NJ 07632

Employment Law in the 50 States: A Reference for Employers
CUE/NAM
1331 Pennsylvania Ave. N.W.
Suite 1500 — North Lobby
Washington, DC 20004-1703

Drug Testing Legal Manual
Kevin B. Zeese, 1988
Clark Boardman Callaghan
375 Hudson St.
New York, NY 10014

Employer's Complete Guide to Immigration
Howard David Deutsch, 1987
Prentice Hall Information Services
113 Sylvan Ave., Rte. 9W
Englewood Cliffs, NJ 07632

Immigration Employment Compliance Handbook
A.T. Fragomen and S.C. Bell, 1991
Clark Boardman Callaghan
375 Hudson Street
New York, NY 10014

Modern Personnel Forms
Deborah Launer, Rev. 1988
Warren Gorham & Lamont
31 St. James Ave., Fourth Floor
Boston, MA 02116

Appendix E   Bibliography and Resources

Current Periodicals

HR Magazine
Society for Human
Resource Management
606 N. Washington St.
Alexandria, VA 22314
(703) 548-3440

Personnel Journal
245 Fischer Ave., Suite B2
Costa Mesa, CA 92626
(714) 751-1883

Bottom Line Business
P.O. Box 2614
Greenwich, CT 06836-2614
1-800-234-3834
(203) 625-5900

Inc.
38 Commercial Wharf
Boston, MA 02110
(617) 248-8000

Employment Practice Reference Sources

Bureau of National Affairs
9435 Key West Ave.
Rockville, MD 20850
1-800-372-1033

Business and Legal Reports
39 Academy St.
Madison, CT 06443
(203) 245-7448

CCH Inc.
4025 W. Peterson Ave.
Chicago, IL 60646
1-800-TELL-CCH

Dartnell Inc.
4660 Ravenswood Ave.
Chicago, IL 60640
1-800-621-5463
(312) 561-4000 (IL)

Equal Employment Opportunity Commission
1801 L St. N.W.
Washington, DC 20507
(202) 663-4900

Personnel Forms

Amsterdam Printing & Litho
Wallins Corner Road
Amsterdam, NY 12010
1-800-342-6116

Dartnell Inc.
4660 Ravenswood Ave.
Chicago, IL 60640
1-800-621-5463
(312) 561-4000 (IL)

Selectform Inc.
P.O. Box 3045
Freeport, NY 11520
(516) 623-0400

Written Honesty Tests

ETS Test Collection
Educational Testing Service
Rosedale Road
Princeton, NJ 08541
(609) 921-9000

McGraw-Hill/London House
9701 W. Higgins Rd.
Rosemont, IL 60018
1-800-221-8378
(708) 292-1900 (IL)

Pinkerton Services Group
6100 Fairview Road, Suite 900
Charlotte, NC 28210
1-800-528-5745

Psychological Assessment Services
900 Jorie Blvd.
Oak Brook, IL 60521
(708) 990-3883

The Reid System
200 S. Michigan Ave.
Chicago, IL 60604
1-800-922-7343

Stoelting Co.
620 Wheat Lane
Wood Dale, IL 60191
(708) 860-9700

Appendix E Bibliography and Resources

Written Personality Tests

Bay State Psychological Associates
225 Friend St.
Boston, MA 02114
1-800-438-2772
(617) 367-8400 (MA)

Consulting Psychologists Press
3803 E. Bayshore Road
Palo Alto, CA 94303
1-800-624-1765
(415) 969-8901

McGraw-Hill/London House
9701 W. Higgins Rd.
Rosemont, IL 60018
1-800-221-8378
(708) 292-1900 (IL)

Personnel Decisions Inc.
45 S. Seventh St.
Minneapolis, MN 55402-1608
1-800-633-4410
(612) 339-0927

Psychological Assessment Services
900 Jorie Blvd.
Oak Brook, IL 60521
(708) 990-3883

Stoelting Co.
620 Wheat Lane
Wood Dale, IL 60191
(708) 860-9700

Employment History Verification

Fidelifacts
50 Broadway
New York, NY 10004
(212) 425-1520

Verified Credentials Inc.
1020 E. 146th St., Suite 200
Burnsville, MN 55337
1-800-473-4934
(612) 431-1811

Index

accents, 29

adverse impact, 26, 28, 32, 104, 105, 180, 181, 184, 186

advertising:
　classified, 15, 87, 92-96
　transit, 269
　personalized recruitment, 66, 68, 87, 88, 273

age:
　Discrimination in Employment Act, 25, 29, 36, 37, 39, 141, 258
　requirements, 29

agencies:
　employment,
　recruitment advertising, 87, 88
　temporary, 16-18, 90

Acquired Immune Deficiency Syndrome (AIDS):
　local ordinances regarding, 40
　overview, 197-199
　policy, 202
　recommendations, 201
　related virus (ARV), 197
　screening for, 178, 197-202

affirmative action, 28, 123

Aid to Families with Dependent Children, 86

airplane banners, 267

alcohol, screening for, 178, 192-195

aliens, employment of, 29

alienage, 29

alternatives to recruiting, 16-21

American Association of Retired Persons, 80, 81

American Bar Association, 23

American Polygraph Association, 188

Americans with Disabilities Act, 24, 25, 30, 84, 163, 193, 198, 258

appearance requirements, 29

application forms:
　development of, 123-125
　review of, 125-126
　sample, 124

applicants:
　sources of, 12
　motivation, 74-76

aptitude testing, 33

arrest record, 30

assessment centers, 160

audit:
　of existing jobs, 49
　forms, 50-51
　job, 46-51
　of new jobs, 49

balloons, hot air, 274

benefits, cafeteria style, 56

bias:
　age, 29
　marital status, 32
　sex, 33

billboards, cinema, 267

blacklisting, 30

body language, evaluating, 157

Bolles, Richard, 151

279

Index

bona fide occupational qualifications, 26, 29, 32, 33, 37

brochures, recruiting, 77, 78, 272

bumper stickers, 66, 267

Bureau of Labor Statistics, 86

bus passes, 271

business necessity, 26, 30, 31, 33, 37

candidate(s):
 notifying, 214-216
 selection forms, 209, 210

career:
 changers, 80, 84
 fairs, 267

Centers for Disease Control, 197

chain of custody, 195, 200, 201

Civil Rights Act of 1964, 24, 26, 28, 29, 31, 32, 36, 37, 39, 191, 193, 258

classified advertising, 92-96

college placement centers, 87, 91-92

commuter rail passes, 271

compensation:
 alternatives, 55-56
 philosophy, 54
 policy, 39, 60
 range, 55
 records, 39
 sales, 59-60
 sample plan, 261-266
 signing bonus, 218
 strategy, 55-56, 217-218

computer-assisted interviews, 161

conciliation process, 36

contests, 272

contracted managers and professionals, 16, 18-20

contractors, independent, 19

cost of living, 55, 64

Council of State Administrators of Vocational Rehabilitation, 84

cover letters, evaluating, 120-122

credentials:
 checking, 173-175
 education, 153, 173
 services, 175

credit:
 checks, 173-174
 requirement, 30

criminal record, 30

cultural diversity, 3, 149

defenses to Title VII and the Age Discrimination in Employment Act, 37

dependability testing, 181-182

dependents' status, 30

disabilities, 30, 40

disabled individuals:
 interviewing, 163
 as labor sources, 80, 84-85

disparate treatment, 29, 31, 32, 37, 193

displaced homemakers, 80, 82

door hangers, 268

dress requirements, 29

drugs, screening for, 192-195

economically disadvantaged, 80, 86

education:
 credentials, 153, 173
 requirements, 31

employee, leasing, 20-21

employment:
 agencies, 72, 89
 of aliens, 29
 laws, 7, 24-28
 records, 39

Enzyme-Linked Immunosorbent Assay (ELISA), 200

Enzyme Multiplied Immunoassay, 194

Equal Employment Opportunity Commission, 25, 26, 28, 29, 33, 36, 39, 40, 105, 120, 182

Equal Pay Act, 25, 39

envelope stuffers, 268, 274

escort services, 271

executive:
    Orders 11246 and 11375, 28, 258
    recruiters, 90
    search firms, 90-91

exempt employees:
    definition, 38
    and Fair Labor Standards Act, 38, 39
    table for determining, 38

experience, work, 33, 118-119

Fair Labor Standards Act, 38, 39, 260

false positive, 192, 194

family:
    hiring of, 103, 104, 107-109
    termination of, 103

federal, contracts, 24, 28, 30, 193, 258, 259, 260

Fair Credit Reporting Act, 173

fingerprinting, 31

flextime, 55, 212

Forty-Plus clubs, 82

friends:
    hiring of, 103, 104, 106-108
    termination, 103

Gas Chromatography-Mass Spectrometry (GC-MS) test, 194

genetic screening, 178, 190-191

hair requirement, 31

handwriting analysis, 183

headhunters, 72, 87, 90-91

health requirements, 31

height requirements, 31

hiring:
    cost of, 7-9
    negligently, 34-35
    procedure, 6

"hold harmless clause," 195, 201

homosexuals, local ordinances regarding, 40

honesty testing, 178, 179, 185-186

housing:
    shared, 271
    subsidized, 271

human immunodeficiency virus (HIV), 197

human T-lymphotropic virus type III (HTLV-III), 197

image, organizational, 10, 76-79

Immigration Reform and Control Act of 1986, 24, 25, 29, 36, 115, 260

incentive, nonmonetary, 56, 218

industry trends, 150

integrity testing, 185-186

internship, 160, 271

interviewing:
    alternative strategies for, 159-164
    candidates, 10
    computer-assisted, 161
    conducting of, 154-158
    disabled candidates, 163
    evaluation form, 155
    process factors, 150-151
    schedule, 151
    self-rating form, 158
    questions, 152-154
    videotape, 161

Jacknis, I. Martin, 4

Index

job:
    audits, 46-51
    descriptions, 9, 43-46, 52-54, 65, 87
    fairs, 46
    notices, 92-96
    offers, 215, 217-219
    relatedness, 29, 31, 32, 33, 104
    services, public, 92
    sharing, 270
    shops, 16, 20
    Training Partnership Act, 85

jurisdictional defect, 37

kiosks, 268

labor:
    leased, 16, 20-21
    pools, 98
    senior pool, 81-82
    sources, 80-87
    temporary, 16-18

language requirement, 31

leaflet distribution, 268

leasing, labor, 16, 20-21

letters:
    cover, 120-122
    offer, 215
    rejection, 216

lie detector (polygraph):
    Protection Act, 24, 180, 186
    requirement, 32
    testing, 186-189

lymphadenopathy-associated virus (LAV), 197

mail, direct, 267

marriage status requirement, 32

military:
    record requirement, 32
    retired, 80, 82

moonlighters, 80, 82-83

National Association of Part-Time Professionals, 17

National Association of Temporary Services, 16, 17

National Labor Relations Board, 193

national origin requirement, 32

negligent hiring, 34-35

nepotism:
    arguments for, 103
    arguments against, 104
    definition of, 102
    legal aspects of, 105
    policy, 106
    requirement, 32

nonexempt employees, table for determining, 38

Occupational Safety and Health Administration, 191, 198

offenders, ex-, 80, 85-86

offers, job:
    making, 214-216
    negotiating, 217-219

open houses, 268

organizational image, 76

paper and pencil testing, 179-184

parking lots, 271

part-time, employment, 82-83, 92

performance-based testing, 196-197

point of sale, 268

polygraph (lie dectector):
    Protection Act, 24, 180, 186
    requirement, 32
    testing, 186-189

portraying the company, 162

posters with tear-off coupons, 81

pregnancy:
    Discrimination Act, 24, 25, 32, 36
    requirement, 32

privacy, invasion of, 178, 180, 192, 196

Projects with Industry, 85

psychological testing, 33, 178

public-private partnerships, 85

questions:
    development of, 152-154
    sample interview, 221-256

radio, 268

Radio Immuno Precipitation Assay (RIPA), 200

reasonable accommodation, 38

records:
    compensation, 39
    criminal, 30, 35
    employment, 39
    military, 32, 35

recruiters, executive, 90

recruiting:
    alternatives to, 16-21
    applicants, 74-76
    brochures, 77, 78
    budget, 71-72
    external, 87-92
    internal, 73-74
    plan, 66-70
    professionals, 90-91
    requirement, 32
    services, 89-92

references:
    checking, 168-172
    questions to ask, 169
    telephone guide, 172

referrals:
    external, 87-92
    internal, 72, 73-74

refusals, 219

Rehabilitation Act of 1973, 25, 30, 36, 193, 198, 259

rejection letters, 216

relatedness, job, 29, 31, 32, 33

relatives:
    hiring, 32, 103, 104, 107-109
    policy, 106

release:
    credit check, 174
    polygraph, 188

religious conviction, 32-33

remedies for Title VII judgments, 37

relocation programs, 272

resumes, evaluating, 113-120, 126-127

requirements:
    accents, 29
    aliens, 29
    alienage, 29
    appearance and dress, 29
    arrest and criminal records, 30
    blacklisting, 30
    age, 29
    credit, 30
    dependent's status, 30
    disabilities, 30
    education, 31
    fingerprinting, 31
    hair, 31
    health, 31
    height, 31
    language, 31
    marital status, 32
    military record, 32
    national origin, 32
    nepotism, 32
    polygraph/lie detector, 32
    pregnancy, 32
    religious conviction, 32-33
    sex, 33
        no-spouse, 33, 104
    strength, 33
    testing:
        aptitude/psychological, 33
        drug, 33
    weight, 31
    work experience, 33

retired military, 80, 83

Retired Persons, American Association of, 80

retirees, 78, 270

right-to-sue notice, 36

salary calculation, 217-219

sales compensation, 59-60

screening:
    AIDS, 178, 197-202
    alcohol, 192-195
    drugs, 192-195
    family, 107-109
    friends, 107-109
    genetic, 178, 190-191
    physical, 178
    polygraph, 186-189
    psychological, 178
    telephone, value of, 131-133

Index

selection:
    law, 29-33
    process, 79, 206-213

seniority systems, 37

senior citizens, 80-82

Senior Corps of Retired Executives, 82

sex requirement, 33

signs, magnetic, 268

skills, evaluation, 153, 154

Small Business Administration, 82, 102

spouse (no-spouse) requirement, 33, 104

state laws, 25, 29, 39-40, 123, 173, 184, 193, 199

strength requirement, 33

Targeted Jobs Tax Credit, 85

targeted selection systems, 154

telecommuting, 270

telemarketing, 268

telephone:
    job line, 273
    screening, value of, 131-133
    screening form, 135
    reference guide, 172

television, 269

temporary labor, 16-18

testing:
    AIDS, 178, 197-202
    alcohol, 178, 192-195
    aptitude, 33, 179, 181
    checklist
    dependability, 181-182
    drug, 33, 192-195
    expense of, 180, 182, 183, 200
    genetic, 178, 190-191
    handwriting, 183
    honesty, 178, 179, 185-186
    integrity, 185-186
    legalities of, 178, 187, 193-194, 198-199
    personality, 179
    performance-based, 196-197
    polygraph, 186-189
    psychological, 33, 178
    recommendations, 184
    skills, 178, 179, 181
    validation, 182-183

Thornton, Robert, 171

Title VII, see Civil Rights Act of 1964

trade associations, 55

trade shows, 269

turnover, employee, 49, 64, 65, 66, 68, 79, 117, 150, 182, 207, 212

Uniform Guidelines for Employee Selection Procedures, 26

U. S. Office of Technology Assessment, 180, 190

validity:
    construct, 182, 183
    content, 182
    criterion, 182

van services, 271

vans, mobile recruiting, 273

Veterans Administration, 85

Vietnam-Era Veterans Readjustment Assistance Act, 28, 259

visiting executives, 273

weight requirement, 31

Western Blot Test, 200

Women Work: The National Network for Women's Employment, 82

work experience:
    evaluation, 153
    requirement, 33

workforce trends, 2

YOUR BACK-OF-THE-BOOK STORE

ORDER FORM

Because you already know the value of National Press Publications Desktop Handbooks and Business User's Manuals, here's a time-saving way to purchase more career-building resources from our convenient "book store."

- **IT'S EASY** ... Just make your selections, then mail, call or fax us your order. (See back for details.)
- **INCREASE YOUR EFFECTIVENESS** ... Books in these two series have sold more than a million copies and are known as reliable sources of instantly helpful information.
- **THEY'RE CONVENIENT TO USE** ... Each handbook is durable, concise and made of quality materials that will last you all the way to the boardroom.
- **YOUR SATISFACTION IS 100% GUARANTEED.** Forever.

60-MINUTE TRAINING SERIES™ HANDBOOKS

TITLE	YOUR PRICE*	QTY.	TOTAL
8 Steps for Highly Effective Negotiations #424	$14.95		
Assertiveness #4422	$14.95		
Balancing Career and Family #415	$14.95		
Change: Coping with Tomorrow Today #421	$14.95		
Customer Service: The Key ... Customers #488	$14.95		
Dynamic Communication Skills for Women #413	$14.95		
Empowering the Self-Directed Team #422	$14.95		
Fear & Anger: Control Your Emotions #4302	$14.95		
Getting Things Done #4112	$14.95		
How to Conduct Win-Win Perf. Appraisals #423	$14.95		
How to De-Junk Your Life #4306	$14.95		
How to Manage Conflict #495	$14.95		
How to Manage Your Boss #493	$14.95		
How to Supervise People #4102	$14.95		
Listen Up: Hear What's Really Being Said #4172	$14.95		
Managing Our Differences #412	$14.95		
Motivation and Goal-Setting #4962	$14.95		
A New Attitude #4432	$14.95		
PC Survival Guide #407	$14.95		
Parenting: Ward & June ... #486	$14.95		
Peak Performance #469	$14.95		
The Polished Professional #426	$14.95		
The Power of Innovative Thinking #428	$14.95		
Powerful Communication Skills #4132	$14.95		
Powerful Leadership Skills for Women #463	$14.95		
Powerful Presentation Skills #461	$14.95		
Real Men Don't Vacuum #416	$14.95		
Self-Esteem: The Power to Be Your Best #4642	$14.95		
SELF Profile #403	$14.95		
Shortcuts to Organized Files and Records #4307	$14.95		
The Stress Management Handbook #4842	$14.95		
Supreme Teams: How to Make Teams Work #4303	$14.95		
Techniques to Improve Your Writing Skills #460	$14.95		
The Write Stuff #414	$14.95		

VIP No. 705-008438-098   *in Canada $16.95

MORE FROM OUR BACK-OF-THE-BOOK STORE

Business User's Manuals — Self-Study, Interactive Guide

TITLE	RETAIL PRICE	YOUR PRICE	QTY.	TOTAL
The Assertive Advantage #439	$26.95	$22.95		
Business Letters for Busy People #449	$26.95	$22.95		
Dealing with Conflict and Anger #5402	$26.95	$22.95		
Hand-Picked: Finding & Hiring ... #5405	$26.95	$22.95		
High-Impact Presentation and Training Skills #438	$26.95	$22.95		
Learn to Listen #446	$26.95	$22.95		
The Manager's Role as Coach #456	$26.95	$22.95		
The Memory System #452	$26.95	$22.95		
Parenting the Other Chicks Eggs #5404	$26.95	$22.95		
Taking AIM On Leadership #5401	$26.95	$22.95		
Prioritize, Organize: Art of Getting It Done #453	$26.95	$22.95		
Sex, Laws & Stereotypes #432	$26.95	$22.95		
Think Like a Manager #451	$26.95	$22.95		

SPECIAL OFFER:
Orders over $75 receive
FREE SHIPPING

Subtotal	$
Add 7% Sales Tax *(Or add appropriate state and local tax)*	$
Shipping and Handling *($3 one item; 50¢ each additional item)*	$
Total	$
VOLUME DISCOUNTS AVAILABLE — CALL 1-800-258-7248	

Name_____ Title _____

Organization _____

Address _____

City _____ State/Province _____ ZIP/Postal Code_____

Payment choices:
❑ Enclosed is my check/money order payable to National Seminars.
❑ Please charge to: ❑ MasterCard   ❑ VISA   ❑ American Express

Signature X _____ Exp. Date_____ Card Number _____

❑ Purchase Order # _____

MAIL: Complete and mail order form
with payment to:
National Press Publications
P.O. Box 419107
Kansas City, MO 64141-6107

PHONE:
Call toll-free **1-800-258-7246**

FAX:
1-913-432-0824

Your VIP No.: 705-008438-098

YOUR BACK-OF-THE-BOOK STORE

ORDER FORM

Because you already know the value of National Press Publications Desktop Handbooks and Business User's Manuals, here's a time-saving way to purchase more career-building resources from our convenient "book store."

- IT'S EASY ... Just make your selections, then mail, call or fax us your order. (See back for details.)
- INCREASE YOUR EFFECTIVENESS ... Books in these two series have sold more than a million copies and are known as reliable sources of instantly helpful information.
- THEY'RE CONVENIENT TO USE ... Each handbook is durable, concise and made of quality materials that will last you all the way to the boardroom.
- YOUR SATISFACTION IS 100% GUARANTEED. Forever.

60-MINUTE TRAINING SERIES™ HANDBOOKS

TITLE	YOUR PRICE*	QTY.	TOTAL
8 Steps for Highly Effective Negotiations #424	$14.95		
Assertiveness #4422	$14.95		
Balancing Career and Family #415	$14.95		
Change: Coping with Tomorrow Today #421	$14.95		
Customer Service: The Key ... Customers #488	$14.95		
Dynamic Communication Skills for Women #413	$14.95		
Empowering the Self-Directed Team #422	$14.95		
Fear & Anger: Control Your Emotions #4302	$14.95		
Getting Things Done #4112	$14.95		
How to Conduct Win-Win Perf. Appraisals #423	$14.95		
How to De-Junk Your Life #4306	$14.95		
How to Manage Conflict #495	$14.95		
How to Manage Your Boss #493	$14.95		
How to Supervise People #4102	$14.95		
Listen Up: Hear What's Really Being Said #4172	$14.95		
Managing Our Differences #412	$14.95		
Motivation and Goal-Setting #4962	$14.95		
A New Attitude #4432	$14.95		
PC Survival Guide #407	$14.95		
Parenting: Ward & June ... #486	$14.95		
Peak Performance #469	$14.95		
The Polished Professional #426	$14.95		
The Power of Innovative Thinking #428	$14.95		
Powerful Communication Skills #4132	$14.95		
Powerful Leadership Skills for Women #463	$14.95		
Powerful Presentation Skills #461	$14.95		
Real Men Don't Vacuum #416	$14.95		
Self-Esteem: The Power to Be Your Best #4642	$14.95		
SELF Profile #403	$14.95		
Shortcuts to Organized Files and Records #4307	$14.95		
The Stress Management Handbook #4842	$14.95		
Supreme Teams: How to Make Teams Work #4303	$14.95		
Techniques to Improve Your Writing Skills #460	$14.95		
The Write Stuff #414	$14.95		

VIP No. 705-008438-098   *in Canada $16.95

MORE FROM OUR BACK-OF-THE-BOOK STORE

Business User's Manuals — Self-Study, Interactive Guide

TITLE	RETAIL PRICE	YOUR PRICE	QTY.	TOTAL
The Assertive Advantage #439	$26.95	$22.95		
Business Letters for Busy People #449	$26.95	$22.95		
Dealing with Conflict and Anger #5402	$26.95	$22.95		
Hand-Picked: Finding & Hiring ... #5405	$26.95	$22.95		
High-Impact Presentation and Training Skills #438	$26.95	$22.95		
Learn to Listen #446	$26.95	$22.95		
The Manager's Role as Coach #456	$26.95	$22.95		
The Memory System #452	$26.95	$22.95		
Parenting the Other Chicks Eggs #5404	$26.95	$22.95		
Taking AIM On Leadership #5401	$26.95	$22.95		
Prioritize, Organize: Art of Getting It Done #453	$26.95	$22.95		
Sex, Laws & Stereotypes #432	$26.95	$22.95		
Think Like a Manager #451	$26.95	$22.95		

SPECIAL OFFER:
Orders over $75 receive
FREE SHIPPING

Subtotal	$
Add 7% Sales Tax *(Or add appropriate state and local tax)*	$
Shipping and Handling *($3 one item; 50¢ each additional item)*	$
Total	$

VOLUME DISCOUNTS AVAILABLE — CALL 1-800-258-7248

Name _____ Title _____

Organization _____

Address _____

City _____ State/Province _____ ZIP/Postal Code _____

Payment choices:
❏ Enclosed is my check/money order payable to National Seminars.
❏ Please charge to: ❏ MasterCard   ❏ VISA   ❏ American Express

Signature X _____ Exp. Date _____ Card Number _____

❏ Purchase Order # _____

MAIL: Complete and mail order form with payment to:
National Press Publications
P.O. Box 419107
Kansas City, MO 64141-6107

PHONE:
Call toll-free **1-800-258-7246**

FAX:
1-913-432-0824

Your VIP No.: 705-008438-098